T0315514

AMC'S BEST DAY HIKES IN
NEW JERSEY

Four-Season Guide to 50 of the Best Trails in the Garden State, from the Skylands to the Shore

2nd Edition // Priscilla Estes and Michael McCormick

Appalachian Mountain Club Books // Boston, Massachusetts

AMC is a 501(c)3 nonprofit, and sales of AMC Books fund our mission to foster the protection, enjoyment, and understanding of the outdoors. If you appreciate our efforts and would like to become a member or make a donation to AMC, visit outdoors.org, call 603-466-2727, or contact us at Appalachian Mountain Club, 10 City Square, Boston, MA 02129.

outdoors.org/books-maps

Distributed by National Book Network.

Front cover photograph of hikers in Delaware Water Gap National Recreation Area © Ryan Smith/Rooted in Light Media
Back cover photograph of Brendan T. Byrne State Forest © Richard Lewis/AMC Photo Contest
Interior photographs by Priscilla Estes (pages iii, xxviii, 6, 15, 18, 33, 38, 45, 52, 64, 78, 83, 88, 92, 94, 103, 108, 120, 124, 130, 137, 140, 148, 157, 162, 174, 186, 192, 203, 206, 228, 236, 244); Michael McCormick (pages 48, 59, 68, 113, 153, 168, 185, 197, 214, 217, 224, 232, 250, 255, 259, 263); Paul Wulfing (pages 28, 99); Siddharth Mallya/Wikimedia Commons (page 10); Susan Bennett (page 23); TomH2323/Creative Commons on Flickr (page 71); Liz D. Imperio/AMC Photo Contest (page 72); Dorian Wallender/Creative Commons on Flickr (page 132); U.S. Fish and Wildlife Service/Creative Commons on Flickr (page 178); John Hoey/Creative Commons on Flickr (page 241)
Maps by Ken Dumas © Appalachian Mountain Club
Cover design by Jon Lavalley
Interior design by Abigail Coyle

Library of Congress Cataloging-in-Publication Data

Names: Estes, Priscilla A., author. | McCormick, Michael (Travel blogger), author. Title: AMC's best day hikes in New Jersey : four-season guide to 50 of the best trails in the Garden State, from the Skylands to the shore / Priscilla Estes and Michael McCormick. Other titles: Appalachian Mountain Club's best day hikes in New Jersey
Description: 2nd edition. | Boston, Massachusetts : Appalachian Mountain Club Books, [2024] | "Distributed by National Book Network"--T.p. verso. | Summary: "A guide to 50 of the best hikes in New Jersey that can be completed in one day or less, for beginner and experienced hikers"--Provided by publisher.
Identifiers: LCCN 2023048565 | ISBN 9781628421705 (trade paperback : acid-free paper) | ISBN 9781628421712 (epub) | ISBN 9781628421729 (mobi)
Subjects: LCSH: Day hiking--New Jersey--Guidebooks. | Hiking--New Jersey--Guidebooks. | Walking--New Jersey--Guidebooks. | Trails--New Jersey--Guidebooks. | Outdoor recreation--New Jersey--Guidebooks. | New Jersey--Description and travel. | New Jersey--Guidebooks. | BISAC: SPORTS & RECREATION / General | TRAVEL / United States / Northeast / Middle Atlantic (NJ, NY, PA)
Classification: LCC GV199.42.N5 E77 2024 | DDC 796.5109749--dc23/eng/20231122
LC record available at https://lccn.loc.gov/2023048565

The paper used in this publication meets the minimum requirements of the American National Standard for Information Sciences-Permanence of Paper for Printed Library Materials, ANSI Z39.48-1984. ∞

Interior pages and cover are printed on responsibly harvested paper stock certified by The Forest Stewardship Council®, an independent auditor of responsible forestry practices.

Printed in the United States of America, using vegetable-based inks.

5 4 3 2 1   24 25 26 27 28

To my born family: Charles, Elizabeth, Patricia, Steven, and Charlie. And to my chosen family: Paul, my husband.
—Priscilla Estes

For my favorite adventurers: Alix, Abe, John, Ben, Michael, and Joseph.
—Michael McCormick

LOCATOR MAP

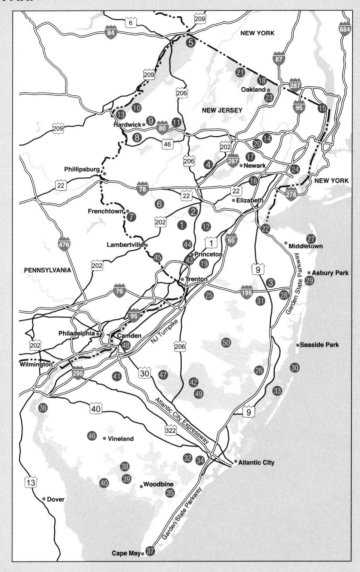

KEY TO ICONS

Exposed ledges (trail crosses an exposed ledge—a consideration in severe weather or in wet or icy conditions; hikes that end at a scenic ledge but do not cross an exposed ledge en route are not marked with this icon)

Steep or difficult terrain

Difficult brook crossing

Good for kids

Dog-friendly

Accessible

Waterfall

Pond, stream, spring, or other water feature

Snowshoeing

Cross-country skiing

Scenic view

Designated tentsite

Swimming

Picnic area

Visitor center

Public transit

Fee

Fishing

Horseback riding

Bicycle trails

Fire tower (although some are more stable than others, all towers should be considered climb-at-your-own-risk)

CONTENTS

ESSAYS

AT-A-GLANCE TRIP PLANNER

Trip number	Trip name and location	Difficulty rating	Round-trip distance	Elevation gain	Estimated time
SECTION 1 // SKYLANDS					
1	Sourland Mountain Preserve *Hillsborough, NJ*	Moderate	6.3 mi	700 ft	3 hrs
2	Duke Farms *Hillsborough, NJ*	Easy	4.9 mi	496 ft	2 hrs
3	Rockhopper and Dry Run Creek Trails *Lambertville, NJ*	Moderate–Strenuous	9.3 mi	1,000 ft	4.5 hrs
4	Morristown National Historical Park: Jockey Hollow Section *Morristown, NJ*	Strenuous	10 mi	1,250 ft	5–6 hrs
5	High Point State Park: Monument Trail to Appalachian Trail *Sussex, NJ*	Strenuous	7.9 mi	1,250 ft	5 hrs
6	Deer Path Park: Round Mountain Section *Flemington, NJ*	Easy–Moderate	6.6 mi	900 ft	3.5 hrs
7	Delaware and Raritan Canal and Horseshoe Bend Park *Frenchtown, NJ*	Moderate–Strenuous	10.6 mi	900 ft	5.5 hrs
8	Jenny Jump State Forest *Hope, NJ*	Strenuous	11.4 mi	1,500 ft	5 hrs
9	White Lake Natural Resource Area *Hardwick Township, NJ*	Easy	4 mi	350 ft	1.5 hrs
10	Delaware Water Gap National Recreation Area: Millbrook Village to Van Campens Glen Loop *Hardwick Township, NJ*	Strenuous	7.1 mi	850 ft	4 hrs
11	Allamuchy Mountain State Park *Byram Township, NJ*	Easy	5.1 mi	450 ft	3 hrs
12	Six Mile Run Reservoir *Somerset, NJ*	Easy	6 mi	400 ft	2.5 hrs
13	Mohican Outdoor Center: Rattlesnake Swamp Trail and Appalachian Trail *Blairstown, NJ*	Moderate	6 mi	600 ft	3–4 hrs

Trip highlights	Trip features (see Key to Icons on page vi)
"Ringing rocks," boulder fields, a stream that roars	
Former Duke estate with lakes, fountains, statues, and orchids	
Boulder-hopping, cardio workout on Continental Army's route	
Rolling terrain on former farm past Continental Army encampments	
Panoramic views of three states from the highest point in New Jersey	
Woods, meadows, historic farms and barns; beehives	
Walk along the Delaware River, then over ravines, streams, and rolling meadows	
Lake and views of Kittatinny Ridge and Valley; dramatic outcroppings	
Peaceful lake, hidden history	
Waterfalls, wildflowers, wooded glens, and steep steps	
Old railroad bed, lake, abandoned mine pits, rock formations	
Zigzag between fields and woods, along a creek	
Spectacular views from Kittatinny Ridge; 100-year-old fire tower	

Trip number	Trip name and location	Difficulty rating	Round-trip distance	Elevation gain	Estimated time
SECTION 2 // GATEWAY					
14	Garret Mountain Reservation *Woodland Park, NJ*	Easy	2.8 mi	400 ft	2 hrs
15	Palisades Interstate Park: State Line Lookout to Peanut Leap Cascade *Alpine, NJ*	Moderate	3 mi	600 ft	1.5–2 hrs
16	Watchung Reservation: White Trail to Feltville *Scotch Plains, NJ*	Easy	3.9 mi	550 ft	2.5 hrs
17	Branch Brook Park *Newark, NJ*	Easy	4.5 mi	160 ft	2 hrs
18	Norvin Green State Forest (South) *Ringwood, NJ*	Strenuous	5.4 mi	1,800 ft	4–5 hrs
19	Plainsboro Preserve *Cranbury, NJ*	Easy	4.9 mi	200 ft	2.5 hrs
20	Mills Reservation *Cedar Grove, NJ*	Easy–Moderate	2.5 mi	300 ft	1.5 hrs
21	Wawayanda State Park *Hewitt, NJ*	Easy	6 mi	425 ft	3.5 hrs
22	Cheesequake State Park *Matawan, NJ*	Moderate	3.3 mi	370 ft	2 hrs
23	Ramapo Mountain State Forest *Oakland, NJ*	Strenuous	5.4 mi	650 ft	3 hrs
24	Liberty State Park *Jersey City, NJ*	Easy	5.2 mi	20 ft	2 hrs
SECTION 3 // JERSEY SHORE					
25	Clayton Park *Imlaystown, NJ*	Easy	4.2 mi	490 ft	2 hrs
26	Wells Mills County Park *Waretown, NJ*	Moderate	8.3 mi	750 ft	4 hrs
27	Hartshorne Woods Park *Locust, NJ*	Strenuous	9.3 mi	1,600 ft	5 hrs
28	Allaire State Park *Wall Township, NJ*	Easy	5.2 mi	250 ft	3 hrs
29	Manasquan to Asbury Park *Manasquan, NJ*	Moderate	9.8 mi	50 ft	4 hrs

Trip highlights	Trip features (see Key to Icons on page vi)
Excellent New York City views; climb Lambert Tower	
Hudson River vistas, steep stone steps to a waterfall	
Explore an abandoned village deep in the woods	
Largest collection of cherry trees in the USA, hike the Lenape Trail	
360-degree views of New York City and Wanaque Reservoir; rock scrambles	
Peaceful lake, secluded woods, Nature Center	
Rocky footing along edge of quarry; dramatic views of New York City	
Lake, large rocks, shady trails	
Good beginner's hike with well-marked trails; boardwalk over Atlantic white-cedar swamp	
Boulder scrambling, castle ruins, lakes, views of New York City	
Flat trail along the Hudson River; excellent New York City views; urban oasis	
Wildflowers, mountain laurels, and cozy, sparsely populated trails	
Scenic pine barrens primer but hilly; excellent Nature Center	
Excellent Navesink River views, deep woods, World War II bunkers	
Working steam railroad, village, nature walk with activities	
Walk the boardwalk and beach through popular shore towns	

Trip number	Trip name and location	Difficulty rating	Round-trip distance	Elevation gain	Estimated time
30	Island Beach State Park: Johnny Allen's Cove Trail and Barnegat Inlet Trail *Seaside Park, NJ*	Johnny Allen's Cove Trail: Easy; Barnegat Inlet Trail: Moderate	Johnny Allen's Cove Trail: 1.2 mi; Barnegat Inlet Trail: 4.1 mi	Johnny Allen's Cove Trail: 100 ft; Barnegat Inlet Trail: 200 ft	Johnny Allen's Cove Trail: 30 mins; Barnegat Inlet Trail: 3.5 hrs
31	Manasquan Reservoir *Howell, NJ*	Moderate	6.6 mi	250 ft	3 hrs

SECTION 4 //GREATER ATLANTIC CITY

32	Estell Manor Park *Mays Landing, NJ*	Easy	5.6 mi	150 ft	2.5 hrs
33	Edwin B. Forsythe National Wildlife Refuge *Galloway, NJ*	Easy	5.3 mi	300 ft	2.5 hrs
34	Birch Grove Park *Northfield, NJ*	Easy	3 mi	50 ft	1.5 hrs

SECTION 5 //SOUTHERN SHORE

35	Belleplain State Forest *Woodbine, NJ*	Moderate–Strenuous	10.3 mi	300 ft	5 hrs
36	Fort Mott State Park *Pennsville, NJ*	Easy	3.1 mi	250 ft	2 hrs
37	Cape May Point State Park and South Cape May Meadows *Cape May Point, NJ*	Easy	3.4 mi	100 ft	1.5 hrs
38	Maurice River Bluffs Preserve *Millville, NJ*	Moderate	5.5 mi	400 ft	3 hrs
39	Glades Wildlife Refuge: Tat Starr Trail and Bald Eagle Trail *Newport, NJ*	Easy	3.9 mi	100 ft	2 hrs
40	Maurice River Bicycle and Walking Trail *Millville, NJ*	Easy	3.2 mi	100 ft	2 hrs

SECTION 6 //DELAWARE RIVER

41	Wenonah Woods *Wenonah, NJ*	Easy	5.7 mi	350 ft	3–4 hrs
42	Mullica River Trail: Atsion to Quaker Bridge *Shamong, NJ*	Moderate–Strenuous	9.9 mi	320 ft	4.5 hrs
43	Princeton Battlefield State Park and Institute Woods *Princeton, NJ*	Easy	4.2 mi	75 ft	2.5 hrs

Trip highlights	Trip features (see Key to Icons on page vi)
Stroll the dunes of a barrier reef surrounded by water toward a lighthouse	
Loop around a massive 770-acre reservoir teeming with birds	
1.8-mi boardwalk through a swamp; World War I munitions plant; South River views	
A birder's paradise with marshes and stunning views of Atlantic City	
Wind among almost two dozen ponds, teeming with wildlife	
Long woods walk past lakes, through wetlands and tunnels of mountain laurels	
Unique history hike; Civil War POW cemetery and 1890s battery; bird refuge	
A mix of sand, sea, woods, and marshes; prime hawk migration area; lighthouse	
Rugged trail through forests and along the bluff of Maurice River	
Salt and fresh water meet in riparian region	
Paved path along Maurice River, wetlands, ruins, eagles	
Footbridges, Japanese tea houses, and beavers	
Quiet hike in the Pine Barrens along a river	
Shady birding oasis, American Revolution battlefield	

Trip number	Trip name and location	Difficulty rating	Round-trip distance	Elevation gain	Estimated time
44	Laurie Chauncey Trail *Princeton, NJ*	Easy	2.7 mi	200 ft	1.5 hrs
45	Washington Crossing State Park *Titusville, NJ*	Easy	3.9 mi	350 ft	2 hrs
46	Parvin State Park *Elmer, NJ*	Moderate–Strenuous	9.3 mi	375 ft	5 hrs
47	Black Run Preserve *Evesham, NJ*	Easy	5 mi	100 ft	2–3 hrs
48	Cooper River Park Loop *Cherry Hill, NJ*	Easy	7.8 mi	200 ft	3.5 hrs
49	Batona Trail: Sand and Water Trail and 1808 Trail *Hammonton, NJ*	Moderate	7.3 mi	350 ft	3 hrs
50	Brendan T. Byrne State Forest *New Lisbon, NJ*	Moderate	9.4 mi	300 ft	4 hrs

Trip highlights	Trip features (see Key to Icons on page vi)
Green oasis along a creek; three-pony bridge	
See where George Washington crossed the Delaware; walk in his footsteps	
Wildflowers, lake, egrets, and a secluded swamp trail	
Surprisingly secluded hike through pine barrens	
Urban and suburban adventure with water, woods, and hawks	
Hike through the heart of a massive cedar swamp in the Pine Barrens	
Wander the pines and cranberry bog to Pakim Pond	

ACKNOWLEDGMENTS

From Priscilla: The biggest thanks go to my husband since 1979, Paul Wulfing, who in 1996 introduced me to the Appalachian Mountain Club (AMC) as a connection to healthy activities we could do together. AMC has been a big part of our lives ever since. Now that we live in western North Carolina, I must add the Carolina Mountain Club (CMC) to the family. And, of course, co-author extraordinaire, Michael McCormick—thank you!

From Michael: Thank you to my wife, Alexandria, for all her support with this book and in life . . . and also for her master's degree in English. Thank you to my five sons—Abe, John, Ben, Michael, and Joseph—for being the best adventure buddies anyone could hope for. Thank you to my mom, Joyce, for teaching me how to set up a tent and to my late father, Dave, for sharing his love of national parks and road trips. Thank you to the Whalens for getting me into Scouting, and thanks to Troop 48—particularly Pat, Tom, Gallagher, Danny, Brian, Paul, and, of course, Gary. Thank you to everyone who's followed my South Jersey Trails blog and our family's adventures over the past decade. Last, thanks go to Priscilla for asking me to join her in this project and to the Appalachian Mountain Club.

Our editors at AMC Books were great and made the book better by improving readability: senior books editor Tim Mudie, senior production manager Abigail Coyle, and copyeditor Lenore Howard. Illustrator Ken Dumas worked his magic on the maps.

INTRODUCTION

More than a century ago, John Muir, the naturalist also known as the Father of the National Parks, wrote, "Thousands of tired, nerve-shaken, over-civilized people are beginning to find out that going to the mountains is going home; that wildness is a necessity; and that mountain parks and reservations are useful not only as fountains of timber and irrigating rivers, but as fountains of life." —*Our National Parks* (1901)

While Muir was certainly thinking of places far away from, far more elevated than, and far wilder than New Jersey, the sentiment of what he expressed has once again thundered across the nation. In the uncertainty of recent years, people have flocked to our state's trails and green places like never before, seeking rest, relaxation, comfort, adventure. They found all of these, along with something else that surprised even life-long residents—they discovered that New Jersey is a remarkable place. It is a beautiful state of glorious contrasts: small but diverse, urban but agricultural, inland and coastal, industrial yet forested.

At 8,723 square miles, it's one of the smallest states, ranked 47th in size. Only Connecticut, Rhode Island, and Delaware are smaller. But New Jersey ranks first in population density, with 1,263 people per square mile, and is eleventh in total population (census.gov/quickfacts/NJ; 2022). New Jersey is the only state in the union in which every county is considered "urban." The U.S. Census Bureau classifies an urban area as a territory that encompasses at least 2,500 people, at least 1,500 of which reside outside institutional group quarters. Yet fully 34 percent of New Jersey's total land area is preserved, and New Jersey is a national leader in open space preservation and in funding park and recreation facilities (nj.gov/dep/greenacres/pdf/2018_draft_SCORP.pdf).

Despite dense population and urbanization, the state has a strong tradition of agriculture. New Jersey is one of the top ten producers of blueberries, cranberries, peaches, tomatoes, bell peppers, eggplants, cucumbers, apples, spinach, squashes, and asparagus in the United States. Productive farmland covers nearly 720,000 acres (nj.gov/agriculture /about/overview.html). Abraham Browning of Camden was remarkably prescient in 1876 at the Centennial Exhibition in Philadelphia (on New Jersey Day) when he nicknamed New Jersey the "Garden State."

Although people may not think of it as such, New Jersey is a peninsula. The Atlantic Ocean hugs the eastern coastline from Sandy Hook to Cape May. Delaware Bay, where the Delaware River meets the Atlantic, cradles the southern and western coastlines from Cape May to Fort Mott and separates New Jersey from Delaware. To the north, the Hudson River forms a boundary between New Jersey and New York. Tributaries of the Delaware and Hudson rivers crisscross the state. Altogether, New Jersey boasts 1,792 total miles of coast.

New Jersey has been an important center of manufacturing since the Industrial Revolution, but today forests cover 40 percent of the state (nj.gov/dep/parksandforests/forest) and provide abundant habitats for wildlife. In fact, the National Audubon Society has designated the Delaware Bayshore area one of Earth's most important stopovers for migratory birds.

Overlaid on this beauty is New Jersey's varied terrain: the rugged Kittatinny Ridge and Valley, Delaware Water Gap, and the Highlands in the north; the forested Ramapo and Watchung mountains in the middle of the state; and the flat expanse of the coast and the Pine Barrens in the south. Within these regions, New Jersey boasts 34 state parks, eleven state forests, one state wildlife management area, five national wildlife refuges, two national parks, a national historic site, a national historic park, a national recreation area, and hundreds of municipal parks (stateparks.com/new_jersey_parks_and_recreation_destinations.html).

Can there be there any doubt that New Jersey is an urban hiker's paradise?

With such a vast array of riches to choose from, selecting the hikes for this second edition was a challenge for the authors.

For the first edition of this book, Priscilla Estes drew upon her rich experiences as a member of and hike leader for the Appalachian Mountain Club (AMC) since 1996, as well as her wide knowledge of the state. Her research involved reading books and online guides and reaching out to leaders of local hiking clubs, such as the AMC Delaware Valley Chapter, the Outdoor Club of South Jersey, the TriState Ramblers, and Metrotrails. She also scoured websites such as the New York–New Jersey Trail Conference, NJ Hiking, and the New Jersey Trails Association, as well as blogs such as Gone Hikin' and South Jersey Trails.

For the second edition of this book, Priscilla approached Michael McCormick, author of the South Jersey Trails blog, and asked him to co-author the update. Michael brought his own experience to the project, including twenty years of leading his Boy Scout troop in Berlin, New Jersey, on the trails of the state, a decade of writing his hiking blog, and a love of adventuring with his wife and five young sons.

Together, the authors have created a book that will help readers explore many of the corners of this varied state. They hope this "best of" guide will be useful for all who love the outdoors, and especially for beginning and intermediate hikers. Keep in mind that the word "best" is fluid and somewhat subjective. Age and physical ability influence perspective, as do experience and mindset. A 10-year-old child hiking the rustic boardwalk of an Atlantic cedar swamp for the first time will have a different sense of wonder about the smells, sounds, animals, and flowers than will a 65-year-old adult who hikes frequently.

Still, this book cannot hope to cover all the wonderful walks this state has to offer. To help lessen that gap, this book again includes a reference section listing other worthwhile trails in New Jersey. Please explore the hikes listed in the appendix (page 265), and if you discover more treks on your own, email amcbooks@outdoors.org to make a suggestion for future inclusion. While the maps included in this book are as comprehensive as possible, trails do change, so check the latest maps listed for each hike before heading out.

Read. Enjoy. Find new adventures. Visit New Jersey's own "fountains of life." You may just find that going out onto the trails is indeed going home.

Thank you to each reader and to AMC for making this journey possible.

HOW TO USE THIS BOOK

With 50 hikes to choose from, you may wonder how to decide where to go. The locator map at the front of this book will help you narrow down the trips by location, and the at-a-glance trip planner that follows the table of contents will provide more information to guide you toward a decision.

Once you settle on a destination and turn to a trip in this guide, you will find a series of icons that indicate whether fees are charged, if the trip is fully or partially accessible, whether the hike is good for kids, whether dogs are permitted, whether cross-country skiing and snowshoeing are allowed, and more. The locator map includes a list of all icons.

Information on the basics follows: location, rating, distance, elevation gain, estimated time, contact information, and maps. The ratings are based on the authors' perception and are estimates of what the average hiker will experience. You may find hikes to be easier or more difficult than stated. The estimated time is also based on the authors' perception. Consider your own pace when planning a trip.

The elevation gain is calculated from measurements and information obtained from U.S. Geological Survey (USGS) topographic maps, landowner maps, and Google Earth. Each hike identifies the relevant USGS maps, if any, as well as where you can find additional trail maps. Most USGS topographic maps can be downloaded for free from store.usgs.gov. The boldface summary provides a basic overview of what you will see on your hike.

The directions explain how to reach the trailhead by car and, for some trips, by public transportation. Global Positioning System (GPS) coordinates for parking lots are also included. Enter these coordinates into your own device for driving directions. Whether or not you own a GPS device, it is wise to consult an atlas before you leave home.

In the trail description, you will find instructions regarding where to hike, the trails on which to hike, and turn-by-turn directions. You will also learn about natural and human history along your hike, as well as information about flora, fauna, and any landmarks and objects you will encounter.

The trail maps that accompany each trip will guide you along your hike, but it would be wise to take an official trail map with you. They are often—but not always—available online, at the trailhead, or at the visitor center.

Each trip ends with a section titled "More Information" that provides details, if needed, about restroom locations, access times and fees, and the property's rules and regulations. The "Nearby" section provides useful information on other sights, hikes, and points of interests in the area.

TRIP PLANNING AND SAFETY

While elevations in and around New Jersey can be relatively low, and the hikes detailed in this guide aren't particularly dangerous, you'll still want to be prepared. Some of the walks traverse moderately rugged terrain along rocky hills, while others lead to ponds and fields where you'll have extended periods of sun exposure and slow walking. Many places in the region have complex trail networks, some of which are unmarked. Allow extra time in case you get lost.

You will be more likely to have an enjoyable, safe hike if you plan ahead and take proper precautions. Before heading out, consider the following:

- Select a hike that everyone in your group is comfortable taking. Match the hike to the abilities of the least experienced person in the group. If anyone is uncomfortable with the weather or is tired, turn around and complete the hike another day.

- Plan to be back at the trailhead before dark. Before beginning your hike, determine a turnaround time. Don't diverge from it, even if you have not reached your intended destination.

- Check the weather. Spring and fall bring unstable air masses to the area; summer features late-afternoon thunderstorms. If you are planning a ridge or summit hike, start early so you will be off the exposed area before the afternoon hours, when thunderstorms most often strike. Temperatures at higher elevations are often significantly lower than they are in the cities and suburbs and tend to fall quickly after sunset. Storms are a potential hazard throughout the area. If rain is in the forecast, bring waterproof gear.

Bring a pack with the following items:

- Water: Two quarts per person is usually adequate, depending on the weather and the length of the trip.

- Food: Even if you are planning a one-hour hike, bring some high-energy snacks, such as nuts, dried fruit, or snack bars. Pack a lunch for longer trips.

- Map and compass: Be sure you know how to use them. A handheld Global Positioning System (GPS) device may also be helpful but is not always reliable.

- Headlamp or flashlight, with spare batteries

- Extra clothing: rain gear, wool sweater or fleece, hat, and mittens

- Sunscreen

- First-aid kit, including adhesive bandages, gauze, nonprescription painkillers, and moleskin

- Pocketknife or multitool
- Waterproof matches and a lighter
- Trash bag
- Toilet paper
- Whistle
- Insect repellent
- Sunglasses
- Cell phone: Be aware that cell phone service is unreliable in rural areas. If you are receiving a signal, use the phone only for emergencies to avoid disturbing the back-country experience for other hikers.
- Binoculars (optional)
- Camera (optional)

Wear appropriate footwear and clothing. Wool or synthetic hiking socks will keep your feet dry and help prevent blisters. Comfortable, waterproof hiking boots will provide ankle support and good traction. Avoid wearing cotton clothing, which absorbs sweat and rain, contributing to an unpleasant hiking experience. Polypropylene, fleece, silk, and wool all wick moisture away from your body and keep you warm even in wet or cold conditions. To help avoid bug bites, you may want to wear pants and a long-sleeved shirt.

When you are ahead of the rest of your hiking group, wait at all trail junctions until the others catch up. This avoids confusion and keeps people from getting separated or lost.

If you see downed wood that appears to be purposely covering a trail, it probably means the trail is closed due to overuse or hazardous conditions.

If a trail is muddy, walk through the mud or on rocks, never on tree roots or plants. Waterproof boots will keep your feet comfortable. Staying in the center of the trail will keep it from eroding into a wide hiking highway.

Leave your itinerary and the time you expect to return with someone you trust. If you see a logbook at the trailhead, be sure to sign in when you arrive and sign out when you finish your hike.

Poison ivy is always a threat when hiking. To identify the plant, look for clusters of three leaves that shine in the sun but are dull in the shade. If you do come into contact with poison ivy, wash the affected area with soap as soon as possible.

Snakes, common in many hiking areas, are cold-blooded. Their body temperature rises and falls with the ambient temperature, and they hibernate during cold months. In summer, snakes may bask on exposed rocks or on open trails, although you also may find them near stone walls, brush piles, or fallen logs. Snakes usually avoid confrontation and are not aggressive toward humans; when surprised or provoked, however, they may bite. Most snakes in New Jersey are harmless, but northern copperheads and timber rattlesnakes have venomous bites that can be painful or, in rare cases, fatal. To reduce the chance of an unpleasant encounter for both parties, use proper snake etiquette, especially when hiking around rocky areas in the warm seasons: look before taking a step or reaching in between rocks; if you see a snake, leave it alone. If you are bitten by a snake, seek medical attention as quickly as possible.

Wear blaze-orange items in hunting season. Hunting seasons vary. Check nj.gov/dep/fgw/hunting.htm.

Ticks, which can carry diseases, are common in many wooded and grassy areas in suburbs and exurbs, although uncommon on mountain ridges, and are active year-round in New Jersey. To reduce the chance of a tick bite, wear pants and a long-sleeved shirt. After you finish your hike, check for ticks on your clothes and body. The deer tick, which can carry Lyme disease, can be as small as a pinhead. Run a lint roller over your clothes. Take a shower when you get home and check for ticks again.

Mosquitoes can be common in the woods in summer and fall. Although some carry diseases, their bite is mostly annoying. As with ticks, you can reduce the chance of bites by wearing long sleeves and pants. A variety of options are available for dealing with bugs, ranging from sprays that include the active ingredient N, N-diethyl-meta-toluamide (commonly known as DEET), which potentially can cause skin or eye irritation, to more skin-friendly products. Head nets, often cheaper than a can of repellent, are useful in especially buggy conditions.

LEAVE NO TRACE

 The Appalachian Mountain Club (AMC) is a national educational partner of Leave No Trace, a nonprofit organization dedicated to promoting and inspiring responsible outdoor recreation through education, research, and partnerships. The Leave No Trace program seeks to develop wildland ethics: ways in which people think and act in the outdoors to minimize their impact on the areas they visit and to protect our natural resources for future enjoyment. Leave No Trace unites four federal land management agencies—U.S. Forest Service, National Park Service, Bureau of Land Management, and U.S. Fish and Wildlife Service—with manufacturers, outdoor retailers, user groups, educators, organizations such as AMC, and individuals.

The Leave No Trace ethic is guided by the following seven principles:

1. **Plan Ahead and Prepare.** Know the terrain and any regulations applicable to the area you're planning to visit, and be prepared for extreme weather or other emergencies. This will enhance your enjoyment and ensure that you've chosen an appropriate destination. Small groups have less impact on resources and on the experiences of other backcountry visitors.

2. **Travel and Camp on Durable Surfaces.** Travel and camp on established trails and campsites, rock, gravel, dry grasses, or snow. Good campsites are found, not made. Camp at least 200 feet from lakes and streams, and focus activities on areas where vegetation is absent. In pristine areas, disperse use to prevent the creation of campsites and trails.

3. **Dispose of Waste Properly.** Pack it in, pack it out. Inspect your camp for trash or food scraps. Deposit solid human waste in cat holes dug 6 to 8 inches deep, at least 200 feet from water, camps, and trails. Pack out toilet paper and hygiene products. To wash yourself or your dishes, carry water 200 feet from streams or lakes and use small amounts of biodegradable soap. Scatter strained dishwater.

4. **Leave What You Find.** Cultural or historical artifacts, as well as natural objects such as plants and rocks, should be left as found.

5. **Minimize Campfire Impacts.** Cook on a stove. Use established fire rings, fire pans, or mound fires. If you build a campfire, keep it small and use dead sticks found on the ground.

6. **Respect Wildlife.** Observe wildlife from a distance. Feeding animals alters their natural behavior. Protect wildlife from your food by storing rations and trash securely.

7. **Be Considerate of Other Visitors.** Be courteous, respect the quality of other visitors' backcountry experience, and let nature's sounds prevail.

AMC is a national provider of the Leave No Trace Master Educator course. AMC offers this five-day course, designed especially for outdoor professionals and land managers, as well as the shorter two-day Leave No Trace Trainer course at locations throughout the Northeast.

For Leave No Trace information and materials, contact the Leave No Trace Center for Outdoor Ethics, P.O. Box 997, Boulder, CO 80306. Phone: 800-332-4100 or 303-442-8222; fax: 303-442-8217; web: lnt.org. For information on the AMC Leave No Trace Master Educator training course schedule, see activities.outdoors.org.

1 // SKYLANDS

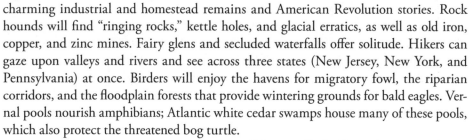

Variety is the key word for the Skylands region, a diverse corner of northwestern New Jersey that comprises five counties: Sussex, Warren, Morris, Hunterdon, and Somerset. Both serious and casual hikers will find journeys here that explore slopes, floodplains, wetlands, ravines, valleys, fields, waterfalls, streams, rugged ridges, and rock outcroppings. Most of New Jersey's section of the Appalachian Trail runs through the Skylands region, which hosts both New Jersey's highest point and some of its flattest terrain. At 1,803 feet, the challenging High Point, in High Point State Park, is the highest elevation in the state. On the other hand, parts of the mainly flat, 70-plus-mile Delaware and Raritan State Park Trail in Hunterdon and Somerset counties are universally accessible.

Not only is the terrain varied, but so is this region's character. History buffs will discover charming industrial and homestead remains and American Revolution stories. Rock hounds will find "ringing rocks," kettle holes, and glacial erratics, as well as old iron, copper, and zinc mines. Fairy glens and secluded waterfalls offer solitude. Hikers can gaze upon valleys and rivers and see across three states (New Jersey, New York, and Pennsylvania) at once. Birders will enjoy the havens for migratory fowl, the riparian corridors, and the floodplain forests that provide wintering grounds for bald eagles. Vernal pools nourish amphibians; Atlantic white cedar swamps house many of these pools, which also protect the threatened bog turtle.

Every area in this region boasts colorful wildflowers. Duke Farms has a greenhouse of cultivated orchids (see Trip 2), and the uplands harbor the small-whorled pogonia, a wild orchid. Deciduous trees blaze in autumn. Rattlesnakes, bats, bears, turtles, and small mammals live in these woods. Timber rattlesnakes especially enjoy the shale cliffs and rock formations. Although typically shy, rattlesnakes can deliver painful, but non-fatal, bites. If bitten, seek medical attention as quickly as possible.

The jewel of the Skylands is the rugged Delaware Water Gap National Recreation Area (Trip 10), hugging 37 miles of the Delaware River (parts of which are designated a Wild and

Facing page: The Skylands region hosts many brooks, streams, and waterfalls, such as this one at Van Campens Glen in the Delaware Water Gap National Recreation Area.

Scenic River by Congress) and sprawling across New Jersey and Pennsylvania. The New Jersey side of the recreation area comprises 31,000 acres and runs along the eastern edge of the Kittatinny Ridge. This section is largely shaped by the Kittatinny Ridge and Valley.

The Kittatinny Ridge and Valley spans 346,838 acres and 35 miles, from High Point State Park in the north to Worthington State Forest in the south. This wooded greenway provides refuge for black bears, bobcats, red-shouldered hawks, and bald eagles.

The verdant Highlands area of New Jersey is part of the Kittatinny Ridge and Valley and occupies about 980 square miles in the state, with major portions in the Skylands. The area is the ancestral home of the Lenni-Lenape people, many of whom live here today. Local iron ore provided munitions during the American Revolution. The Highlands Trail, when complete, will stretch 180 miles from the Delaware River in New Jersey to the Hudson River in New York, with more miles in Pennsylvania (maintained by AMC). Plans include extending the trail into Connecticut. Volunteers from the hiking clubs and organizations that make up the New Jersey Regional Trails Council maintain the trails. The Highlands Conservation Act, heavily supported by AMC, protects this valuable land. To learn more, visit outdoors.org/resources/amc-outdoors /conservation-and-climate/conserving-the-highlands.

The Sourland Mountain Preserve—90 square miles of wetlands and forest, and a major source of drinking water—is a unique ecological island of unbroken habitat. Migratory birds, rare plant species, and vernal pools for reptiles and amphibians are found here. The New Jersey Conservation Foundation and its partners—including the dedicated Sourland Conservancy, which offers excellent maps—maintain this section.

Along with the Delaware and Raritan Canal (see "From Mules to Multiuse: Today's Delaware and Raritan Canal State Park" on page 40), another notable route is Patriots' Path, covering roughly 90 miles, including side trails, primarily in Morris County. Patriots' Path links several federal, state, county, and municipal parks, along with watersheds, green open spaces, and historical sites. Some of the route is universally accessible.

The hikes in this section cover parts of all the areas described above for a diverse taste of the Skylands region. Visitors find no shortage of adventure in the fourteen state parks, one national park, three state forests, one natural wildlife refuge, one national historical park, and many natural areas—including 9-mile-long Lake Hopatcong, New Jersey's largest—that occupy more than 100,000 acres in this corner of paradise.

1 SOURLAND MOUNTAIN PRESERVE

Be amazed by huge boulders, fantastic trees that grow from rocks, a hidden stream that roars, "ringing rocks," and spotted salamanders in vernal pools.

Features 👨‍👧 🐕 💧 🌿 🎿

Location Hillsborough, NJ

Rating Moderate

Distance 6.3-mile loop

Elevation Gain 700 feet

Estimated Time 3 hours

Maps USGS Rocky Hill; somersetcountyparks.org/sites/g/files/vyhlif8281/f/uploads/sourland_mountain_preserve_map_0.pdf

GPS Coordinates 40° 28.428′ N, 74° 41.655′ W

Contact Somerset County Park Commission, 355 Milltown Road, Bridgewater, NJ 08807; somersetcountyparks.org; 908-722-1200

DIRECTIONS

Take I-80 west to Exit 43 and proceed south on I-287. Take Exit 17 and continue south on US 206 about 7.2 miles. Turn right onto Amwell Road (County Route 514; do not turn right at New Amwell Road) and proceed 2.8 miles to East Mountain Road. Turn left onto East Mountain Road and follow it 1.9 miles to the entrance to Sourland Mountain Preserve, which is on the right and has at least 50 parking spots.

TRAIL DESCRIPTION

The Sourland region of New Jersey covers 90 square miles. Despite its name, the 3,025-acre Sourland Mountain Preserve is a sweet hike, with 10 miles of blazed trails to choose from, most of which are easy to moderate. This trip explores a longer, more scenic, and challenging route: a perimeter journey through a deciduous forest. Numbered green markers denote trail intersections, and arrows indicate trail direction. (Use connecting trails, marked with a black dot in the middle of the color trail blazes, to shorten your hike, if desired.) Deciduous trees make Sourland beautiful in fall and shady in summer. Critters in vernal pools and wildflowers charm in spring, and icy rocks provide an extra challenge in winter.

Head toward the forest and the well-marked trailhead. The preserve is dog-friendly and provides "mutt mitt" dispensers to clean up after your pet. Take advantage of the chemical toilet in the parking lot, if needed, before heading out.

Start on orange-blazed Maple Flats Trail, which follows the streambed on the left. Continue straight at 0.2 mile. At a bridge with railings, veer slightly right (keeping the bridge on your left) to get onto yellow-blazed Devil's Half-Acre Trail, which heads to the boulder field. Enjoy the flat, easy stepping-stones before the trail becomes rockier as you near the boulder field. The drone of summer insects and loud chuuree of the yellow Kentucky warbler provide comforting background noise. At 0.6 mile, pass one of many connecting trails to your left, this one blazed yellow with a black dot. Keep straight and ascend, still on rocky Devil's Half-Acre Trail. Shadows of birds flit over the rocks, urging you higher in the bushy woods. Stop at the impressive boulder field. This amphitheater of diabase, or rock formed from molten magma that cooled far below the earth's surface, has

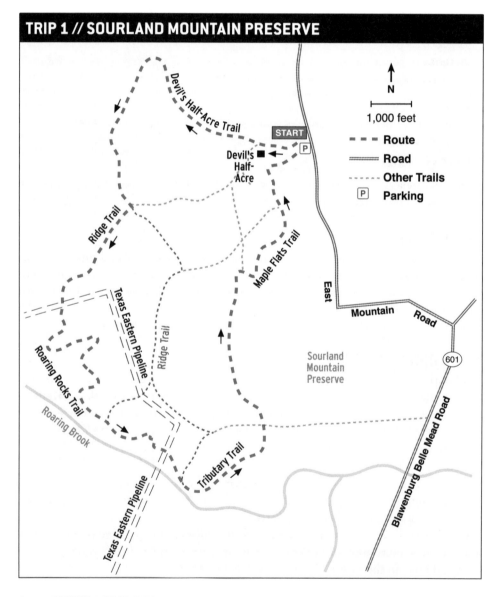

TRIP 1 // SOURLAND MOUNTAIN PRESERVE

presence. Tap on rock fragments to discover musical "ringing rocks." The trail leads to its namesake, a section of car-sized boulders known as Devil's Half-Acre, which you can go around on the right or slip through via a person-sized gap. Linger for a trail break.

Lots of footpaths exist near the rock formations, so be sure to stay on the yellow-blazed trail that cuts around the boulders on the right. If you walk through the boulders' gaps, be sure to pick up the trail. Maneuver past the tree growing in the path and keep going straight. Soon a rhinoceros-shaped rock appears, wallpapered with lichens. Marvel at the tree growing in the rock, one of several such trees in Sourland. The boulder field ends, and the walk in the woods begins.

Enjoy the narrow, leafy trail, which is cool and refreshing most months of the year. You will see fewer people now. Walk along a ridge of hardened magma, or igneous rock, with views obscured by leaves. At about 1.9 miles, follow the fork to the right at marker 3, getting onto white-blazed Tributary Trail. After only about 100 yards, turn right onto red-blazed Ridge Trail. (The trail passes through a floodplain and is often flooded and wet in rainy months.) Look for vernal, or spring-only, breeding pools for amphibians, such as frogs and salamanders. The trees cohabit with the rocks, roots splaying and grasping. If these trees could talk, they would tell some amazing survival stories. Rock-hop for 50 yards, watching out for bounding deer.

Go through a fallen metal fence. Note the many trees with interesting animal burrows. Walk through a gap in a rock wall into a grassy pipeline clearing, picking up the trail on the other side in the cooling woods. Enter another boulder field, not as dramatic as Devil's Half-Acre, populated by "sleeping" rocks—large and low to the ground, as if curled up in slumber. Lichens splash the rocks like black-and-white paint. At the fork, go left onto the red-with-black-dot-blazed connector trail. This well-maintained path gradually descends through a moderate boulder field. At the next fork, veer right to stay on the red-with-black-dot connector trail. After 3.6 miles, at marker 4, reach a rock cairn. Turn left onto blue-blazed Roaring Rocks Trail.

As you head downhill, pass the famous Roaring Rocks. Unlike most rock fields in New Jersey, this one was not left by glaciers, which did not stretch down quite this far. Instead, this formation is the result of a stream eroding the soil and smaller rock from around these large boulders, exposing them over the ages. After a heavy rain on this sparsely traveled trail, you can hear the roaring of that stream, almost invisible beneath the boulders. After walking less than 10 minutes downhill (staying right to remain with the blue blazes and away from the connector trail), watch for a fence on the left. Go through the gate. At marker 5 (4.0 miles), proceed straight (not left) onto white-blazed Tributary Trail, going away from the fence.

A pleasant boardwalk meanders over a creek bordered by soft green grasses. Cross other boardwalks, still in the shade, and reach marker 7 at 4.4 miles. Go straight to continue on white-blazed Tributary Trail and onto another boardwalk. Listen for birdsong and fussing squirrels; other wildlife includes pileated woodpeckers, bobcats, wood turtles, barred owls, Cooper's hawks, and bobolinks. At marker 10 (5.5 miles), the rock shapes once again become amazing—amateur geologists should look for hornfels, or heat-altered rocks—and give way to roots on the path. Turn right onto orange-blazed Maple Flats Trail toward the parking lot.

This fantastically twisted tree has grown over a rock in Sourland Mountain Preserve.

At 5.9 miles, pick some raspberries in the meadow and then traverse a boardwalk into the woods. Look for ghost pipes, trout lilies, and wood anemones in season. Solitude gives way to dogs and people. At the T intersection (6.1 miles), turn right to stay on orange-blazed Maple Flats Trail to a beautiful pond nestled in a meadow, complete with a bench beneath a tree. At 6.3 miles, reach the parking lot and journey's end.

DID YOU KNOW?

John Hart, a signer of the Declaration of Independence, hid in these hills during the American Revolution. The name Sourland comes from the Dutch *sauer landt*, probably because settlers found the rocky soils difficult to farm or perhaps because of the sorrel-colored dirt.

OTHER ACTIVITIES

Turn right out of the Sourland parking lot, and in about 10 minutes (within 5 miles), you will see a lavender farm and food stop. Hike the 70-mile linear Delaware and Raritan Canal (see Trip 7). The entrance is 15 minutes away (about 8 miles), where Amwell (County Route 514) and Millstone roads meet. To reach canal parking, head east on East Mountain Road and turn right on County Route 514 to Millstone Road. Look for the Stoutsburg Sourland African American Museum, at 189 Hollow Road, Skillman, NJ 08558; ssaamuseum.org.

MORE INFORMATION

No fee. Open dawn to dusk. Leashed dogs allowed. Bicycle trails are separate from hiking trails. Sourland is part of two nonprofits: D&R Greenway Land Trust and the Sourland Conservancy. The Sourland Conservancy has detailed hiking maps of the entire region at sourland.org/sourland-trail-maps, as well as the Sourland Region Hiking Atlas. The Watersheds of Sourland Mountain map is available directly from Kevin Burkman, kevinburkman@gmail.com. For information on the Sourland Conservancy, visit sourland.org. For information on D&R Greenway Land Trust, contact 609-924-4646; drgreenway.org.

2 DUKE FARMS

Take an easy stroll on the former estate of tobacco heiress Doris Duke, following mostly paved paths through woods and around lakes, fountains, an orchid greenhouse, a pet cemetery, and statuary.

Features 👫 🌊 💧 🔍 🎿 ⛱ ⛺ 🚴

Location Hillsborough, NJ

Rating Easy

Distance 4.9-mile loop

Elevation Gain 496 feet

Estimated Time 2 hours

Maps USGS Bound Brook, USGS Raritan; dukefarms.org/visiting-duke-farms/property-map; also see the Duke Farms trails app: dukefarms.org/dukefarmsapp

GPS Coordinates 40° 32.722' N, 74° 37.397' W

Contact Duke Farms, 1112 Dukes Parkway West, Hillsborough, NJ 08844; 908-722-3700; dukefarms.org

DIRECTIONS
From US 206 (Bayard Lane), turn left onto Dukes Parkway West. (If you reach County Route 583, you've gone too far.) After 0.7 mile, take the third left. In 0.1 mile, turn right. Take the first left, and the marked entrance is in about 100 feet. The parking lot has space for about 100 cars and offers car-charging stations.

TRAIL DESCRIPTION
James Buchanan (J. B.) Duke, an American tobacco grower and electric power industrialist, originally transformed these 2,742 acres of farmland and woodlot into the estate known as Duke Farms. The landscape consists of an astonishing 9 human-made lakes, 18 miles of trails, more than 45 buildings, and one of America's largest indoor botanical displays. After J. B.'s death in 1925, his fortune passed to his daughter, Doris Duke. She was an avid traveler, horticulturist, and philanthropist, doing much to protect and conserve Duke Farms, her primary residence. After her death in 1993, more than a decade passed while trustees of the Doris Duke Foundation decided how to fulfill her wish to promote conservation via Duke Farms. Eventually, in May 2012, Duke Farms opened to the public with the goal of teaching visitors to be good stewards of the environment. A variety of educational programs for children and adults, many held in the old coach barn building (restored in 2015), help fulfill this goal.

Duke Farms offers 18 miles of well-marked trails through woodlands and meadows, passing lakes, lagoons, fountains, and sculptures—all clearly explained by signs. Beginning hikers, children, and those with limited mobility will appreciate the tram stops and paved paths. Numbered markers indicate all intersections. The farm is most

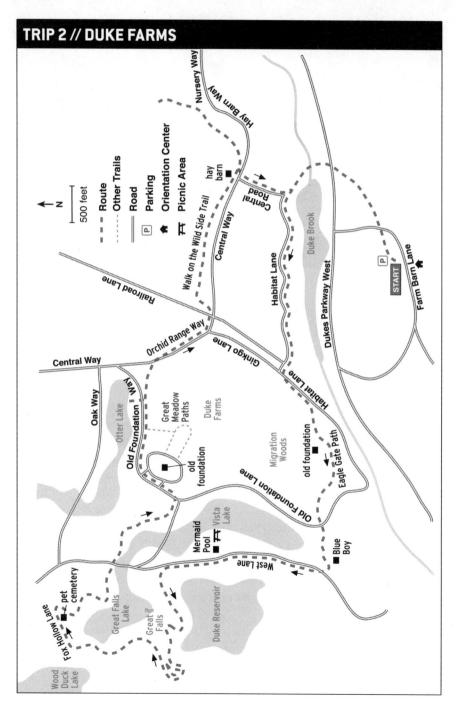

TRIP 2 // DUKE FARMS

The hay barn on Duke's property burned down in 1915. It was later converted to a statuary garden by Doris Duke, with the original walls still standing.

crowded and flower-filled from April through September but is open all year. In winter snow, look for tracks of deer, rabbit, fox, coyote, bobcat, mink, skunk, and badger. In fall, the blazing colors of the trees (maple, oak, beech, black cherry, and more) reflect in the lakes and other waters.

From the parking lot, make your way to the Orientation Center. Inside, grab a map, watch a short film, and visit the educational displays on conservation and preservation. The building itself is powered by a 2.6-acre solar array and geothermal wells. The Farm Barn Café offers locally sourced organic meals. With a driver's license for collateral, borrow an Eco-Kit: binoculars, compass, field guide, and nature journal for recording notes.

This hike goes through the middle of the park and Migration Woods, past five lakes, the site of an unfinished mansion at Old Foundation, the Orchid Range, and other interesting sites, with scads of butterflies and dragonflies in season, plus bunnies and wood ducks. Look out for trams as you walk.

To start, take the pedestrian path from the right of the Orientation Center, turn right at the tram stop and sunflower field, pass the bluebird houses on the right, and head to marker 7. There, at the South Gate entrance, a guard will stop traffic so you can cross the road into the park.

Pause to admire Duke Brook—a minor tributary of the Raritan River—and the elegant falls. Watch for a great blue heron or a great egret. Continue on paved and level Habitat Lane. Note the raspberries, black-eyed Susans, and cell phone "dial and listen" stops that provide audio information about the plants, landscaping, and historical buildings. Take a break on one of the stone benches and admire the enormous trees.

Turn right onto Woods Lane, a gravel path, and then immediately left onto Eagle Gate, a path over a charming stone bridge. After Eagle Gate, get back onto paved Habitat Lane at the darling Blue Boy (1.2 miles), a statue of a lad who eternally examines his bare foot for an offending stone or thorn. Turn right onto West Lane toward Duke Reservoir on the left, which used to gravity-feed the farm's seven-lake system via a canal above the Raritan River. Today, new wells supply the water. (Lake elevations are listed on the hiking map.) Wheelchair-accessible bathrooms are on the left. Tables next to Mermaid Pool, a former swimming pool, make a perfect picnic spot where you can admire the stone balustrade that runs the length of the pool and lake (1.5 miles). Stone steps invite you down to a meadow to explore bird habitats, waterfalls, and flowers.

When you are ready, turn left onto Fox Hollow (1.6 miles), a dirt/gravel path through woods, to Great Falls Lake with a terraced, human-made 30-foot waterfall that "turns on" at certain hours in season (check with staff). Stroll flat ground to Wood Duck Lake on the left, complete with Canada geese and wood ducks, and a solar panel on the right (2.1 miles).

Climb a gentle, tree-lined grade to a large ravine on the right, where an unannounced pet cemetery surprises atop a knoll. Here are the grave markers for about 60 birds, dogs, and cats—mostly Doris Duke's pets, including a camel named Baby who died on September 13, 1994.

Continue downhill, passing through a stone tunnel with a resounding echo, until you reach marker 18 (2.7 miles). Turn left onto paved Old Foundation Way, where another surprise awaits: a deep pit with the jutting footers of an unbuilt mansion. Take a minute to read the explanation on a nearby plaque.

Head down into the woods and toward the gazebo on the left. Follow the gravel path a few hundred yards left of the gazebo to view a giant clamshell sculpture, a statue of a little boy, and educational signs about orchids of the Northern Piedmont Range. At marker 21 (3.0 miles), you can turn right to take a side trip onto Great Meadow Path and explore the wildflowers and native grasses of Great Meadow, once a high-maintenance lawn.

On the way back from Great Meadow, turn right at marker 22 onto Orchid Range Way (3.1 miles) to explore the Orchard Range, a series of greenhouses with mind-boggling arrays of tropical and subtropical orchids. At the end, a 9/11 memorial sits beneath a tree on the left.

From Orchid Range Way, turn right onto paved Central Way toward the Hay Barn and then turn left onto crushed-stone Railroad Path. After just 250 feet, turn right onto crushed-stone Walk on the Wild Side Trail (look for a sign labeled "trail" with an arrow), where a narrow spur path leads to Research Way, which travels through an ecotone field (a transitional area between two communities of plants and animals) and past the Farnese Bull statue (3.7 miles). Turn left past the statue onto paved Hay Barn Way to visit a statue garden ensconced in the shored-up stone ruins of the old hay barn (3.8 miles). Past the statue garden, a tiny dirt path on the left leads to Research Woods, a gated enclosure you can explore, if you'd like. Double back to Hay Barn Way and go left past the wheelchair-accessible Sugar Shack on the right and then left onto paved Nursery Way, past restrooms on the left.

You can keep going straight and explore the upper part of the farm or, at the statue of Athena (4.2 miles), double back through the statue garden and turn left onto Central Way toward the South Gate entrance, passing Duke Brook on the right. If it's after 6 P.M., the guard will be off duty, so push the button on the left of the gate to release it and walk past the sunflower field back to your car.

DID YOU KNOW?

A seasonal weekly farm-to-table market on the premises offers cheeses, wines, meats, vegetables, fruits, and more. The farm also has bike shares at selected locations. Obtain a geocaching trail brochure at the front desk of the Orientation Center.

OTHER ACTIVITIES

Duke Island Park in nearby Bridgewater is part of the Raritan River Greenway and features trails and summer concerts. See the Wallace House in Somerville, which served as George Washington's headquarters from 1778 to 1779. Visit the Sri Venkateswara Temple in Bridgewater (check venkateswaratemple.org for hours), which has a cafeteria. US 206 also offers many dining options.

MORE INFORMATION

Hours of operation are generally 8:30 A.M. to 6:00 P.M., Tuesday through Saturday. The free Accessibility Shuttle is available, weather permitting, between the Orientation Center and the Orchid Range for those with limited mobility, but reservations are required; call 908-566-8865. Two-hour bike rentals are available at a bike tent 0.75 mile from the Orientation Center ($8 for adults and $5 for children younger than 18; ID required). An advance parking pass (free) is required for Saturdays from April to October. The parking lot closes when full, which often happens on weekends in nice weather, so check X (formerly known as Twitter) @dukefarmsnj or call 908-722-3700 for updates. For information on workshops and festivals, visit dukefarms.org.

3 ROCKHOPPER AND DRY RUN CREEK TRAILS

Walk the woodsy road used by the Continental Army under General George Washington en route to battle at Monmouth and get a boulder-hopping cardio workout.

Features

Location Lambertville, NJ

Rating Moderate to Strenuous

Distance 9.3-mile loop

Elevation Gain 1,000 feet

Estimated Time 4.5 hours

Maps USGS Bound Brook; sourland.org/maps; njtrails.org/trail; Sourland Region Hiking Atlas

GPS Coordinates 40° 21.831′ N, 74° 56.786′ W

Contact Dry Run Creek Trail is maintained by D&R Greenway Land Trust, One Preservation Place, Princeton, NJ 08540; 609-924-4646; drgreenway.org

DIRECTIONS

From I-95, take the NJ 29 exit and follow NJ 29 about 10 miles. At a light, turn left onto NJ 179. In 0.2 mile, turn left at unused railroad tracks before a bridge to Pennsylvania. Drive through the parking lot of Lambertville Station Restaurant and Inn to the Delaware and Raritan Canal (D&R Canal) lot behind the inn, with parking for about 25 cars.

TRAIL DESCRIPTION

A 10-minute walk through historic Lambertville takes you to the solitude of Rockhopper Trail and onto an old road used by soldiers during the American Revolution. Keep going and in 3.2 miles, cross County Route 518 to pick up Dry Run Creek Trail on the other side. Both trails are blazed blue and are in the Sourland region, a 90-square-mile section of contiguous forest that is an important breeding ground for migratory songbirds and home to rare and endangered plant species. This hike includes a break at Howell Living History Farm. The trail markings are a little tricky to spot sometimes, but if you don't see a blaze for a while, simply backtrack. Rockhopper Trail undulates, and Dry Run Creek Trail is hilly. It's a choice route for summer due to the heavy, almost continuous shade of oaks, beeches, and sycamores; the length of the combined trails makes this a great cardio workout.

From the D&R Canal parking lot overlooking the Delaware River, walk past Lambertville Station Restaurant and Inn, turn right to cross the old railroad tracks behind Lambertville Station Restaurant (separate from Lambertville Station Restaurant and Inn), and take the small bridge over the D&R Canal to Ferry Street (0.2 mile), stopping to admire the adorable houses. Cross NJ 29 and then NJ 179 (be careful on this busy road), and turn left onto Quarry Street (0.4 mile). Here, the charming houses on the right face a massive rock wall. Pass a stream, some apartment buildings, and woods on the right. Then turn right onto Stymiest Road–Rock Road (0.8 mile), cross a one-lane bridge, and veer left uphill onto a shaded gravel road. Climb the gravel road, bearing to the right. Look carefully for the next left—a house is at the intersection—and for the orange and blue trailhead markers at the edge of the woods. Take the orange-blazed trail, which soon meets blue-blazed Rockhopper Trail. Pause a moment to consider that many people think this is a historic colonial road used by General George Washington's Continental Army during the American Revolution on a march to Monmouth to do battle in 1778. The road was then called Bungtown Road because alcoholic spirits,

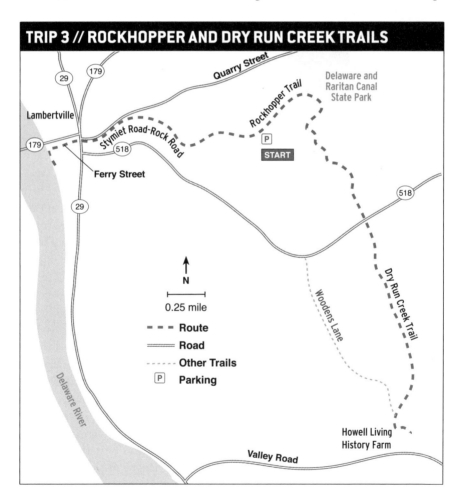

TRIP 3 // ROCKHOPPER AND DRY RUN CREEK TRAILS

AMC's Delaware Valley Chapter explores these historic woods.

contained by a bung (or cork) in the barrel, were trudged to New York on this route. Toast the past with a drink of water.

Today, the level dirt path leads into a welcoming mature hardwood forest and over several wooden footbridges. Briefly pop out into an open field with wildflowers on your left and walk under a set of power lines. The trail crosses the dirt road just after the power lines, but do not follow the orange trail on the other side of the power-line cut, as it's flooded out. Instead, turn right here and follow the power lines, keeping an eye on the blue blazes on the left side of the woods. About 500 feet up the power lines, Rockhopper Trail turns left to enter the woods again and becomes rooty and rocky, living up to its name. This traprock, or blue-gray diabase, was used in the past for railroad ballast, concrete aggregate, and gravel roadbeds. Note the scattered shallow pits where stone was quarried in the nineteenth century. At the next clearing, the blue-blazed trail meets back up with the orange-blazed trail; bear right to follow the blue blazes.

Trees with interesting shapes enchant in this green oasis, which feels miles away from Lambertville and the twenty-first century. To the right are the Lambertville Lower and Middle reservoirs; you can't see them in summer when trees are in full leaf. Cross a wooden footbridge and pass an open field on the left. Go right at the fork and watch for blue trail markers in a few yards. A lovely old stone bridge and stream are to the right (2.2 miles) before another footbridge. The rocks are in earnest now and will indeed have you hopping! Be careful in wet weather. Rockhopper Trail stays in the cool woods as it goes through a low stone wall that dates back to 1792. Cross a stream and then a boulder field. At the fork, keep straight to remain on the blue-blazed route (2.6 miles). Pass houses on the right as the path widens and becomes gravel. Note the picturesque old barn and group of buildings on the left—a nice spot for a photograph. The smell of crushed wild onions carries on the gentle breeze. Cross paved County Route 518 (Brunswick Pike) and enter the woods (3.2 miles).

You are now on blue-blazed Dry Run Creek Trail in the D&R Greenway Land Trust Nature Preserve. (The creek itself is a tributary of Moore's Creek.) Formed in 1989, the D&R trust has permanently preserved more than 22,000 acres of watershed, farm, and canal lands.

The rocks magically disappear as you take the narrow dirt path into the dappled shade, crossing one (3.6 miles) of several wooden footbridges over dry streambeds, which can be very wet in spring. The route winds downhill, past a large, dry creek bed to the left. A bench marks the beginning of some wooden steps that lead down through a low, well-constructed rock wall. The woods have a soft, hushed quality as you descend, smelling the sweet, hot green. Turn left onto paved Valley Road (4.4 miles) at a large trail signage area; it leads to Howell Living History Farm for a fantastic picnic-table lunch stop under giant trees. Flush toilets are available inside the visitor center, as well as honey, syrup, crafts, and more. Maintained by the Mercer County Park Commission, the farm is an educational facility that preserves and interprets farm life from about 1890 to 1910. Pigs, sheep, chickens, and oxen roam the grounds and are part of many educational programs for children. The farm also connects to the trails at Baldpate Mountain, for hikers who want to explore.

Throw away your trash and go back to the trail signage area. Enter the woods at the blue blaze, cross County Route 518 (6.2 miles), and stay on the blue-blazed trail. (Be careful not to take the private drive to the left.) Retrace your steps: blue-blazed trail to stone bridge (7.2 miles) to Quarry Street (8.7 miles). Carefully cross NJ 179 to Ferry Street. Traverse the bridge over the canal and the railroad tracks. Turn left to go behind Lambertville Station Restaurant, past the separate Lambertville Station Restaurant and Inn, and back to the D&R parking lot.

DID YOU KNOW?

The Road Along the Rocks 1758: "The Bungtown Road," second edition, by John P. and Barbara J. Hencheck (independently published, 2016), is a book about the historical significance of this route (now part of Rockhopper Trail).

OTHER ACTIVITIES

Lambertville is rich in galleries, antique shops, and restaurants. Walk a section of the approximately 70-mile D&R Canal that runs through town. The museum at nearby Monmouth Battlefield State Park, on the site of one of the largest battles of the American Revolution, is well worth visiting. If you'd care to drop in on another state, walk across the Delaware River via the car/pedestrian bridge to vibrant New Hope, Pennsylvania. Be sure to look for turtles sunning themselves on the river rocks below.

MORE INFORMATION

Rockhopper Trail's canopy of white oaks might date to the 1700s. In spring, the forest floor dances with rue anemone, tiny orchids, ferns, bloodroot, toothwort, and jack-in-the-pulpit. Take a peek up a snag (dead tree) and look for large, shelflike polypore mushrooms. Various fungi sprinkle the woods, growing on dead wood and decaying plant matter.

FUNGI PUT THE FUN IN HIKING: MUSHROOMS

Mushrooms are beautiful, prolific, tasty, and even medicinal. Foraging for the fruiting bodies (the part you see) of these fabulous fungi is entrenched in popular culture. And New Jersey's woods produce many of the commonly recognized edible and medicinal mushrooms in the United States.

Top culinary mushrooms include morel, chanterelle, oyster, black trumpet, and chicken of the woods. Prized medicinal mushrooms are lion's mane, turkey tail, shiitake, chaga, and reishi. Mushrooms generally thrive in moist, shady conditions and can appear almost magically after a hard rain.

Mushroom growth can vary based on local weather conditions, but some general rules apply. Morels and shiitakes shoot up in spring and grow well in areas recently ravished by forest fires. Chicken of the woods pops up in summer, while lion's mane loves fall. Winter mushrooms include witch's butter and turkey tail. Reishi and chaga grow all year long.

While hiking in spring, look for beige, brown, or black morels with their honeycomb-pitted skin on the forest floor near hardwoods such as ash and tulip popular. Keep an eye out also for curving, umbrella-shaped clusters of shiitakes on hardwood logs. In summer, search oak trees for overlapping rosettes of velvety chicken of the woods. Lion's mane, which thrives in fall, resembles a white beard and grows on trunks, logs, and stumps of decaying hardwoods. In winter, spy bright yellow witch's butter growing in gelatinous clusters on hardwood logs, branches, and stumps, especially

Witch's butter fungus, also called yellow brain fungus, grows on dead wood.

beech and oak. Turkey tail grows in multicolored, fan-shaped rows on a variety of woods. Chaga, a hard, black fungus, primarily grows on beeches.

Interest in medicinal fungi is mushrooming. Chaga, turkey tail, and reishi in particular have been the subjects of extensive research and seem to help support immune function. Reishi, known by the Chinese as the "mushroom of immortality," is an antiviral, an antioxidant, and a blood pressure modulator. Chaga is being investigated for anticancer properties and is known as a chelator—or reducer—of heavy metals in the body. Studies have shown that turkey tail has immune-boosting properties and suggest future hopes for use in fighting cancer.

Never eat a mushroom you can't positively identify as they can be highly poisonous, even deadly. And never forage on private land without asking first. Generally speaking, mushroom foraging is prohibited in New Jersey on state park lands and on property owned, managed, and/or under the control of the Division of Fish and Wildlife. Some locations have different rules, so check before you seek. A knife and paper bag are usually sufficient for gathering. Plastic bags tend to create moisture that may spoil the mushroom.

Buy a book about mushrooms and learn how to identify different species. Popular choices are *The Fungal Pharmacy* (North Atlantic Books, 2011) and *Medicinal Mushrooms: The Human Clinical Trials* (independently published, 2020), both by Robert Dale Rogers; and *Mushrooms of the Northeastern United States and Eastern Canada* (Timber Press, 2017), by Timothy J. Baroni. If your appetite is whetted, consider joining a mushroom foraging group, either a formal or an informal one. The New Jersey Mycological Association is a good place to start: njmyco.org. Experiment with online mushroom apps to identify the results of your searches.

Hiking is a great way to find mushrooms. But if you'd like to raise them yourself, you can learn how to plug logs: drill 1.5-inch holes in freshly cut wood, plug with mushroom spawn (available commercially or from your friendly local mushroom dealer), seal with wax (use cheese wax or paraffin mixed with a little oil to keep it pliable), water well, and watch your mushrooms sprout and grow for years. Cultivating mushrooms in bags, like many commercial growers do, is also an option; you can buy kits online.

Fungi appeared on land at least 440 million years ago. Experts estimate that a minimum of 611,000 species of mushrooms exist. Start your search with the common, prevalent mushrooms found in New Jersey and enjoy the delicious, healthy journey.

4 MORRISTOWN NATIONAL HISTORICAL PARK: JOCKEY HOLLOW SECTION

Maximize the miles with an aerobic hike through the heart of Jockey Hollow over rolling terrain, and experience American Revolution–era history as you visit reconstructed soldier huts.

Features 🐕 💧 🍃 🏃 ❄️ ⛺ ⬆️

Location Morristown, NJ

Rating Strenuous

Distance 10-mile loop

Elevation Gain 1,250 feet

Estimated Time 5–6 hours

Maps USGS Mendham; nps.gov/morr/planyourvisit/maps.htm

GPS Coordinates 40° 45.691′ N, 74° 32.561′ W

Contact Jockey Hollow Visitor Center, 586 Tempe Wick Road, Morristown, NJ 07960; 973-543-4030; nps.gov/morr/index.htm

DIRECTIONS

From I-287, take Exit 30B (Bernardsville exit). Turn right at the top of the ramp. At the traffic light, turn right onto US 202 North. At the next traffic light, turn left onto Tempe Wick Road (County Route 646). Continue on Tempe Wick Road for about 1.5 miles. The entrance to Jockey Hollow is on the right and has a large parking lot.

TRAIL DESCRIPTION

The 27 miles of trails on what used to be the 1,400-acre Wick Farm are easy to follow if you keep a sharp lookout (which may be difficult with the wonderfully distracting historical markers). The 10-mile meander on the yellow, white, green, blue, and red trails gets the most distance possible out of the park while covering the historical highlights. Some trails overlap with Patriots' Path, a cross-county trail system (morrisparks.net). On sunny winter days, enjoy clear, excellent views of New York City (Empire State Building and One World Trade Center). Spring and summer bring out the water plants, wildflowers, and vernal-pool amphibians.

Stop at the Jockey Hollow Visitor Center and pick up a map for $1 (or download one beforehand). Be sure to view the exhibits and short film about the Continental Army's winter encampments in Jockey Hollow, and check out the Junior Ranger Program for kids. When finished, walk out the back of the visitor center and follow the paved path toward Wick House. Pass the house and walk through the parking lot, past a red barn on your right, toward a beautiful fenced flower garden. Pass the first trail sign for yellow-blazed Soldier Hut Trail (the wrong direction) and walk straight down the mown trail to where the parking lot rejoins the park road. Just past this point, veer right into the woods on yellow-blazed Soldier Hut Trail. The pretty path with tall grasses slopes down crunchy gravel.

Keep straight, staying on Soldier Hut Trail; enter a field and cross paved Grand Parade Road (1.0 mile). Pass a sign for the Pennsylvania Line Encampment site, where the First and Second Pennsylvania brigades were the backbone of Washington's army under General Anthony Wayne.

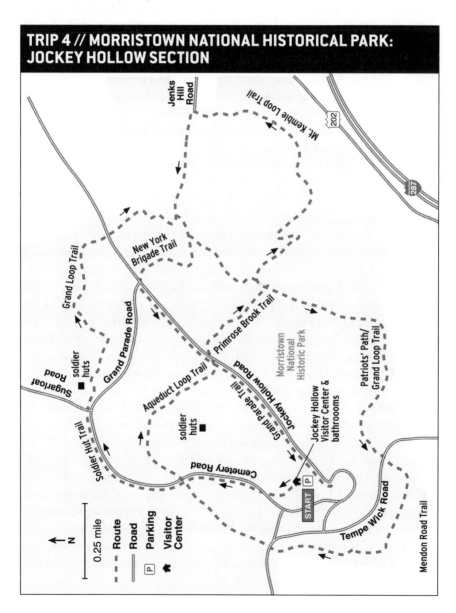

TRIP 4 // MORRISTOWN NATIONAL HISTORICAL PARK: JOCKEY HOLLOW SECTION

Soon reach the replicas of the soldiers' huts (1.1 miles). The original huts, built of timber from Wick Farm, were 14 by 16 feet and 6.5 feet high. They each housed up to twelve soldiers. Markers along the trail relay more information about the historical aspects of this hike.

Continuing on Soldier Hut Trail, bear right toward white-blazed Grand Loop Trail and Grand Parade Road. When you reach this junction, turn left toward white-blazed Grand Loop Trail (1.3 miles). Follow a dirt path as it wanders through the woods. At marker 8, turn right onto the official Grand Loop Trail (1.5 miles), which descends and turns rocky before leveling off and widening into a lovely, small, green valley. After a slight ascent to a hilltop and a "Park Open" sign, cross paved Jockey Hollow Road (1.9 miles), heading into the woods again at a metal gate.

Go right at the junction onto the blue-and-white-blazed trail, where Grand Loop Trail temporarily merges with New York Brigade Trail (2.3 miles). (Do not go straight onto blue-blazed Mt. Kemble Loop Trail at marker 10.) Here, the trail widens; watch for roots and rocks. Pass a beautiful, calm pond on the left, with a bench for rest and contemplation. Turn left at the next junction onto white-blazed Grand Loop Trail (2.4 miles), which follows a sweet, meandering stream before widening and sloping down. Stay on Grand Loop Trail at marker 21 and cross a pretty footbridge over another stream. Cross two more footbridges and go uphill.

At the trail junction with Patriots' Path (2.8 miles), go straight. Watch your footing on this downward, rooty path. Do not take the feeder trail to the left after the stepping-stones. Keep straight as Patriots' Path/Grand Loop Trail begins to ascend, passing the sign for the Connecticut Line Encampment Site on the right. Stay on the white-blazed trail at marker 55. (It overlaps with Patriots' Path during some of this section.)

Descend a rocky hill and cross paved Mendham Road Trail (3.7 miles, not on map) to marker 56. Still on Grand Loop Trail, walk carefully across Tempe Wick Road (3.8 miles). Continue on a footbridge over a trickling stream at marker 57. At the trail junction, go straight on Grand Loop Trail at marker 58. (Do not take New Jersey Brigade Trail/Patriots' Path; 4.0 miles.) The rocky trail leads up and narrows; bushes brush your thighs. At marker 59, the trail splits. Head toward a "Green Acres" sign and the picnic tables at the Boy Scout camp (4.7 miles), where you can pause for lunch or snacks. After a break, return to the woods and turn left to continue on lightly graveled Grand Loop Trail. Go downhill, pass an iron gate, and cross Tempe Wick Road (5.0 miles).

Take the path on the left into the woods, past old split rail fences. Continue straight up Grand Loop Trail (or go to the right and take the footpath back to the visitor center). The trail levels off for a delightful walk on a ridgeline and then slopes downhill into loose rocks and roots, so watch your step. At marker 3, take the fork to the right onto green-blazed Aqueduct Loop Trail (5.5 miles). Cross small paved Cemetery Road.

Go downhill on loose pebbles as the path widens. Pretty rocks are scattered on the rise to the right. Pass an area enclosed by a 6-foot wire fence and keep winding through a beautiful forest. At the trail junction, turn right at marker 53 and continue on a soft, flat dirt path with lacy overhanging trees. Boulders in the streambed on the left look like bowling balls. Cattails wave in the marsh. Stay on the trail, which veers to the left before an iron gate. Cross a bridge over a brook and follow the "To Trail Center" sign at marker 34.

Come out at a paved parking lot with the Aqueduct Loop Trail sign on the left (6.2 miles). Take a moment to read a marker about Nathanael Greene, George Washington's quartermaster. Then turn left (in the opposite direction of the one-way sign) onto paved Jockey Hollow Road (no blaze) at the Trail Center kiosk. Turn right onto red-blazed Primrose Brook Trail, which parallels Patriots' Path, at marker 28. The trail descends and becomes narrow, winding, and very rooty in the deep woods. Use a series of footbridges and stepping-stones to cross a meandering stream. (*Note*: The water can get high in the rainy season.)

Turn left at marker 30 onto white-blazed, wide gravel Grand Loop Trail (6.6 miles). Turn right at marker 20 onto blue-blazed Mt. Kemble Loop Trail (6.7 miles). At a junction atop the incline, go left at marker 19 into the woods. Stay right at marker 17, still on well-worn Mt. Kemble Loop Trail.

Vista alert: Stop at the sign at Jockey Hollow View and admire the New York City skyline and the Watchung Mountains, a natural defense. Read the marker about Stark's Brigade Encampment. Back on blue-blazed Mt. Kemble Loop Trail, pass another iron gate and a house to the right. At marker 14, go left (8.0 miles), still on Mt. Kemble Loop Trail (blazed aqua here). Go right at a fork and head down a rocky dark-blue-blazed trail (still Mt. Kemble Loop Trail); then turn left (mostly straight) onto a slightly graveled

Replicas show the cramped quarters in which Continental Army soldiers lived, twelve to a hut, during the American Revolution. By 1780, there were 1,200 huts in Jockey Hollow.

path. At a culvert and marker 10, take the light-blue-and-white-blazed unnamed trail to the left (8.4 miles), where Grand Loop and New York Brigade trails merge.

You'll revisit the pond and bench from earlier. At marker 22, take light-blue-blazed New York Brigade Trail on the right (8.5 miles), going past a beautiful grassy meadow, to the restrooms (8.8 miles). At marker 23, read about the New York Brigade Encampment.

Head toward marker 24 and then 26, following signs to orange-blazed Grand Parade Trail (not Grand Loop Trail) and Wick House. It's a straight shot and only 1.2 miles to the parking lot where you started.

DID YOU KNOW?

Just minutes south of the park is Scherman Hoffman Wildlife Sanctuary, a New Jersey Audubon sanctuary, on 11 Hardscrabble Road in Bernardsville. Fort Nonsense in downtown Morristown provides great views of the Watchung Mountains without any of the effort. Bat lovers can travel 20 miles north to a hibernaculum to see more than 26,000 of these furry mammals, at the Hibernia Mine in Wildcat Ridge Wildlife Management Area in the Highlands region. Entrance to the hibernaculum itself is prohibited. (Take I-80 to Exit 37. Go north on County Route 513 toward Hibernia for 2.8 miles; turn right on Sunnyside Road. The parking area is 0.1 mile on the left.)

OTHER ACTIVITIES

See Cross Estate Gardens at the south end of the park. Visit Washington's Headquarters Museum and the Ford Mansion at the east end of the park (30 Washington Place). From here, walk part of the Washington–Rochambeau National Historic Trail, "only" 680 miles long from Massachusetts through Virginia. Morristown has a variety of shops and restaurants. Other attractions include the Frelinghuysen Arboretum, New Jersey's largest horticultural park (353 East Hanover Avenue), and Historic Speedwell, a National Historic Landmark musuem, known as the "birthplace of the telegraph." The Factory Building at this site has three floors of exhibits devoted to the development of Samuel F. B. Morse's telegraph, which was first successfully demonstrated here in 1838. (333 Speedwell Avenue).

MORE INFORMATION

Park grounds are open from 8 A.M. to sunset. Building hours and days of operation vary seasonally. The Jockey Hollow Visitor Center is open Thursday through Sunday, 10 A.M. to 4 P.M., and is accessible to wheelchair users. The 1.5-mile self-guided Aqueduct Loop Trail traces the history of New Jersey's first water company, built in 1799.

5 HIGH POINT STATE PARK: MONUMENT TRAIL TO APPALACHIAN TRAIL

This challenging trek offers panoramic views of three states from the highest point in New Jersey. Spot hawks and grouse in the world's highest Atlantic white cedar swamp.

Features

Location Sussex, NJ

Rating Strenuous

Distance 7.9-mile loop

Elevation Gain 1,250 feet

Estimated Time 5 hours

Maps USGS Port Jervis South; nj.gov/dep/parksandforests/maps/highpoint-trail.pdf; Delaware Water Gap & Kittatinny Trails, Map 123, eighth edition, New York–New Jersey Trail Conference

GPS Coordinates 41° 18.176′ N, 74° 40.051′ W

Contact High Point State Park, 1480 Route 23, Sussex, NJ 07461; 973-875-4800; state.nj.us/dep/parksandforests/parks/highpoint.html. Friends of High Point State Park, P.O. Box 817, Wantage, NJ 07461; friendsofhighpointstatepark.org

DIRECTIONS
From all points southeast in New Jersey, take I-80 West to NJ 15 North, and then take NJ 15 North to County Route 565 (Ross Corner Sussex Road). Take County Route 565 to NJ 23, just north of Colesville. Park in the Appalachian Trail parking lot, marked with a brown sign, on the left. It holds about twenty cars.

TRAIL DESCRIPTION
Get ready to summit New Jersey's 1,803-foot-high point, appropriately named High Point. Climb even higher on the 220-foot High Point Monument (small fee may apply), which boasts spectacular vistas of the Catskill Mountains to the north, the Pocono Mountains to the west, and the Wallkill River valley to the southeast. Thirteen marked trails cover more than 50 miles, over ridges, fields, and wetlands, through forests and an Atlantic white cedar swamp. Stop by the park office (just 1.2 miles north of the parking lot) and pick up a free map. You'll hike part of the Shawangunk Ridge Trail (SRT), named after the rugged, rocky range—also called "the Gunks"—that extends north to New York and south to Virginia. The Appalachian Trail (AT) runs for 9.0 miles through the park, 884 miles from the AT's northern terminus at Katahdin in

Maine and 1,330 miles from its southern terminus at Springer Mountain in Georgia. The park is spectacular in fall with blazing colors from oak, hickory, and birch trees; the cedar swamp is peaceful in winter. Enjoy blooming rhododendrons in spring and blueberries and huckleberries in summer.

Directly from the parking lot, take the blue-blazed connector path at the trail sign. The path becomes rooty and rocky as it progresses. After a turn to the right, it becomes Iris Trail (red dot on white background; 0.2 mile) and slopes up gradually. This dirt path was originally built to be a bridle trail by the Civilian Conservation Corps between 1933 and 1941.

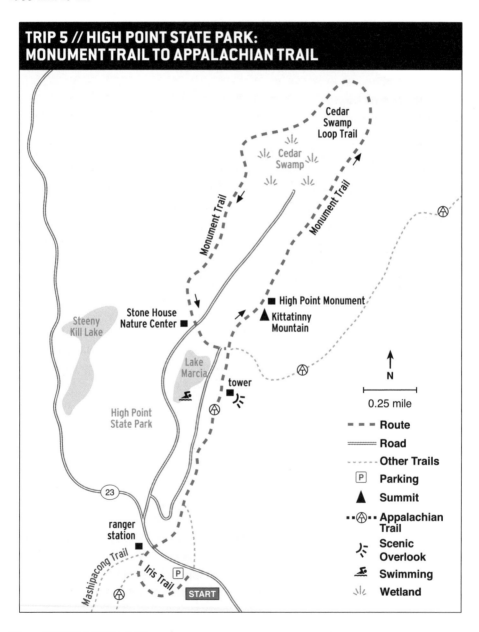

TRIP 5 // HIGH POINT STATE PARK: MONUMENT TRAIL TO APPALACHIAN TRAIL

Cedar Swamp Loop Trail

Cedar Swamp

Monument Trail

Monument Trail

High Point Monument

Stone House Nature Center ■

▲ Kittatinny Mountain

Steeny Kill Lake

Lake Marcia

tower

High Point State Park

N

0.25 mile

- - - Route

Road

Other Trails

P Parking

▲ Summit

Appalachian Trail

Scenic Overlook

Swimming

Wetland

23

ranger station

Mashipacong Trail

Iris Trail

P

START

At the four-way intersection, turn right onto the white-blazed Appalachian Trail (0.4 mile). (Do not go straight onto yellow-blazed Mashipacong Trail.) At the park office and kiosk, veer right into the woods, staying on the AT. Cross NJ 23 (0.6 mile) and stay on the AT northbound—the sign is apparent across the road. Traverse a field and enter the woods at the AT sign.

Gradually ascend rocky terrain before entering a shady grove of tree tunnels. Big rocks give way to smaller rocks before you pop out on the ridgeline into open sky and welcome breezes. Enjoy the scene and then descend about 1 mile to the raised observation platform (1.6 miles) with a 360-degree view of High Point Monument and the Delaware Water Gap to the south, the Catskills to the north, and Pennsylvania and Lake Marcia to the west.

Head through the woods toward the obvious monument by curving left onto red-and-green-blazed Monument Trail, which overlaps just a bit with blue-blazed SRT. Cross a boulder field and a park road (1.8 miles; watch for cars) and then head into the woods again, still on Monument Trail. Go right at a fork, climbing steeply uphill over large wooden water bars to reach the monument and the spacious parking lot with wheelchair ramp (1.9 miles).

Visit the small museum to learn about the Kuser family—who donated the land—and about the formation of the Kittatinny Mountains. The museum offers coin-operated observation binoculars, a snack bar, and bathrooms.

Walk away from the monument to the end of the parking lot, where Monument Trail descends into the woods and goes up and down past beautiful oak trees, traverses challenging rocks, passes a scenic overlook to the right, and then steadily descends. At a trail junction, go straight after the footbridge (3.1 miles), still on Monument Trail, which levels off briefly. Turn left at the next junction (3.6 miles) for a detour onto the magnificent but unmarked 1.2-mile Cedar Swamp Trail loop. (*Note*: Protect against chiggers—tiny red mites that bite and cause skin irritation—here in warm weather by wearing long pants, a long-sleeved shirt, socks and boots, and insect repellent all over, including the entire foot.) Very soon, a sign reassures that you are on Cedar Swamp Trail, which is unblazed. Turn right at a bench to continue on Cedar Swamp Trail. At an elevation of 1,500 feet, the Atlantic white cedar swamp here is believed to be the highest in the world.

High Point State Park's website offers the Cedar Swamp Trail Guide, with eleven pages of more in-depth information on the Atlantic cedar swamp. The trail also has nature signs to help visitors enjoy the flat dirt path and rich air, dense with green particles from hay-scented and bracken ferns, spongy sphagnum mosses, highbush blueberries, spruces, black gums, hemlocks, black birches, red oaks, carnivorous plants, and irises and callas (in spring). The rhododendrons are tall and dense.

Turn left at the stone wall with an embedded metal plaque that reads "John Dryden Kuser Memorial Natural Area" to continue on unmarked Cedar Swamp Trail (4.3 miles). Turn left at the next junction, still on Cedar Swamp Trail (4.6 miles), and cross a magnificent boardwalk over a bog.

Back at the bench, turn right onto the SRT (4.8 miles), walk for about 100 yards, and then go left at a junction to return to red-and-green-blazed Monument Trail. Ascend,

High Point Monument, as seen from the observation platform on the AT.

passing a turnoff on the right for the SRT, and travel through gorgeous woods before you pop out on a ridge for a pleasant view of Port Jervis (New York) and Pennsylvania on the right.

Continuing to ascend, pass a boulder field on the right and cross a footbridge, where you can hear, but not see, the thundering falls to the left. Keep straight (do not take the blue-blazed trail to the right). Curving stone stairs lead to the top of the hill and a large "resting rock," shaped to the contours of a human back.

Turn left onto the paved road at the Stone House Nature Center (6.0 miles) toward Lake Marcia, a pretty spring-fed glacial pond at 1,570 feet, where you can swim in summer months when a lifeguard is on duty. Head toward the brown building on the wide cinder path to the left of the lake, keeping the lake to your right. Turn left at the next intersection (6.2 miles) onto an unmarked trail, which becomes red-and-green-blazed Monument Trail in about 200 feet. Ascend over broken rocks, then cross the road and head straight into the woods. At a trail junction, turn right, going uphill onto the AT (6.3 miles).

Soon you'll see the observation platform; retrace your steps the 1.6 miles back to the parking lot, staying on the white-blazed AT. Cross NJ 23, pass the kiosk on the left of the park office, and head into the woods. Turn left at the next two junctions to reach the parking lot.

DID YOU KNOW?

The park was landscaped by the sons of Frederick Law Olmsted, who designed New York City's Central Park. Anthony R. and Susie Dryden Kuser donated the land. The High Point Monument is a 220-foot obelisk that honors all war veterans. Tri-States Monument, where New York, New Jersey, and Pennsylvania meet, is in Laurel Grove Cemetery in Port Jervis, New York, beneath the I-84 underpass; for help in finding the monument, see roadsideamerica.com.

OTHER ACTIVITIES

High Point State Park offers swimming in season. Stokes State Forest (33 miles of trails, including the AT) connects to High Point State Park via light-green-blazed Parker Trail; hike Sunrise Mountain there, the second-highest point in New Jersey. Also nearby is Wallkill River National Wildlife Refuge in Sussex. Visit the Sterling Hill Mine Museum in Ogdensburg, the "fluorescent mineral capital of the world." Within 10 miles is Grey Towers National Historic Site in Milford, Pennsylvania, the former home of Gifford Pinchot, founder of the U.S. Forest Service.

MORE INFORMATION

Seasonal entrance fees may apply from Memorial Day to Labor Day—check the park's website to see if fees are currently in effect before you go. During the season, visitors may climb the interior of High Point Monument (291 steps) from 8:30 A.M. to 3:30 P.M. Wednesday through Sunday. The free AT parking lot is at 1396 NJ 23 in Sussex. The park office is 1.2 miles north on NJ 23, but parking is limited to 2 hours.

6

DEER PATH PARK:
ROUND MOUNTAIN SECTION

This township park features paths that wind in and out of rustic woods and beautiful meadows, past historical farms and barns, a museum, and beehives.

Features 🚶 🐕 🍦 🏃 🏕

Location Flemington, NJ

Rating Easy to Moderate

Distance 6.6-mile loop

Elevation Gain 900 feet

Estimated Time 3.5 hours

Maps co.hunterdon.nj.us/Facilities/Facility/Details/Deer-Path-Park-11

GPS Coordinates 40° 33.208′ N, 74° 50.315′ W

Contact Township of Readington, 509 County Route 523, Whitehouse Station, NJ 08889; 908-534-4051; readingtontwpnj.gov. Hunterdon County Division of Parks and Recreation, 1020 Route 31, Lebanon, NJ 08833; 908-782-1158; co.hunterdon.nj.us/479/Parks-Recreation

DIRECTIONS

From all points south, take NJ 31 North and turn right onto West Woodschurch Road, following signs for Deer Path Park and the YMCA. Proceed about 0.7 mile on West Woodschurch Road to the park entrance on the right. Drive past the YMCA entrance to the parking lot on the left, with space for about 30 cars.

TRAIL DESCRIPTION

This hike explores the Round Mountain section of Deer Path Park. Deer Path Park is one of 28 parks in Hunterdon County. Round Mountain is 600 feet above sea level, and the Lenni-Lenape used to camp here. The area has one of the finest mature forests in Hunterdon County, with oaks, ashes, maples, and beeches.

Rolling terrain, sometimes rocky, slips repeatedly from meadows to woods, creating variety and interest. You'll visit a working farm and a historical farmstead on Bouman-Stickney Loop (orange diamond), Woodschurch Farm Loop (yellow diamond), and Round Mountain Loop (white diamond). Following the blazes in and out of the woods can be a bit tricky; keep a sharp lookout. In spring and summer, flowers bloom and birds are active. In fall, the meadows are bright with goldenrod and rimmed with a brilliantly colored forest. In winter, frozen grasses catch the sun, and bare tree branches lace the sky.

Grab a Round Mountain trail system map from the kiosk in the parking lot. Then head toward the bathrooms and take the paved path behind them. The path goes past brown buildings, through the soccer fields, and across open fields before veering left to parallel the road on your right (West Woodschurch). Turn right to cross the road (0.4 mile) and enter the Round Mountain section of Deer Path Park.

Bear to the right, walking along a beautiful blooming meadow. As you stroll the many meadows and fields on this hike, be sure to stop and look up for hawks. You may even spot an eagle. When you are almost at the top of the meadow, turn right into the woods on the first path you see, which is orange-blazed Bouman-Stickney Loop (0.6 mile). Go over a bridge that parallels a field. (Be sure to wear a hat or have sun

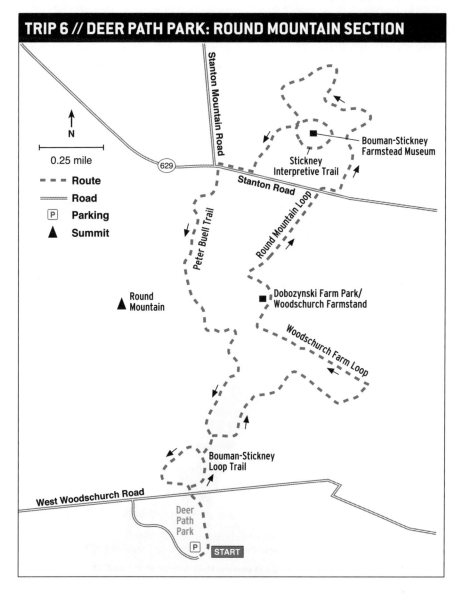

TRIP 6 // DEER PATH PARK: ROUND MOUNTAIN SECTION

N

0.25 mile

- - - **Route**
───── **Road**
P **Parking**
▲ **Summit**

Stanton Mountain Road

629

Stanton Road

Peter Buell Trail

Round Mountain Loop

Stickney Interpretive Trail

Bouman-Stickney Farmstead Museum

▲ Round Mountain

Dobozynski Farm Park/ Woodschurch Farmstand

Woodschurch Farm Loop

Bouman-Stickney Loop Trail

West Woodschurch Road

Deer Path Park

P START

protection in this exposed area.) Take an uneven path uphill into lush green woods—watch your footing. Still on the orange-blazed trail, veer left into another lovely meadow with soft, colorful grasses and seasonal flowers. Toward the end of the meadow, take the first path on the right into the cool woods. The rocky dirt path slopes down, soft grasses lining the way. At the intersection marked by a public lands sign (0.9 mile), bear right. Then bear left at a junction marked by posts onto Woodschurch Farm Loop. Follow yellow-blazed Woodschurch Farm Loop (maintained by the Readington Trail Association) across another bridge.

You'll reach Dobozynski Farm Park/Woodschurch Farmstead (1.4 miles) on the yellow-blazed trail. Take time to inspect the house and historical barns. In the animal pens, chickens and usually a large tom turkey are fun to observe. The trail becomes a gravel road through the farm and then turns left at the "Dobozynski Farm" sign and goes uphill.

Turn left onto the first road, and follow it to a gate and fence. Go through the gate and walk slightly uphill around another beautiful meadow. Enter the woods, then walk along a field, turning right into woods again on a dirt path (1.9 miles); note houses for orientation to your right. You are now on white-blazed Round Mountain Loop. Stay on this trail (eroded and rocky in spots) as it goes gradually up and in and out of fields and meadows. At 2.6 miles, Round Mountain Loop crosses County Route 629. Turn right on the road, walk on the shoulder for 100 yards, and then cross the road and turn left to continue on Round Mountain Loop.

The Bouman-Stickney Farmstead Museum is in a stone building on the right. Take some time to visit the museum and learn about Howard Lindsay and Dorothy Stickney. This thespian couple entertained many luminaries at their retreat, including Julie Andrews, Shelley Winters, and Oscar Hammerstein, before Dorothy's death in 1998 at age 101. The reconstructed New World Dutch barn is worth exploring. Walk light-orange-blazed Stickney Interpretive Trail, which circles the property. Go right and pass two footbridges to get back on white-blazed Round Mountain Loop. (If you go left, you'll be backtracking.) As you enter a field, look for County Route 629; head toward it, and when you reach it, turn right and walk on the shoulder for 0.2 mile until you see Stanton General Store, a restaurant on the opposite side of the road. Stop for a drink or a meal.

Backtracking slightly, leave the restaurant, cross County Route 629, and turn left to walk on the shoulder, keeping the wire fence on your right. When the fence ends, turn right and then almost immediately left into the woods, still on the white-blazed trail, which here is a very rutted dirt path, rooty and rocky. Turn left at the junction onto a white-and-red-blazed connector trail (5.0 miles), which widens and slopes downhill. Turn right onto orange-blazed Bouman-Stickney Loop; a wooden sign labels this stretch Peter Buell Trail, in honor of a park employee. Hike down through the woods (5.3 miles).

Emerge in an open field, under power lines, and continue on Peter Buell Trail. Cross a path and go straight downhill into the woods. Do not take the trail on the left. Step over water bars and cross the creek bed (the creek is sometimes dry, sometimes wet, but easy to cross either way). Turn right at the field and walk the perimeter, visiting the active beehives and honey trays on the left. Turn right at the fork to go toward the gate and cross West Woodschurch Road (6.3 miles). Stay straight. A soccer field is on the right and buildings and bathrooms are on the left as you make your way back to the parking lot.

DID YOU KNOW?

Some say Oscar Hammerstein wrote the score for *The Sound of Music* at what is now Bouman-Stickney Farmstead. Round Mountain is a rest stop for migratory birds; look for eastern bluebird and American kestrel nesting boxes. Wild turkeys are a common sight. Watch for white-tailed deer and red foxes.

OTHER ACTIVITIES

Myriad shops and restaurants crowd the area, especially along NJ 31. Visit the Hunterdon County Arboretum, less than 3 miles (5 minutes) away at 1020 NJ 31. About 22 miles west (25 minutes), park at 182 Dennis Road in the town of Bloomsbury to explore 524-acre Musconetcong Gorge Preserve, especially the moderate-to-difficult Ridge and Highlands trails. Cushetunk Mountain Preserve (106 Old Mountain Road, Lebanon) has nesting bald eagles.

MORE INFORMATION

Deer Path Park, a former summer camp, was acquired by Hunterdon County in 1977. The park features a fifteen-station fitness circuit and running trails. Round Mountain was formed by volcanic activity and reaches 600 feet above sea level. Bouman-Stickney Farmstead (Stanton section) has programs for children (for information, call 908-236-2327). The Round Mountain trail system map is a combined effort of employees and volunteers of Readington Township and the Hunterdon County parks department.

In fall, goldenrod lines the path through beautiful meadows.

NEW JERSEY HIGHLANDS

The Highlands region of New Jersey is large, both in physical dimensions and in ecological importance. Physically, the Highlands stretches for about 60 miles, from Milford in the southwest to Mahwah in the northeast, and encompasses more than 850,000 acres in New Jersey. The region lies within the boundaries of seven counties: Sussex, Warren, Morris, Hunterdon, and Somerset in the Skylands region; and Bergen and Passaic in the Gateway region (see hikes in the Skylands and Gateway regions).

In terms of ecological importance, the Highlands is a giant. This belt of green protects the drinking water resources on which 70 percent of the state's population depends. The Highlands supplies potable water to 5.4 million people, only 821,000 of whom live in the region itself. More than 200 threatened, endangered, or rare plants and animals live here as well. Wetlands, forests, lakes, and streams protect the blue-spotted salamander, the osprey, the silver-bordered fritillary butterfly, and the bog turtle, among others. The tiny bog turtle achieved distinction in June 2018, when Governor Phil Murphy designated it the official state reptile.

Given the Highlands' importance, it's no wonder serious attention was finally given to this geological region in the 1980s. Many conservation organizations, state and local governments, and local businesses are now involved. The Appalachian Mountain Club (AMC) leads the four-state Highlands Coalition, an alliance of nearly 200 nonprofit, municipal, state, and federal organizations that advocate for federal funding to protect the region. Today, the entire Highlands encompasses 3.5 million acres, from Pennsylvania through New Jersey and New York and into Connecticut.

AMC has long been a key advocate for the Highlands. In 2004, AMC led the Highlands Coalition's advocacy efforts to secure passage of the Highlands Conservation Act, a tremendous milestone for the long-term protection of the Highlands, allowing Congress to allocate $10 million a year on open-space projects in the region. When the program expired in 2014, AMC led the charge to reauthorize the Highlands Conservation Act. After much dedicated toil, success came twice, with reauthorization through 2021 and now through 2029. Passage of this reauthorization ensures the protection of Highlands resources that are critical in combating and preparing for climate change, supporting environmental justice, conserving wildlife habitats, and protecting open space.

AMC long advocated for full and permanent funding of the Land and Water Conservation Fund (LWCF), and in 2020, the Great American Outdoors Act finally accomplished this. AMC continues to encourage allocation of money from Congress to projects in the AMC region, specifically the Highlands, as well as to ask for increased overall funding for the LWCF. The LWCF is a visionary and bipartisan federal funding program designed to protect special places. AMC also oversees the Pennsylvania Highlands Coalition.

Work on the currently 168-mile-long Highlands Trail (HT) began in 1995 with an inventive co-alignment of both established and new trails. When complete, the HT will stretch 180 miles from the Delaware River in New Jersey to the Hudson River in New

York, with more miles in Pennsylvania (maintained by AMC). Plans include extending the trail into Connecticut. In New Jersey, the HT is a rugged, sometimes challenging footpath that follows the spine of northwest New Jersey, crosses rolling hills and mountains, cuts through deep forests, and passes waterfalls, small rural communities, and land remnants of historical features, such as iron works, transport canals, and mansions.

Some sections where it aligns with other trails can be confusing. But if you pay attention to the trail's distinctive diamond-shaped teal blazes, especially at intersections, you will be amply rewarded.

One of the best ways to help protect the Highlands is to get out and hike it! Each footstep honors those who fight for it and brings awareness to this vibrant area. According to the New Jersey Highlands Coalition, every $1 invested in state preservation programs returns $10 in economic value to the state. So while you're hiking, invite a buddy, take pictures, and share on social media with #NJHighlands and #LWCF. You'll impress your friends, and Mr. Bog Turtle, the state reptile of New Jersey, will thank you.

For maps, see *Northern New Jersey Highlands Trails* from the New York–New Jersey Trail Conference, as well as the online Highlands Trail Guide (nynjtc.org/book /highlands-trail-guide). For more information on AMC's role in the Highlands, visit outdoors.org/highlandsact.

7

DELAWARE AND RARITAN CANAL AND HORSESHOE BEND PARK

A flat walk along the Delaware River becomes a woodsy ramble through lush forests, over streams, and across rolling meadows.

Features

Location Frenchtown, NJ

Rating Moderate to Strenuous

Distance 10.6-mile loop

Elevation Gain 900 feet

Estimated Time 5.5 hours

Maps USGS Frenchtown; Horseshoe Bend Park: dandrcanal.org/trails#hunterdon; njtrails.org/trail/horseshoe-bend-park

GPS Coordinates 40° 31.493' N, 75° 03.785' W

Contact Delaware and Raritan Canal State Park, 145 Mapleton Road, Princeton, NJ 08540; 609-924-5705; state.nj.us/dep/parksandforests/parks/drcanal.html. Horseshoe Bend Park, 178 Horseshoe Bend Road, Frenchtown, NJ 08825; 908-996-4276; kingwoodtownship.com/recreation-page-list/264-parks-and-recreation

DIRECTIONS

From the direction of Trenton, take NJ 29 toward Frenchtown. Turn onto Bridge Street (NJ 12) toward the Delaware River. Go 0.11 mile and turn left before you cross the bridge (just past Front Street). A free parking lot on River Road holds 20 to 30 cars.

TRAIL DESCRIPTION

This fun adventure combines major trails in two parks: Orange and White trails in Delaware and Raritan Canal State Park and Flagg-Kirkland Trail in Horseshoe Bend Park. Enter the southern end of Horseshoe Bend Park through a little-used access point off the Delaware and Raritan (D&R) Canal towpath. You'll hike only 2.5 miles along the D&R Canal, although the entire route extends for 70 (mostly flat) miles. (For more information on the canal's history, see "From Mules to Multiuse: Today's Delaware and Raritan Canal State Park" on page 40.) The section in Frenchtown is known as a "feeder," supplying water to the main canal. Today, the canal is lined with homes, woods, and whimsical garden creations. Horseshoe Bend Park (736 acres) has three trails spanning 11.5 miles, with Cooley Preserve in the northwest corner and a 7-acre dog park in the northeast corner. Ravines, streams, and forests provide homes for pileated woodpeckers, hawks, and amphibians. Butterfly spotting is best from May to October when swallowtails, hairstreaks, fritillaries, skippers, and more float through the air. Foliage makes this a lovely fall hike; the flat trails are good in snow. Spring brings the running of the shad, the largest fish in the herring family, when they migrate from salt water to the Delaware River to reproduce. (Don't miss the two-day shad festival in Lambertville, usually in late April.)

Start in the parking lot next to the bridge in Frenchtown. With your back to the parking lot and the beautiful Delaware River, walk to the D&R towpath and turn right (south) on the loose-gravel trail. As you begin the hike, note the family of gnomes and a cemetery from the 1800s on the left. On your right is the mighty Delaware River, with Pennsylvania just across the water. Soon traverse a field and walk through a green tunnel of trees, with an inviting bench on the left. As you continue along the towpath,

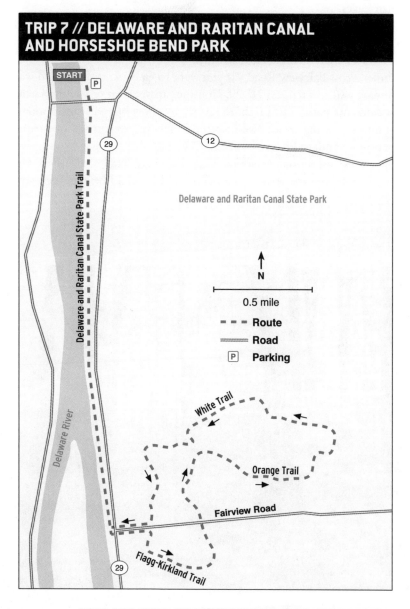

be sure to pause and admire the river. Scan the banks for a bald eagle, red-tailed hawk, or northern goshawk. (*Note*: Be careful of speeding bicycles on this popular route.)

At 2.5 miles, turn left at a gated area onto a paved road (NJ 29). Turn left on the paved road and walk on the shoulder for about 30 yards; then cross the road to get to Fairview Road (green road sign). Walk on paved Fairview Road, immediately crossing a road bridge. Just before the second bridge, turn right onto the yellow-diamond-blazed path, which is Flagg-Kirkland Trail in Horseshoe Bend Park (2.9 miles).

Wide dirt Flagg-Kirkland Trail in this wooded area winds slightly uphill; note the impressive ravine to the right. Go over another ravine, still ascending, and then in and out of a large ditch (may be wet in spring). In fall, be careful of roots and rocks hiding under fallen leaves.

Stroll on a wooden boardwalk for a hundred yards or so. Then meander downhill through oak, beech, and hemlock trees, which offer brilliant foliage in fall. In wet seasons, you'll traverse a few small, clear streams.

At 4.2 miles, cross Fairview Road. (If you want to go back, turn left and walk down the paved road, which intersects NJ 29. Continue to your car or wander farther south on the flat canal towpath.) Turn right to return to yellow-blazed Flagg-Kirkland Trail. Go uphill into a clearing to see awe-inspiring, massive, overturned tree trunks. (The trail skirts private land, so be careful not to trespass.)

Turn right onto appropriately orange-blazed Orange Trail (5.0 miles). Cross two wooden bridges. Ignore the trail to the left after the second bridge; keep straight on

Foliage and butterflies make this an ideal fall hike.

Orange Trail. A wire fence runs along the right, as well as a picturesque stone wall. Turn left onto a paved road in the park and head to a covered pavilion for lunch or a rest stop (5.8 miles).

Refreshed, go back down the paved road and past the trail on the right that you saw earlier. After 100 yards, turn left at the kiosk onto white-blazed White Trail. Veer right into the woods on White Trail, being careful of rocks underfoot. At the fork, turn right to continue on White Trail. The trail then loops off to the right, but keep left (straight). White Trail follows Burke's Run for a while, making for a pretty and lush path. At the intersection with Orange Trail (6.3 miles), turn right onto Orange Trail. The narrow route goes uphill and is exposed to the elements; then it plunges down a steep, rooty hill (use caution). At 6.9 miles, turn right onto yellow-blazed Flagg-Kirkland Trail. At the intersection with Fairview Road (7.5 miles), turn right onto Fairview Road, which soon intersects NJ 29. Turn left on NJ 29 and walk on the shoulder for a few dozen yards. Cross the road carefully as you head back to the canal. Turn right on the canal and go 2.5 miles back to the parking lot, enjoying the Delaware River on your left. Take a good look at 2-mile-long Marshall Island in the middle of the river; perhaps you'll glimpse an otter.

DID YOU KNOW?

Many of the Irish workers who helped build the D&R Canal died during an Asiatic cholera pandemic in 1832 and are buried in unmarked graves along the canal. Visit a memorial, made from a 2-ton granite stone taken from a lock in the New Brunswick section, in front of the Bull's Island Recreation Area office (2185 Daniel Bray Highway, Stockton).

OTHER ACTIVITIES

Small, charming Frenchtown has a bookstore, antique stores, and upscale as well as more affordable shops. Rent skates (inline or quads) at an old-fashioned roller-skating rink just south of town on NJ 29. In summer, companies set up in the parking lot to offer trips down the river on tubes or in canoes. Walk across the bridge, with seriously impressive river views sweeping north and south, and visit Pennsylvania on the other side.

MORE INFORMATION

Hunting is permitted in Horseshoe Bend Park September through February, except for Sundays. The park complex offers a 10,000-square-foot event center, a leash-free dog area, and mountain biking and horseback riding. Fishing is permitted the entire length of the canal.

FROM MULES TO MULTIUSE: TODAY'S DELAWARE AND RARITAN CANAL STATE PARK

This linear park comprises 4,000-plus acres and crosses 5 counties (Middlesex, Mercer, Burlington, Somerset, and Hunterdon) and 22 municipalities. Part of the East Coast Greenway (see "Follow the Super Green Road: The East Coast Greenway" on page 115), the site hosts 160 species of birds and is a source of water for nearly 1 million people. As you hike some of the 70-plus miles of trails in New Jersey's Delaware and Raritan Canal State Park, which runs from Milford to New Brunswick, consider the area's more than 400-year history.

In the early 1600s, during British colonization, canals and other transportation systems between colonies were discouraged because Britain wanted access to all the colonies' raw materials, rather than having colonies trade with one another. Even though officials in New Jersey knew that a canal connecting the Delaware and Raritan rivers would circumvent the poor roads and shallow rivers that inhibited (forbidden) intercolonial trade, it took winning the American Revolution (1775–1783) and the opening of the Erie Canal in 1825 to bring "canal fever" to New Jersey. The Delaware and Raritan (D&R) Canal was built from 1830 to 1834 and was the final link in the intercoastal waterway that runs from Massachusetts to Georgia.

Often referred to as "the Big Ditch," the original canal was 66 miles long, had fourteen locks to raise and lower boat traffic, cost almost $3 million (roughly $73 million today), and was hand-dug by workers, including 3,000 Irish laborers. The workers, mostly recruited from Ireland during a U.S. labor shortage, were paid $1 a day (roughly $25 today) and could earn an additional 25 cents for each tree stump they removed. Passage from Ireland was expensive—$27 for food and transportation—so many laborers borrowed the money from their employers, paying them back by working for "free" for a period of time, usually six months. With shovels, pickaxes, and wheelbarrows, they worked from sunrise to sunset, six days a week, living in tents, with no medical facilities or sanitation. Many died due to these conditions, and in 1832, an outbreak of Asiatic cholera killed hundreds more. Most are buried in marked and unmarked graves at Bull's Island and Griggstown Cemetery, and along Ten Mile Run (a tributary) and the canal banks. Paul Muldoon's Pulitzer Prize–winning collection of poetry, *Moy Sand and Gravel* (Farrar, Straus and Giroux, 2002), honors these "navvies." A 2-ton carved granite stone, taken from a lock in the New Brunswick section of the canal, stands in front of the Bull's Island Recreation Area office (2185 Daniel Bray Highway, Stockton) and pays tribute to the workers.

Mules towed boats on the newly built canal and were kept moving by "mule tenders." The tenders, mostly children, some younger than 9 years old, were tied to the barge so they could be hauled up if they fell in the water. The Mule Tenders Barracks Museum in Griggstown provides an excellent history of this era. Today, you can take a 1-hour mule-drawn canal ride starting in New Hope, Pennsylvania, to enhance your experience. Just walk over the Delaware River on the bridge that connects Lambertville, New Jersey, to New Hope.

By the end of the nineteenth century, railroads put the canals virtually out of business. The D&R Canal closed in 1932, and the state of New Jersey repurposed it to serve as a water supply system. By 1973, after some portions of the canal had been filled in and turned into highways, activists sought to save the canal from total destruction, and it was placed on the National Register of Historic Places. From 1974 on, the canal and corridors of land on both sides were made into a state park. In 1992, the park's trail system was designated a National Recreation Trail.

Museums, historical buildings, and picnic tables and grills stand along this magnificent trail that's perfect for hiking and biking. Several towns on the New Jersey side are worth a special trip. In Stockton, Prallsville Mills contains a sawmill, a gristmill, and a linseed-oil mill. Kingston has Lock 8 and the lockkeeper's house and station. View bridgetenders' homes in Griggstown and Blackwells Mills. Visit old homesteads at Six Mile Run Reservoir in Somerset County (see Trip 12).

Wherever you go on this 70-mile trail, history nudges you, slows your step, and brings a thoughtful and grateful dimension to your hike.

For more on the D&R Canal, see two books by Linda J. Barth: *The Delaware and Raritan Canal* (Arcadia Publishing, 2002) and *The Delaware and Raritan Canal at Work* (Arcadia Publishing, 2004). Also contact Delaware and Raritan Canal State Park, 145 Mapleton Road, Princeton, NJ 08540; 609-924-5705; dandrcanal.org.

Enjoy open views of the Kittatinny Ridge and Valley, plus dramatic rock outcroppings and boulders in rolling terrain.

Features 🏃🚶🐕🐾💧🔵🗺️⛷️✳️🏕️🏔️🎣

Location Hope, NJ

Rating Strenuous

Distance 11.4 miles round-trip

Elevation Gain 1,500 feet

Estimated Time 5 hours

Maps USGS Blairstown; nj.gov/dep/parksandforests/maps/jennyjump-trail.pdf

GPS Coordinates 40° 54.708′ N, 74° 55.507′ W

Contact Jenny Jump State Forest, 330 State Park Road, Hope, NJ 07844; 908-459-4366; nj.gov/dep/parksandforests/parks/jennyjumpstateforest.html

DIRECTIONS

At the blinking light in the village of Hope, turn onto County Route 519 north. At the third right, turn onto Shiloh Road. Drive approximately 1 mile and turn right onto State Park Road. Limited parking is available at the park office, so go a few hundred yards uphill past the office and park in the lot there, which has space for about twenty cars.

TRAIL DESCRIPTION

Jenny Jump State Forest is in the New Jersey Highlands region and has 14 miles of trails. For rock lovers, light-blue-blazed Jenny Jump Trail is a fun hike over moraines (rocky mounds made by glacial deposits) and past unusually shaped glacial rock outcroppings and boulders. (Be sure to wear sturdy boots.) Enjoy views to the west of the Highlands and the Kittatinny Mountain Ridge and Valley. If you climb to the top of Jenny Jump Mountain, you can see Great Meadows to the east. The forest is mainly hardwoods and white pines. A winter hike showcases excellent views of the Delaware Water Gap and is mercifully bug-free.

Head to the park office and pick up a map. Geology enthusiasts should grab the brochure for a self-guided tour of the forest's moraines, kettle holes, and large rocks called erratics that were transported by glaciers. (The geology tour is not covered in this description, but you can see two erratics outside the park office.) From the office parking lot, get on light-blue-blazed Jenny Jump Trail, a beautiful boulder-lined path, and head south. (*Note:* The trail can be icy in winter, so be prepared with poles or traction cleats.) Keep straight on Jenny Jump Trail. Do not turn left onto the yellow-blazed trail.

Enjoy the undulating hills and a lovely ridge to the left. In winter, bare trees allow a pleasant view of the village of Hope, named in an optimistic moment by early Moravian settlers from Germany in 1769, a Protestant sect who believed in education for both boys and girls (unusual for the late 1700s). After almost 40 years, the Moravian planned community "experiment" in Hope ended. The main culprits were smallpox and financial troubles. The entire village was sold for $48,000 to Nicholas Kramer and Abraham Horn, and the Moravian community moved to Bethlehem, Pennsylvania.

Turn right at a large glacial erratic, still on Jenny Jump Trail. Cross a path that appears after 20 yards and stretch your muscles by going straight up a hill (watch your

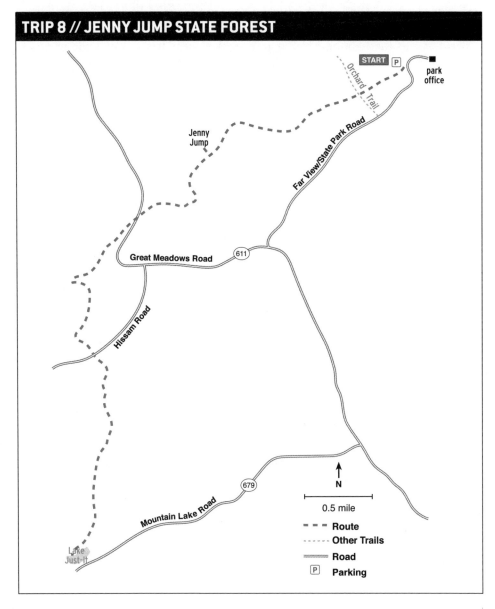

TRIP 8 // JENNY JUMP STATE FOREST

START · P · ■ park office

Orchard Trail

Jenny Jump

Far View/State Park Road

Great Meadows Road · 611

Hissam Road

679

Mountain Lake Road

Lake Just-It

N

0.5 mile

- - - **Route**
..... **Other Trails**
=== **Road**
P **Parking**

footing on the rocks). Cross white-blazed Orchard Trail (0.3 mile), but stay on the light-blue-blazed trail. Enjoy views of the village of Hope and the Delaware Water Gap, as well as Mount Tammany (New Jersey) and Mount Minsi (Pennsylvania). Routes 611, 521, and 519 crisscross below.

Keep walking past impressive rocks along a ridge exposed to the elements, admiring the views. At a fork, a faded blaze of nondescript color on your right indicates a side path toward an excellent vista of the Delaware Water Gap (1.7 miles). Legend has it that this vista marks the spot where Jenny jumped, hence the name Jenny Jump State Forest. Hundreds of years ago, according to the story, 9-year-old Jenny was gathering berries with her father near this ridge. When her father saw Lenni-Lenape people approaching, he became frightened and yelled at her to jump. Some say she died and her small ghost wanders the cliffs forever; others say she survived.

Backtrack to the light-blue-blazed trail, which meanders through the woods to another hilltop. Get ready for a rugged trek over boulders; be sure you are wearing sturdy boots. At the top of the hill, pause to catch your breath, and then follow steep switchbacks down into the valley. In winter, wet, icy leaves and rocks make tricky footing; however, this is the sunny side of Jenny Jump Mountain. The beauty of the brown leaves and white snow are worth it. Cross a boulder- strewn stream and turn right at the light blue blaze at a fork (2.2 miles) to stay on Jenny Jump Trail. Keep a sharp eye out for the blazes as the trail here is winding. Look for a lovely valley with a gorge to the right. You may see some tom turkey tracks here.

Go down over boulders; green moss lines the path. You are on the ridge road, and the valley is to the right. Go down rock steps to County Route 611 (2.7 miles); Jenny Jump Trail cuts right across the road and is prominently blazed (light blue) on the guardrail. Cautiously cross the road, stepping over the guardrail, for a short, steep, rocky descent (poles come in handy). A very narrow, fern-lined path winds across the gently rolling contours of the hill, beneath the roar of traffic. A valley stretches imperially to the right, with an open field at the bottom that glows like a heavenly footprint. Remains of a massive stone wall are to the left.

Carefully traverse a stream, usually partially frozen in winter (3.1 miles). A stone wall near the stream provides a convenient snack spot. It's quite the climb out of this small valley, almost 250 feet over a little more than a half-mile to reach Hissam Road. After crossing the road, climb another 130 feet until the trail mercifully turns south and begins to drop in elevation. It's a rocky half-mile down, over a few old farm walls along the way, to the one-lane woods road. Turn right and follow this road for a little less than a mile until you reach pretty Lake Just-It (5.7 miles). This is a great spot for lunch and rest.

After the break, backtrack up and down the hills toward the parking lot. In the warmer months, listen for kids enjoying themselves on the rides at the Land of Make Believe.

DID YOU KNOW?

The ghoulishly named Shades of Death Road skirts the forest. A former peat mining company there supplies pitcher's mound material for all major league and most minor league ballparks.

Rambling stone walls along this hike offer a welcome resting place or lunch stop.

OTHER ACTIVITIES

The village of Hope is on County Route 512, 1.0 mile south of Exit 12 on I-80. The Greenwood Observatory, off Fairview Road (open April to October), is 0.4 mile south of the park entrance, via State Park Road. Pequest Trout Hatchery and Natural Resource Education Center is 13.0 miles south in Oxford. The Delaware Water Gap National Recreation Area (100 miles of trails, including 27 on the Appalachian Trail) is 12.0 miles northwest (see Trip 10); great hikes include Mount Tammany and Sunfish Pond. About 10 miles east is 9,000-acre Allamuchy Mountain State Park (see Trip 11).

MORE INFORMATION

The park office has information on the surrounding area and local attractions, including the Greenwood Observatory, and offers an interesting selection of taxidermy and plaster animal tracks. No bathrooms are available, but turn left out of the office parking lot, and a bathhouse with flush toilets and showers is on your left. The park is partially accessible for people with disabilities; call 800-852-7897 for details.

9 WHITE LAKE NATURAL RESOURCE AREA

A hike around a peaceful lake with much history hiding out along the trail.

Features

Location Hardwick Township, NJ

Rating Easy

Distance 4-mile loop

Elevation Gain 350 feet

Estimated Time 1.5 hours

Maps USGS Blairstown, USGS Flatbrookville; warrenparks.com/park/white-lake-resource-area

GPS Coordinates 41° 00.120′ N, 74° 55.010′ W

Contact White Lake Natural Resource Area, 97 Stillwater Road, Hardwick, NJ 07825; 908-453-2650; warrenparks.com/park/white-lake-resource-area

DIRECTIONS

From I-80, take Exit 19 toward County Route 517 North. Turn right onto County Route 517 at the light, and then immediately turn left onto Old Hackettstown Road. In 0.2 mile, turn left onto County Route 612 (Johnsonburg Road). In 4.9 miles, turn right onto County Route 519 (Johnsonburg Bypass) and follow it for 1.8 miles; then turn left onto NJ 94 South. In 1.9 miles, turn right onto Spring Valley Road. After 1.3 miles, turn right onto Stillwater Road. A small parking lot (twelve or fewer cars) is on the right in 0.4 mile.

TRAIL DESCRIPTION

White Lake Natural Resource Area is a 394-acre park owned by Warren County, featuring a beautiful lake surrounded by a path through a hardwood forest. The lake gets its name from its unusual white bottom, which is composed of marl, a mixture of clay, sand, and limestone that was often used as fertilizer as far back as the first century. White Lake is a popular spot for kayaking, so feel free to bring your kayak or canoe to get some upper body exercise after your hike!

Beginning at the parking lot, walk down the short road toward the lake to a fishing dock by a boat launch (nonmotorized craft only). Stroll onto the dock for the clearest view of the lake on this 4-mile loop.

Off the dock, head west, away from the lake, on Blue Trail toward Stillwater Road (the road you drove down to enter the parking lot). As you wander through meadows that are filled with yarrow and other flowering plants in summer, enjoy the sweet smells that float through the air among the buzzing bees. Keep left to stay on the trail after about 0.1 mile. (Heading right will take you back to the parking lot.) The route curls around to run parallel to the road and enter the woods. Turn left 0.3 mile into the hike to stay on Blue Trail. Farther along, sit on a bench to admire a new angle of the lake before continuing to the intersection of Red Trail and Blue Trail. Follow the blue blazes across a rock wall.

Blue Trail soon emerges from the woods into another open meadow a half-mile into the hike. Keep an eye out for deer, rabbit, turkey, or—once in a great while—a bear, along with sparrows, meadowlarks, and other birds. Butterflies also love the meadows here. Reenter the woods; a view of the lake soon appears a few steps to the left of the trail (0.9 mile).

Continuing down, keep to the left at 1.5 miles to turn onto Ridge and Valley Trail, which is marked with yellow blazes. Near this turning point, watch for a large wall in the woods to your left. Head over to check out the remains of an old icehouse. In the days before electric refrigerators, people sawed blocks of ice from lakes across New Jersey

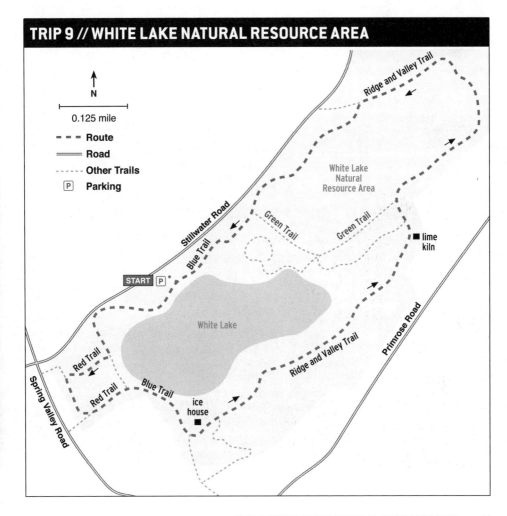

The imposing walls of the old icehouse.

during winter. The blocks were stored in icehouses and then used to stock iceboxes across the region in the warmer months. You won't find much ice here today, only towering stone walls and impressive archways. Remember to practice Leave No Trace: take only pictures; leave only footprints.

At 2.1 miles, the trail passes the remains of a lime kiln that produced quicklime, which was used to improve soil and in construction. It was also used to create white-wash, a waterproofing paint most memorably described in Mark Twain's *The Adventures of Tom Sawyer*.

At 2.2 miles, keep right at the intersection with Green Trail to stay on Ridge and Valley Trail (yellow blazes). From here, the trail narrows as it loops around from north-east to southwest. At the intersection with Blue Trail at 2.5 miles, turn left onto Blue Trail. At 2.9 miles, cross a small access road. The treadway here is mostly level and edged by ferns and the invasive silt grass as it heads through the forest. Continue south past another intersection with Green Trail (3.3 miles) and emerge from the woods shortly before returning to the fishing dock and boat launch (4.0 miles). Walk back up the access road to the parking lot.

DID YOU KNOW?

The use of marl and lime to improve soil goes back to at least the first century. Marl is also interesting because it contains fossils. While today folks usually think of the western states as being the location to go look for fossils in the United States, the earliest American paleontology focused heavily on the marl pits of New Jersey. The most famous New Jersey fossil find, "Haddy the Hadrosaurus," was discovered in a marl pit in Haddonfield in 1858.

OTHER ACTIVITIES

The Blairstown Diner is just 3.0 miles down the road in Blairstown. This diner was a shooting location for the 1980 film *Friday the 13th* and offers some fun movie-related food choices—like the Slasher Burger—plus all the regular diner options. Blairstown and nearby Hope feature many other locations seen in the film. The camp used in *Friday the 13th* is also nearby but is only open to outside visitors on special ticketed tour days. Check crystallaketours.com for days and tickets.

MORE INFORMATION

The property is open from 30 minutes before sunrise to 30 minutes after sunset. Maps are available at the kiosk in the parking area. Leashed dogs are allowed. Nonmotorized boating is allowed; the boat launch is just past the parking area for this hike.

10 DELAWARE WATER GAP NATIONAL RECREATION AREA: MILLBROOK VILLAGE TO VAN CAMPENS GLEN LOOP

Delight in river views, old foundations, waterfalls in a wooded glen, wildflowers, and historical buildings in the middle of the Delaware Water Gap National Recreation Area.

Features 🥾 🐕 🌊 ♨️ 🗺️ ⛷️ ⬆️

Location Hardwick Township, NJ

Rating Strenuous

Distance 7.1-mile loop

Elevation Gain 850 feet

Estimated Time 4 hours

Maps USGS Flatbrookville; nps.gov/dewa/planyourvisit/maps.htm; Delaware Water Gap & Kittatinny Trails, Map 121, eighth edition, New York–New Jersey Trail Conference

GPS Coordinates 41° 04.442' N, 74° 57.785' W

Contact Millbrook Village and Van Campens Glen are operated by Delaware Water Gap National Recreation Area, with headquarters at 1978 River Road, Bushkill, PA 18324 (mailing address is P.O. Box 2); 570-426-2452; nps.gov/dewa

DIRECTIONS

To the Millbrook Village parking lot (capacity at least 40 cars): Take I-80 West to Exit 12, turn right onto County Route 521 North (Hope Blairstown Road/Hope Road), and drive about 5 miles to NJ 94. Turn left and go 0.25 mile to the first traffic light, making a 60-degree turn onto Bridge Street (do not turn onto County Route 521). From here, drive 0.25 mile on Bridge Street uphill to the end of the road, turn right, proceed 50 yards on High Street, and then turn left onto Millbrook Road (County Route 602) toward Millbrook. Continue 7.5 miles to Millbrook Village, which offers parking in the lot on the right (near the intersection of Old Mine Road and Millbrook Road in Hardwick). A Global Positioning System (GPS) device may show Columbia or Blairstown.

TRAIL DESCRIPTION

This hike is in the middle part of the Delaware Water Gap National Recreation Area (DWGNRA) and goes from historic Millbrook Village via orange-blazed Pioneer Trail and blue-blazed Hamilton Ridge Trail to yellow-blazed Van Campens Glen Trail in rugged Van Campens Glen. It connects with Watergate Recreation Area on a brief road walk and enters the rear of Millbrook Village past historical buildings. Along the way, hikers pass an old lime kiln, the Delaware River, an 1800s cemetery, and a glen with waterfalls, rhododendron, mountain laurel, and hemlock. Spring brings high water and a profusion of yellow-blooming spicebush and wildflowers. Pastel bluets, white rue anemones, trout lilies, blue violets, white daffodils, and many others gild the paths. Summer brings crowds and bugs but also kaleidoscopic shades of green: emerald moss, vivid barberry bushes, asparagus ferns, and more. In fall, colorful foliage and red spicebush berries delight. Winter creates a world of frozen solitude with open views.

Begin in the parking lot at Millbrook Village, which boasted a gristmill in 1832 and grew to a community of 75 inhabitants and several noteworthy buildings by 1875. On summer weekends some buildings are open, and Millbrook Village Society volunteers give living history demonstrations. With the parking lot and buildings to your back, walk to the right out of the lot, cross Old Mine Road, and enter orange-blazed Orchard Trail in the woods. (*Note*: Old Mine Road is sometimes closed to cars in winter.) The path is uphill, rocky, and rooty, with many wildflowers in spring as a reward for your efforts. It soon turns grassy and mossy as you follow an attractive rock wall on your

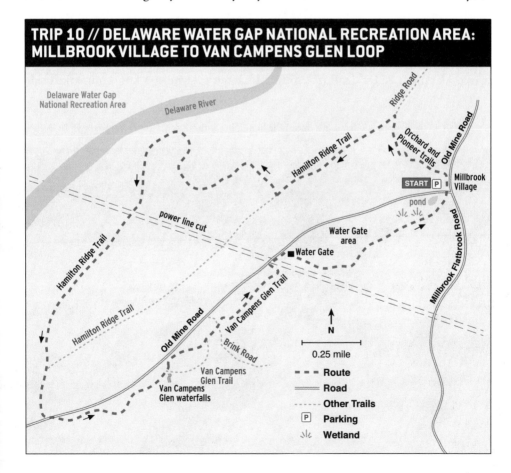

TRIP 10 // DELAWARE WATER GAP NATIONAL RECREATION AREA: MILLBROOK VILLAGE TO VAN CAMPENS GLEN LOOP

left. Enjoy fresh woods smells as you carefully walk downhill. At paved Ridge Road (0.6 mile), turn left and continue on the trail (this is not the road walk), admiring the mayapples and dogwoods, the white rue anemones, and the bluets. (*Caution*: The flat trail is slippery when wet.)

Soon, turn right onto Pioneer Trail, also blazed orange (1.3 miles), and enter a pine glen where the terrain is alternately flat and soft, then rooty and rocky. Veer right to stay on Pioneer Trail for a gradual descent. Begin looking for the old lime kiln on the right at 1.4 miles, about 50 feet off the path. Notice the beautiful, small valley to your right as you slip through gaps in old stone walls. Burgeoning young ferns unfurl in spring. Switchbacks lead you down. The ravine to the left is home to a gorgeous stream and yellow violets. The path rolls up and down to follow views of the majestic Delaware River on your right through the trees. Watch for former homesteads—old foundations and clearings left when residents relocated to accommodate Tocks Island Dam (see "Delaware Water Gap National Recreation Area: Divided It Stands" on page 55), which was never built; instead, the DWGNRA sprang from the seized lands. The trail flattens out and showcases spring violets. Go through a clearing under power lines at 2.8 miles and back into the woods, where a forest of invasive Japanese barberry bushes cluster. At the junction, go straight, following the orange-blazed trees along a flat stone-and-gravel road lined in greenery. Take time to look around and pick out foundations and clearings where houses used to be.

At the intersection of Hamilton Ridge Trail and Pioneer Trail, go straight onto blue-blazed Hamilton Ridge Trail (3.7 miles). In about 0.15 mile, a faint, unmarked side

A waterfall in Van Campens Glen is just one of the highlights of this 7-mile hike through the DWGNRA.

path to the right leads to a nearby 1800s cemetery for the Depue family that is worth the short detour.

If you are lucky, you'll see some orange witch's butter (also known as yellow brain fungus) growing on dead wood. (For more information on mushrooms, see "Fungi Put the Fun in Hiking: Mushrooms" on page 18.) At the intersection with two-lane Old Mine Road (County Route 606, 4.0 miles), turn left onto the road, and walk about 100 feet before turning right at the sign for Van Campens Glen. Chemical toilets are in the small parking lot. (*Note*: This place is very popular and crowded in summer.)

Start climbing yellow-blazed Van Campens Glen Trail at the end of the parking lot along Van Campens Brook. Because of the brook, the trail can be rocky and wet, with slippery footing, so be careful. The water cascades powerfully over the rocks, creating churning pools and mighty falls. The path widens and flattens, level with the brook. Enjoy the large rhododendrons and hemlocks lining the route; the rhodies may be in glorious bloom from mid-May through June. Cross a bridge to a beautiful lunch spot across from a waterfall, with flat boulders for seats. Then climb the steps, still on the yellow-blazed trail, out of the ravine. (*Caution*: The trail is narrow, slippery, and rocky.) In April and May, weeds have not yet overtaken the route, and the water flows strongly. Follow Van Campens Glen Trail as it again becomes level with the brook. Turn left at the junction with an unnamed trail. At the next bridge, turn right just before the bridge to follow the path out (5.27 miles). You are now on unmarked trails, so stay alert. The brook slows to a gentle flow to your left along a soft, straight path.

Cross Brink Road (5.4 miles) and then turn left over a bridge onto a paved path. At an iron gate, the path intersects Old Mine Road (5.9 miles). Turn right onto the road, watching for traffic. After a brief (0.15 mile) road walk, turn right at a gorgeous stone gate etched with the words Water on one column and Gate on the other (6.1 miles). Go around the gate and over a bridge. Admire the pretty lake to the left, where wild strawberries bloom in spring. A stream and a clearing with a picnic area are on the right (6.3 miles). Past the picnic tables, to the left, lies the grave of George Busch's beloved pup Bozo, who died in 1956. Busch was a jeweler, and Watergate was his estate back in the 1950s.

Continue to a swamp on the left. The gravelly path used to be a road, with a stream on the right. A pond emerges on your left; keep a lookout for snapping turtles. At the junction with an unnamed path, go straight. The gravel path changes to grass. Stroll past the historical buildings of Millbrook Village, including the old schoolhouse on the left, and peek in the windows. (Look for the old cemetery rumored to be at the top of the hill behind the schoolhouse.) Here, the trail becomes eroded. Check out the garden to the right, behind the wooden fence, and then cross Old Mine Road. Turn left to go back to the parking lot where you began.

DID YOU KNOW?

The Van Campen in Van Campens Glen refers to Colonel Abraham Van Campen, a settler who built a home in 1725 along the waterway now known as Van Campens Brook and later built a mill nearby. In 1756, his home was used as a frontier fort during the French and Indian War.

OTHER ACTIVITIES

The DWGNRA has dozens of trails: some highlights are Buttermilk Falls, Beulahland, the Appalachian Trail, Sunfish Pond, Dunnfield Creek, and Mount Tammany. AMC's southernmost facility—Mohican Outdoor Center—is here on a beautiful glacial lake. Mohican provides meals, cabins, camping, swimming, kayaking, snowshoeing, and hiking, as well as guided activities. Mohican Outdoor Center, 50 Camp Mohican Road, Blairstown, NJ 07825; 908-362-5670; reservations 603-466-2727; outdoors.org /destinations/new-jersey-new-york/mohican-outdoor-center. In Layton, visit Peters Valley School of Craft and the community of Walpack Center. Cross the river to Pennsylvania to hike two waterfalls on the popular and accessible Dingmans Creek Trail. While in Pennsylvania, visit the Pocono Environmental Education Center, one of the largest and longest-running residential environmental education centers in the northeastern United States (peec.org/programs/school-programs).

MORE INFORMATION

Millbrook Village is open seasonally, but the trails are always open. Call 908-841-9531 for information. Most of the DWGNRA is open 24 hours a day. Many day-use areas within the park are open sunrise to sunset (such as trailhead parking lots, Millbrook Village, and all picnic areas). Camping, fishing, boating, biking, swimming, and dogs are allowed in designated areas. The primary visitor center is in Pennsylvania at 1978 River Road, Bushkill, PA, 18324.

DELAWARE WATER GAP NATIONAL RECREATION AREA: DIVIDED IT STANDS

The Delaware Water Gap National Recreation Area (DWGNRA) has two sides. This 70,000-acre parcel, part of the National Park Service, is split down the middle by the mighty Delaware River, which flows 330 miles from New York through Pennsylvania, New Jersey, and Delaware on its way to the Atlantic Ocean. The DWGNRA nestles along either side of the Middle Delaware River, a section that is generally more peaceful, smooth, and secluded than the upper and lower parts.

To the west of the river lies the Pennsylvania side of the DWGNRA and to the east, the New Jersey side. The Jersey side is split lengthwise by two-lane Old Mine Road, which runs north to south, becoming part of US 209 at Port Jervis, New York. New Jersey farmers relied on Old Mine Road, constructed in the mid-1600s, to bring crops to market. Today, the road is a popular driving and biking route, leading to historical buildings, areas of natural beauty, and hiking trailheads.

A variety of hiking guidebooks further split the DWGNRA into northern, middle, and southern trails. The National Park Service provides a good basic grouping of which trails fall in these three divisions (nps.gov/dewa/planyourvisit/maps.htm).

The Water Gap itself is another divide, created by the Middle Delaware River as it powers through the low, forested mountains and rocky cliffs of the Kittatinny ridgeline, thus forming a gap of water, or a "water gap."

The Appalachian Trail (AT) crosses the river at the Water Gap and follows the eastern perimeter of the DWGNRA. The AT continues northward through Worthington State Forest, a 6,660-acre park adjacent to the DWGNRA. When visitors hike the popular Dunnfield Creek and Sunfish Pond natural areas, they are actually in Worthington State Forest, which is part of the Water Gap but not part of the DWGNRA. If this is confusing, visit the Kittatinny Point Visitor Center on the Jersey side for a map that shows the geography more clearly. North of the Kittatinny Visitor Center lies the Millbrook Visitor Center, near Walpack Bend, where the Delaware River makes a long, lazy S.

The recreation area was also formed by a split—of the political kind. In 1955, Hurricane Diane wreaked havoc along the Delaware. Seeking to control flooding, the U.S. Army Corps of Engineers asked Congress to authorize the building of a dam at Tocks Island, a small island on the Jersey side of the Delaware River, just north of what is now the DWGNRA. Congress complied, and soon about 600 families and property owners were displaced to make way for the dam. Then came the 1960s, a politically and socially charged era that galvanized several causes: Vietnam War protests, the civil rights movement, and a newly energized environmental push. Finally, in 1975, after many years in which squatters and hippies staked their claims on abandoned houses, the Delaware River Basin Commission voted to shelve the Tocks Island Dam project. No one saw any wisdom in turning a beautiful river into a lifeless body of water. The result was the Delaware Water Gap National Recreation Area, with 40 miles of protected, free-flowing river.

Today, whether you visit the Kittatinny Ridge, the AT, or the area's waterfalls, ponds, lakes, and ravines, the DWGNRA is a playground paradise for hikers, cyclists, and paddlers.

Dingmans Falls Visitor Center, 224 Dingmans Falls Road, Delaware Township, PA 18328; nps.gov/dewa/planyourvisit/visitorcenters.htm; 570-828-2253 (call for hours, but generally open in summer). DWGNRA park headquarters and visitor center, 1978 River Road, Bushkill, PA 18324; 570-828-6125 (generally open Monday through Friday, 9 A.M. to 4 p.m, but check first); nps.gov/dewa/index.htm.

ALLAMUCHY MOUNTAIN STATE PARK

An old railroad bed, abandoned mine pits, a pretty lake, and some interesting rock formations make this a popular trail.

Features 🐕 💧 🔍 ⛷ 💲 🔦

Location Byram Township, NJ

Rating Easy

Distance 5.1-mile loop

Elevation Gain 450 feet

Estimated Time 3 hours

Maps USGS Stanhope; nj.gov/dep/parksandforests/maps/allamuchy-trail.pdf

GPS Coordinates 40° 55.320′ N, 074° 44.354′ W

Contact Allamuchy Mountain State Park, Waterloo Road, Stanhope, NJ 07874; 908-852-3790; nj.gov/dep/parksandforests/parks/allamuchymountainstatepark.html

DIRECTIONS

From I-80, take Exit 25 for US 206 North toward Stanhope/Newton. After 0.4 mile, take the exit on the right for International Drive, and then turn right onto Continental Drive. Continue 1.1 miles, and cross Waterloo Road/County Route 604 into the parking lot, which can hold approximately 50 vehicles.

TRAIL DESCRIPTION

Allamuchy Mountain State Park occupies more than 9,000 acres of woodlands and mountains. It's known statewide for rock climbing but is also a great spot for mountain biking, fishing, kayaking, snowshoeing, sledding, and cross-country skiing and includes historic Waterloo Village. The park is home to 14 miles of marked hiking trails and about 20 miles of unmarked trails.

This hike begins at the Sussex Branch trailhead off Waterloo Road. The full Sussex Branch Trail runs 21.2 miles along an old railroad right of way. It begins by heading north along the old rail bed, now a wide trail that allows hiking, biking, horseback riding, and cross-country skiing. Keep an eye out along your journey for evidence of the old railroad; it's there for those who look closely!

A quarter-mile into the hike, past a pair of trail junctions, walk along the western edge of Jefferson Lake. To the west are some boulders along the slopes that children (or children at heart) may enjoy taking a brief side trip to explore, and the area makes for a great photo spot, particularly at sunrise over the lake. Continue past the summer camp that has hugged the north side of the lake for more than 60 years. Watch for mallard ducks, red-winged blackbirds, and other fowl in the marshy lands on either side of the trail. A split to the left near a small waterfall was a siding—a short side track for trains not actively being run—used to load ice from an icehouse on Lake Jefferson to haul to market in the days before electric refrigerators.

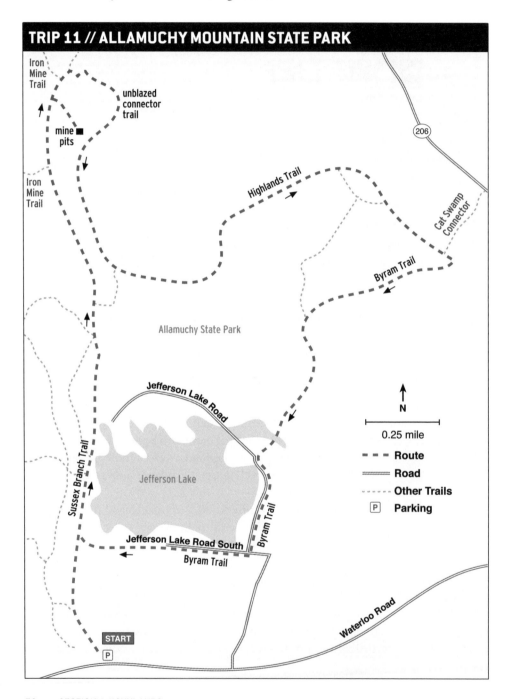

Pass blue-blazed Iron Mine Trail on the left as you continue along the rail-trail. At 1.4 miles in, turn right onto a short, unblazed side path, which winds through some marshlands down to a pretty view of the creek. Along the way, keep an eye out for remains of iron-mine pits. The Sussex Branch Railroad that the main trail now follows emerged from the Sussex Mine Railroad of the 1840s, which used mules to haul iron ore to the Morris Canal.

Head back to Sussex Branch Trail and turn right to continue north. Within 0.1 mile, pass blue-blazed Iron Mine Trail for a second time (the back end of a horseshoe that ends each time on Sussex Branch Trail) before a large wetlands area appears on your left. Keep a sharp eye to the right and quickly (at 1.7 miles in) turn right onto an unblazed, but well-traveled, side trail, which curves right before cutting back sharply to the left as it scales the side of a hill. At the top of the rise, the side trail forks. Stay right as the trail curves back on itself to follow the stream almost due south at 2.0 miles, just after a large glacial erratic and a sign warning visitors to stay out of an area with abandoned mine openings. Light-blue blazes appear at the point (although not on the official map) that takes you south along another well-traveled trail until it runs into an intersection with teal-blazed Highlands Trail at 2.3 miles. Turn left to head east on Highlands Trail.

This part of the route is closer to a moderate hike than the very easy beginning sections along the rail-trail; it features several short inclines past rock formations and through old farm walls. Along the way, skirt more old mine pits, see another warning sign, and pass a "tripod rock"—a large glacial erratic—sitting on top of smaller stones.

An early morning sunrise over Jefferson Lake.

Cat Swamp Connector, at 3.6 miles in, leads to a now-closed restaurant. About 100 yards past this, turn sharply right to hike east along the gray-blazed Byram Trail. The treadway is now wide and flat again. Walk down over an old car bridge to reach a T intersection at a paved road at 4.4 miles. Turn left along paved Jefferson Lake Road, past a boat launch for the lake, and reach an intersection at the southeast corner of the lake. Turn right here to walk the paved road, which dead-ends at a trail sign. Pass the sign and arrive at Sussex Branch Trail 5.0 miles into the hike.

Turn left and you'll soon be back at the parking lot.

DID YOU KNOW?

In the days before refrigeration, icehouses were important businesses. When lakes froze over in winter, workers would cut huge blocks of ice that would be stored in an icehouse. When warm weather came, the ice would be shipped to market, where it would be delivered to homes for folks to put in what we now call an icebox or cold closet: a nonelectric refrigerator.

OTHER ACTIVITIES

Allamuchy Mountain State Park offers many more miles of trails, plus rock climbing (permit required). Camping and picnic facilities are in adjacent Stephens State Park. Just 3 minutes down the road is Waterloo Village. This historic town grew up along the Morris Canal, which connected the Delaware and Hudson rivers. Today, the site is open for walking year-round, has a visitor center open on Saturdays and Sundays from May to October, and offers programs on Saturdays and Sundays from June through September. Mars Wrigley, the parent company of M&M's, is based in nearby Hackettstown and has been in New Jersey since the 1940s. While tours are not available, the property features giant M&M's characters and M&M's crosswalk signs that make for great photos.

MORE INFORMATION

Wear blaze orange during hunting season, as hunting is allowed along many stretches of this hike. Be aware that bears frequent the property. The park is popular for hiking, horseback riding, cross-country skiing, mountain biking, rock climbing, and other activities. It even has designated sledding areas.

12 SIX MILE RUN RESERVOIR

Zigzag between pastoral fields and welcoming woods, stroll along a creek, cross streams (with a stop at a lunch-worthy bridge), and traverse rolling terrain for a soul-lifting experience.

Features 👨‍👧 🐎 💧 🎣 🐎 🚴

Location Somerset, NJ

Rating Easy

Distance 6-mile loop

Elevation Gain 400 feet

Estimated Time 2.5 hours

Maps USGS Monmouth; dandrcanal.org/images/maps/SixMileRun_map.pdf

GPS Coordinates 40° 28.404′ N, 74° 33.929′ W

Contact Administered by the Delaware and Raritan Canal State Park, 145 Mapleton Road, Princeton, NJ 08540, 609-924-5705, nj.gov/dep/parksandforests /parks/drcanalstatepark.html; and by the New Jersey Department of Environmental Protection, Division of Parks and Forestry, P.O. Box 402, Trenton, NJ 08625, 609-777-3373, njparksandforests.org/parks/listserv.html

DIRECTIONS

Take US 1 south if coming north, or take US 1 north if coming south, to Ridge Road. In 1 mile, Ridge Road becomes Heathcote Road. In 0.3 mile, Heathcote Road becomes County Route 603. In 1.8 miles, County Route 603 becomes Canal Road. After 5.4 miles, turn left to stay on Canal Road. In 1.0 mile, turn into the parking lot on the left (625 Canal Road), which has room for 30 cars.

TRAIL DESCRIPTION

The blue-blazed trail in Six Mile Run Reservoir is part of the 70-mile Delaware and Raritan Canal system (see "From Mules to Multiuse: Today's Delaware and Raritan Canal State Park" on page 40) and thus has two names: D&R Canal Trail and Blackwells Trail. The route intersects red-blazed Creek Trail, a rugged, fun hike with impressive views of Six Mile Run Creek. You'll take these three trails (and one unmarked trail) and pause on a shaded, picturesque bridge spanning Six Mile Run Creek. Rolling terrain and small bridges over streams keep the journey interesting. The area is the largest agricultural district in New Jersey and is listed in the National Register of Historic Places. The 3,037 acres were intended to be a reservoir site, but alternative water supplies were located, much to hikers' delight. The presence of many deciduous trees makes this a glorious fall trip. Green shade and sparkling water are cooling in summer. Spring brings a profusion of woodland wildflowers. Snow-covered open fields in winter are stunning. (*Note*: To preserve the easily eroded soil, do not hike here during mud season, usually April and May in New Jersey.)

Start in the parking lot at Canal Road. A few picnic tables promise a rest at hike's end. Be aware that this area is quite popular on the weekends, so those tables may be occupied throughout your visit. Facing Canal Road, turn right and cross the paved access road to enter the woods on blue-blazed Blackwells Trail. The pleasant path winds for a while through woods and open fields with birdhouses. In summer, daisies are prolific; goldenrod and milkweed attract butterflies and birds in season. Note the shagbark

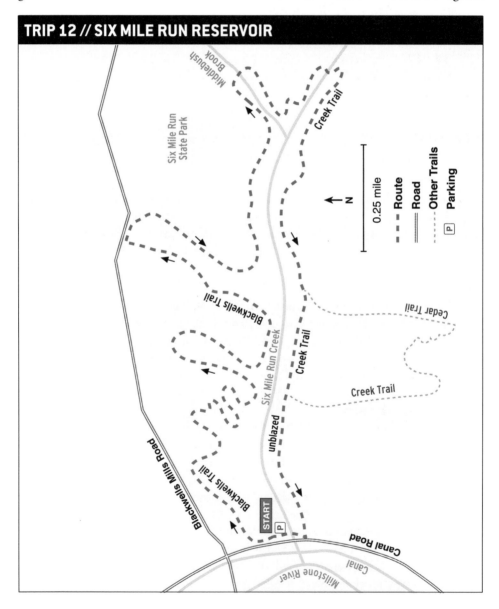

TRIP 12 // SIX MILE RUN RESERVOIR

hickory trees and spicebush. You may smell honeysuckle that blooms near the trail's edge. The terrain becomes rooty and a bit muddy with gentle ups and downs. Be sure to walk in the middle of the treadway; do not skirt the edges and expand the trail. Go through a field briefly and then stroll a boardwalk in a woodsy wetland. Briefly enter an open field again before heading back into the woods.

You'll continue to go in and out of fields and woods throughout the hike. Enjoy the winding trail, cool and green, despite the roots. At the blue trail marker on an iron post, take a rocky downhill trek under a graceful tree canopy. Mayapples and wild strawberries fringe the way. March through a tree tunnel, and skip over a stream on a boardwalk. In late June, blackberry bushes show ripening fruit. Small, steep hummocks (rounded knolls) keep the path interesting as it narrows onto a lovely footbridge.

Go around an open field, with a housing development on the left, following the trail sign. The blue sky frames a golden-grained wheat field to the left, the stalks close enough to brush against you.

Hike gradually uphill and reenter the woods at the trail sign. Watch your footing on the following rocky downhill section. The route heads toward the road, still following blue-blazed Blackwells Trail. Take the footbridge over a clear stream (2.6 miles), and the treadway becomes wider as you walk the woods' edge with the wheat field again to the left. Go straight, ignoring the path on the right, but then turn right at the blue Blackwells Trail sign. The trail forks again; go left into the woods. Enjoy the lovely temperature contrasts between shaded woods and open fields.

Soon briefly leave the woods and enter an open field. At the Blackwells Trail sign, turn right and go back into woods, over yet another footbridge. Watch out for blackberry bush thorns as you move from woods to field and onto a wooden boardwalk over a heavily eroded area. Eventually reach a sunny clearing, where a long, dramatic boardwalk slices through the tall green grasses. Cross another bridge (3.7 miles) over a stream and go gradually downhill to a rather lengthy bridge over Six Mile Run Creek. The bridge is fun to sit on, legs dangling high above the water, and offers an opportunity for lunch or a rest.

Say goodbye to the bridge and go onto the well-marked but rugged red-blazed Creek Trail (4.4 miles) and over a hill. (*Caution*: You may encounter mountain bikers on weekends.) Turn sharply right on the red-blazed trail at the sign for Creek Trail (it's really a U-turn). Walk uphill through a lovely tunnel of cedar trees and down a steep bank. The creek is nearly eye level on your right. At the Y intersection (4.6 miles), go right to stay on Creek Trail (white-blazed Cedar Trail is to the left). Walk a hiking bridge over a stream, parallel to a high, curved mountain-bike bridge. Veer right at the next Y. You are now on a wide, grassy path with naturalist signage for eastern red cedar and black walnut trees. Read about forest succession, whereby a disturbed natural area rebuilds.

Turn right onto an unmarked trail (5.2 miles). Cross a watery ditch and follow the sign for red-blazed Creek Trail. The treadway here is narrow, shaded, and rooty. Enjoy an elevated walk between a field on your left and Six Mile Run Creek on your right. The contrast is one of the loveliest parts of this hike.

Some fencing begins on the left, and then you plunge into a steep descent, where the ground can be rutty. Look for spots where you can walk down and visit Six Mile Run

Creek. The rolling route undulates, wandering in and out of the woods, even going through a cutout log. At a T intersection with a paved road (5.9 miles), turn right for a brief 175-yard road walk (*caution*: no shoulder). Cross the river on a stone bridge and then turn right into the parking lot.

DID YOU KNOW?

Nearby are eighteenth-century farmhouses, Dutch-framed granaries, and barns that tell the story of the first settlers in this region in the 1700s. Local eastern red cedars produce cedar oil, obtained from the wood and leaves, which can repel insects and provide antiseptic properties.

OTHER ACTIVITIES

Browse farmers markets and visit Davidson's Mill Pond Park in South Brunswick for the EARTH Center, a horticultural education facility operated by Rutgers Cooperative Extension of Middlesex County. Walk along the Raritan River for 2.5 miles at Johnson Park in Piscataway. The 20-acre Elmer B. Boyd Park in New Brunswick has views of the city skyline and a historical swing bridge. Colonial Park in Somerset features outstanding horticultural displays.

MORE INFORMATION

Open dawn to dusk. Be aware that biking and horseback riding is allowed on the trails. Leashed pets are permitted. For other trails in the Six Mile Run Reservoir site, see nj.gov/dep/parksandforests/maps/trailguides/six_mile_brochure_text.pdf.

Boardwalks aid in the trek across Six Mile Run Reservoir's marshy terrain.

13 MOHICAN OUTDOOR CENTER: RATTLESNAKE SWAMP TRAIL AND APPALACHIAN TRAIL

Walk through Rattlesnake Swamp before climbing to Kittatinny Ridge to enjoy spectacular views and a fire tower built in 1922.

Features

Location Blairstown, NJ

Rating Moderate

Distance 6-mile loop

Elevation Gain 600 feet

Estimated Time 3–4 hours

Maps USGS Bushkill, USGS Flatbrookville; Delaware Water Gap & Kittatinny Trail, Map 121, eighth edition, New York–New Jersey Trail Conference

GPS Coordinates 41° 02.144′ N, 74° 59.990′ W

Contact Mohican Outdoor Center, 50 Camp Mohican Road, Blairstown, NJ 07825; front desk: 908-362-5670; reservations: 603-466-2727; outdoors.org /destinations/new-jersey-new-york/mohican-outdoor-center. Delaware Water Gap National Recreation Area, 1978 River Road, Bushkill, PA 18324; 570-426-2452; nps.gov/dewa/index.htm

DIRECTIONS

Take NJ 31 North to US 46 in Buttzville. Go left on US 46 West for 1.6 miles to Hope-Bridgeville Road/County Route 519 and continue 6.4 miles to County Route 521 North in Hope. From there, take County Route 521 North 6.4 miles to NJ 94; turn left to head south. Take NJ 94 South for 1.1 miles through Blairstown to Mohican Road; turn right on Mohican Road and follow it 3.5 miles to Gaisler Road (bear right at forks on the winding road). Turn left and follow Gaisler Road for 0.5 mile, then turn right onto Camp Road, which becomes a dirt road. Drive across the Appalachian Trail, passing Mohican Outdoor Center on your left as you pull into the large dirt parking lot on your left, which has room for about 30 cars.

TRAIL DESCRIPTION

In the early decades of the Appalachian Trail, backpacking pioneers such as Earl Schaffer, Grandma Gatewood, Ed Garvey, and New Jersey's own Peace Pilgrim came looking to commune with nature, to get away from the bustle of modern life, to escape their troubles, or just to experience the sheer adventure of it. The AT, as the Appalachian Trail is affectionately known, travels more than 2,100 miles from Georgia to Maine.

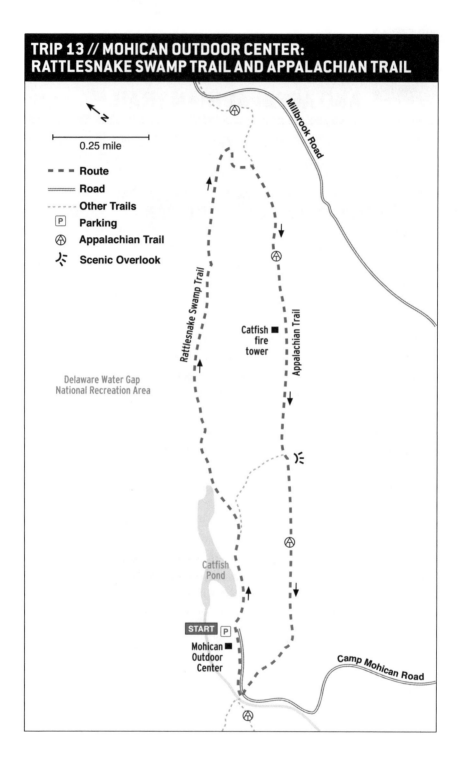

TRIP 13 // MOHICAN OUTDOOR CENTER: RATTLESNAKE SWAMP TRAIL AND APPALACHIAN TRAIL

N

0.25 mile

- - - Route
===== Road
----- Other Trails
P Parking
Ⓐ Appalachian Trail
⋏ Scenic Overlook

Millbrook Road

Rattlesnake Swamp Trail

Appalachian Trail

Delaware Water Gap
National Recreation Area

Catfish ■
fire
tower

Catfish
Pond

START P

Mohican ■
Outdoor
Center

Camp Mohican Road

Seventy-two of those miles run through New Jersey and include some spectacular views, the longest footbridge on the trail, a walk across a swamp, and a chance to hike next to cows. The beauty of the AT in New Jersey often catches thru-hikers (people who try to hike the entire AT in one year) by surprise, as their ideas of New Jersey rarely include things like mountain views or bears.

This hike offers a taste of the adventure and the beauty of the New Jersey section of the AT in any season. The new flowers and calls of returning birds greet hikers in spring; trees show off an explosion of color in autumn. Summer provides a leafy roof along much of the trail, and the bare trees of winter allow almost constant views. Be sure to wear gaiters and waterproof boots right after the spring thaw when the streams are full. Also be bear-aware, as the AT in New Jersey offers one of the largest concentrations of bears anywhere along the AT.

Start your hike by turning right out of the Mohican Outdoor Center parking lot and walking 100 yards down Camp Mohican Road to pick up a map at the lodge. Then backtrack down Camp Mohican Road past the parking lot and down past the campsites and cabins, passing Catfish Pond. Just to the left of a cabin, look for the trailhead sign for Rattlesnake Swamp Trail 0.25 mile into your hike. Step up on the puncheon bridges almost immediately. Within a short distance, a split in the trail gives you the choice of orange-blazed Rattlesnake Swamp Trail or a connector path with the AT. Stay to the left to get onto Rattlesnake Swamp Trail. Despite the name, rattlesnakes are no more or less common on this trail than along the ridgeline, according to the Delaware Water Gap National Recreation Area website.

The trail winds past Catfish Pond, which slowly turns into a swamp. Near the end of the pond, look out over the water for a trio of beaver lodges and, if you are fortunate, some beavers. Shortly after the lodges is the first stream crossing of the hike. Roughly half a dozen stream crossings exist over the next 1.5 miles. Most of the time, you can safely hop from stone to stone to cross, but be very careful during wet weather or when the streams are running high. This stretch also contains areas of tricky footing away from the water. In fact, much of the terrain of the AT and surrounding trails in New Jersey is very rocky. However, contrary to the stated beliefs of many thru-hikers, trail maintainers in certain sections do not make sure during trail maintenance that the rocks stick upward to trip unwary visitors.

Rattlesnake Swamp Trail slowly climbs out of the wetlands, offering a workout to legs and lungs, along with several opportunities to walk through tunnels created by mountain laurels. At mile 2.5, Rattlesnake Swamp Trail ends at a gravel road. Turn right on this road and make a breath-stealing steep climb up a pair of switchbacks. When you cut back to the right for your third switchback, you join with the white-blazed AT. At the end of that switchback, the AT leaves the road; make sure to follow it. Just a short distance down the trail, the AT rejoins the road (make sure to head southwest) along the Kittatinny Ridge. The hardest work of the hike is done now.

Head down the AT, enjoying the hints of views off to the left side of the ridge, and reach the Catfish fire tower (3.2 miles). A picnic table provides the perfect spot for lunch or a snack. With permission (call the New Jersey Forest Fire Service at 973-786-6350),

The AT skirts the edge of a cliff while heading south from the Catfish fire tower.

you can climb the tower to take in a spectacular 360-degree vista. The tower was built in 1922 and is 60 feet high!

Continuing southbound on the AT, you will have a few more opportunities to check for views. At 4.2 miles, on the right, you may notice the other trailhead along the AT for Rattlesnake Swamp Trail, which you can take back to the intersection near the beginning of the hike. However, you very likely won't see that intersection at all because to your left is an eye-catching, wide-open scene of the valley below. For the next half-mile or so, be careful as the trail skirts the edge of a steep drop, offering beautiful views to go with the tricky footing. Eventually, the trail begins to descend, meeting up with Camp Mohican Road (5.6 miles). Here, sadly, you leave your AT adventure. Turn right and walk down the road, past the MOC sign, until you reach the parking lot and the end of the hike.

DID YOU KNOW?

The Dutch discovered copper in the Kittatinny Mountains in the seventeenth century and built a 100-mile-long road to transport the ore to Kingston, New York. The mine was not profitable, but Old Mine Road continues to be used and maintained by the Delaware Water Gap National Recreation Area. Pahaquarry Copper Mine (a side trip off Kaiser Trail) is a bat hibernaculum, one of at least twenty known bat hibernation refuges in New Jersey. A gate across the entrance protects bats from people and from contact with the fungus that causes white-nose syndrome, a disease discovered in 2006 that has killed 90 percent of little brown bats. For more bat-finding, visit Hibernia Mine (see "Did You Know?" in Trip 4).

OTHER ACTIVITIES

Canoe and swim in MOC's crystal-clear Catfish Pond. Hike south from MOC to make a lovely loop of 5.7 miles with the AT, Kaiser Trail, and Coppermine Trail, which includes views of the Delaware Water Gap. Tour Lakota Wolf Preserve in Columbia (must make online reservations in advance; see lakotawolf.com) and Hidden Brook Ranch Alpaca Farm in Blairstown. Stroll the 665-acre White Lake Natural Resource Area in Hardwick (Trip 9). Explore Blairstown's shops and restaurants, and visit the Blairstown Museum to learn about regional history. The Blairstown Theatre (Roy's Hall), a former silent movie theater built in 1913, now features films and live performances.

MORE INFORMATION

Mohican Outdoor Center is the Appalachian Mountain Club's southernmost property. It offers self-service cabin options, as well as opportunities for camping. For more information, see outdoors.org/destinations/new-jersey-new-york/mohican-outdoor-center/.

NEW JERSEY'S BLACK BEARS

Black bears are the largest land mammal in New Jersey, and New Jersey has a lot of them. A 2013 study put New Jersey's human population at 8,791,894 and its black bear population at 3,400. Estimates in 2020 by Fish and Wildlife biologists calculated a population increase in the region north of Interstate 78 and west of Interstate 287, with about 3,000 bears projected to live in the northwestern portion of the state, including Sussex, Passaic, Warren, and Morris counties. Large litters and high survival rates mean black bears have been sighted in all of New Jersey's 21 counties. The black bear's natural life span is about 33 years or more, while the average life span in unprotected black bear populations is only 3 to 5 years. Given that New Jersey is the most densely populated state for both humans and black bears, hikers and bears will probably overlap.

Statistically, a hiker is most likely to encounter a bear in northwestern New Jersey, such as in the Kittatinny and Appalachian mountains or the Delaware Water Gap National Recreation Area, all of which feature the ideal bear habitats of mixed hardwood forests, dense swamps, and forested wetlands. You won't necessarily see the bears, however. Black bears are shy, timid creatures and often wary of people. But they can be oblivious when on the trail of a tasty smell (they can detect scents more than 2 miles away) and can cross paths unintentionally with hikers. If the bear is curious, it may stand on its hind legs to see and smell better, which many people falsely take as a sign of aggression.

If you do see a black bear, it's smart to have a healthy fear, but don't panic and run. Instead, make noises to scare it, avoid eye contact, and slowly back away. Don't approach it for that once-in-a-lifetime photo, and never feed it.

As the overall bear population increases, New Jersey's southern and eastern regions have seen bear populations rise. Humans and bears are often drawn to the same habitat, such as wooded suburbs, forested parks, and developments in former agricultural areas that have retained some degree of wildness. Black bears favor forested slopes and riparian corridors where urban areas meet wildlands, and they thrive there. Female bears who live in close proximity to human development actually have more cubs than those living in the wild, although the suburban cub survival rate is lower. As the black bear population increases, suburban encounters between bears and humans are more likely to occur.

Human suburbanites who live in areas where there is known bear activity must properly manage outdoor food and garbage. Even though bears are shy, they are dedicated foodies. A bird feeder, an improperly managed compost pile, pet food left outside, or a smelly garbage container (even if empty) might attract investigation by a curious bear. And this bears repeating: Never intentionally feed a bear. Trouble arises when bears associate humans with food.

Please don't report a bear as a problem if it is simply passing through your neighborhood, doing no harm. Bears that wander into residential areas, usually attracted by food smells, often end up in trees because they are confused and scared, as are the homeowners. If you do need to alert law enforcement, an officer will usually tranquilize and relocate the bear, typically to state-owned land, such as a wildlife management area. Bears are aversely conditioned with rubber buckshot or killed on the rare occasions when they pose a public safety threat. ("Averse conditioning" modifies undesirable bear behavior so the animals don't need to be killed.)

Keep in mind that predatory attacks by black bears are extremely rare. Only one documented bear fatality has occurred in New Jersey's history, the death of a hiker in West Milford, Passaic County, in September 2014.

Unfortunately, bear populations cannot be effectively controlled by relocation or birth control. Bear harvesting (i.e., bear hunting), although controversial, has been shown to control bear populations and to reduce human–bear conflicts by creating a "landscape of fear"—or looked at another way, by creating a healthy respect for humans. We should return the favor and develop a healthy fear of and respect for bears.

Don't contribute to poor human–bear relations by being ignorant and overreactive. Black bears are large land mammals, native to New Jersey, who are gracious enough to share their home with day-hikers, even as we share our suburbs with them. Whether you are in their forested homes or they are in your suburban ones, be a good neighbor. In the woods, announce yourself by singing, talking, clapping, and making other noises. Bears, being shy and ever so polite, will simply try to stay hidden, leaving you to enjoy your hike. When bears are in your territory, don't tempt them with food, and never tease or approach them.

With the ever-increasing human population, it's important to remember we share this planet with animals. Being a good neighbor is more important than ever.

For bear safety tips at home and in the outdoors, see *Know the Bear Facts: Black Bears in New Jersey* at state.nj.us/dep/fgw/pdf/bear/bearfacts_know.pdf.

Black bears are the largest land mammal in New Jersey, but due to their shy nature, hikers are unlikely to see them.

The Gateway region of New Jersey is home to part of Ellis Island, the "gateway" through which many immigrants entered the United States. (The other part of the island belongs to New York State, according to a 1998 Supreme Court ruling.) Of the six geographic regions in New Jersey, Gateway best exemplifies the contrasts between this state's urban and rural bounties. With a population of more than 4 million, Gateway is the most urban part of the state and yet is home to some of its most beautiful and even secluded trails. The largest shopping mall in New Jersey is in Bergen County, but the same county also boasts 4,269-acre Ramapo State Forest and 2,500-acre Palisades Interstate Park. Ramapo State Forest is a stream-crossed and hilly sanctuary for wildlife, with views of the New York City skyline, and Palisades Interstate Park offers 30  miles of hiking on the uplands and cliffs of the Hudson River shorefront, tucked incongruously just off the Palisades Interstate Parkway. You could easily have dinner in Manhattan after hiking in Palisades Park.

Gateway encompasses New Jersey's six largest municipalities (Newark, Jersey City, Paterson, Elizabeth, Woodbridge Township, and Edison) and four major rivers (Hudson, Hackensack, Passaic, and Raritan). The urban/rural sprawl includes the Meadowlands and the Palisades in the northeast, the valleys and hills of the Watchung Mountains in the west, the Ramapo Mountains in the north, and the tidal plains of the Raritan River to the south. The Watchung Mountains are a group of three long, low ridges, the product of volcanic activity 200 million years ago, that range from 400 to 500 feet high. The Watchungs are known for scenic vistas of New York City and parts of New Jersey, traprock areas, and isolated ecosystems that contain rare plants, endangered wildlife, and rich minerals. The Ramapo Mountains, a forested chain of the Appalachians, range in height from 900 to 1,200 feet. The Ramapos are known for their nature preserves and their concentrations of gneiss, granite, and marble. New

Facing page: Autumn colors the steep basalt cliffs of the New Jersey Palisades.

York's Harriman State Park is in these beautiful mountains and is home to the Appalachian Mountain Club's Stephen & Betsy Corman AMC Harriman Outdoor Center.

Long ago, the Lenni-Lenape people resided in what is now called Gateway. In 1609, Henry Hudson sailed into what is now Sandy Hook and Weehawken Cove; by 1660, the first chartered village was established at Bergen Square on the North River. Many of today's hiking areas bear Lenape-derived names, such as Ramapo, Watchung, and Cheesequake State Park. "Cheesequake" is anglicized from the Lenape word *chichequaas*, meaning "upland," or *chiskhakink*, meaning "at the land that has been cleared." Cheesequake is a transitional zone between two ecosystems: coastal salt marshes and upland forest.

Industry came in earnest to this region in 1755 with the first steam engine, and Alexander Hamilton helped found the Society for the Establishment of Useful Manufactures, which used water from the Great Falls of the Passaic River, which is near one of the hikes in this section (see Trip 14). Thomas Edison also left his impression here: visit his laboratories in Edison and his home in West Orange to learn more about the Wizard of Menlo Park.

The Central Railroad of New Jersey Terminal, a symbol of immigration and industry, is featured in the Liberty State Park hike (Trip 24). You can visit historical displays here. The railroad was chartered in 1838 and accommodated 30,000 passengers a day at its peak in 1900. It ceased passenger operations in 1967.

Gateway boasts 26 parks, including 3 state forests and 5 state parks; 11 are covered in hikes featured in this section.

14 GARRET MOUNTAIN RESERVATION

Expect excellent views of New York City in all seasons—especially from 75-foot-tall Lambert Tower—and a beautiful urban walk in fall.

Features 🚶 🐕 📷 🎿 ❄️ ⛱️ 🚌

Location Woodland Park, NJ

Rating Easy

Distance 2.8-mile loop

Elevation Gain 400 feet

Estimated Time 2 hours

Maps USGS Paterson; nynjtc.org/sites/default/files/GarretMtnRes_Map_v1-1.pdf; passaiccountynj.org/home/showpublisheddocument/4468/637702593922800000

GPS Coordinates 40° 53.999′ N, 74° 10.178′ W

Contact 8 Mountain Avenue, Woodland Park, NJ 07424; 973-881-4833; passaiccountynj.org/Home/Components/FacilityDirectory/FacilityDirectory/44/316

DIRECTIONS

Driving: Take I-80 west to Exit 56. Turn left at the bottom of the ramp onto Squirrelwood Road. (If you are coming from the west, take Exit 56A and proceed south on Squirrelwood Road.) Continue along Squirrelwood Road for 0.7 mile, then turn left onto Weasel Drift Road. Go approximately 0.5 mile to the entrance to the park, on the left. Turn left into the park and proceed north on Benson Drive/Park Drive (pass the equestrian center on your right). In about 0.3 mile, parking is on your left, across from the observation tower (Lambert Tower). About twelve parking spots are available here, but bigger lots dot the park; see online map.

Public Transportation: From New York City's Port Authority Bus Terminal to Lambert Castle at Garret Mountain Reservation, take NJ Transit bus 192 (Clifton–New York). Get off the bus at the intersection of Valley Road, Mountain Park Road, and Fenner Avenue (if unsure, ask bus driver). Walk one block east (toward Paterson Avenue); the entrance to the castle's driveway is on the left. Walk up the driveway. From the Lambert Castle parking lot, take Morris Canal Greenway (yellow octagon) to the top of mountain (0.15 mile). At the top, with the observation tower on the left, turn right on Morris Canal Greenway. For more information, please contact NJ Transit at 973-275-5555 or visit njtransit.com. Travel time from New York City to Lambert Castle is 48 minutes. You can reach trails from Lambert Castle.

TRAIL DESCRIPTION

Hikes in 560-acre Garret Mountain Reservation combine history, city views, rocky cliffs, and paved and dirt paths. The area is especially beautiful in fall. December brings festivities at Lambert Castle, which serves as headquarters for the Passaic County Historical Society and is also a library and art museum (check posted hours and admission fees). Spring brings the return of a wide array of warblers, vireos, thrushes, sparrows, flycatchers, swallows, and wrens. Summer can be crowded, with lots of activity at the picnic groves and basketball courts.

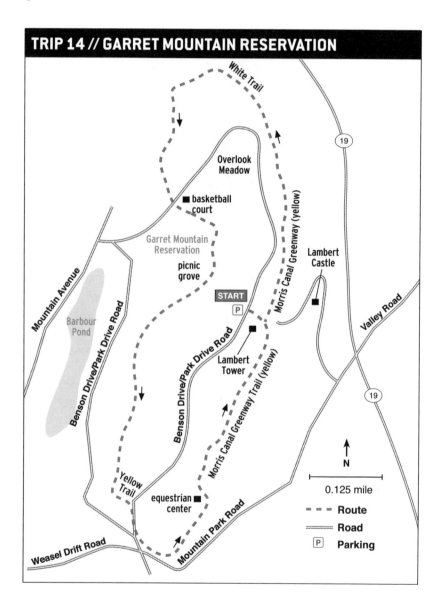

TRIP 14 // GARRET MOUNTAIN RESERVATION

From Lambert Tower, take Morris Canal Greenway (MCG), blazed with yellow octagons, to White Trail to Yellow Trail (blazed with white rectangles and yellow rectangles, respectively). This route along the eastern edge of the reservation and down through the middle is easy to follow, even though minor unblazed trails branch off.

Walk across Mountain Park Road to the marker for Watchung Ridge; you are on the third-highest peak (about 500 feet) of the Watchung Mountains. Enter the gray stone Lambert Tower, marked by a green sign and named for Catholina Lambert, who emigrated from England in 1834 and founded a silk dynasty in Paterson (the Silk City of the New World). Lambert lived in Lambert Castle and used the tower as an observatory and summer house. He died in 1923, and his son Walter sold the castle and land to the city of Paterson. (Lambert had eight children. Seven predeceased him, leaving Walter as the only heir.)

Climb the 75 steps of the 75-foot tower (with interior historical signage), which is 502 feet above sea level, for excellent views of the George Washington Bridge and, in New York, Bear Mountain State Park and the Verrazzano-Narrows Bridge, as well as New York City. Leave the tower, perhaps walking to the protected edge of the 150-foot sheer cliff to look down on the now-blocked "Devil's Staircase," a dangerous fissure once explored by adventurous young visitors.

Facing the view toward New York, with your back to the tower, turn left (north) onto the cinder path, rimmed by a massive stone wall, with Lambert Castle visible below. You are on yellow-octagon-blazed MCG. This 1-mile path was reclaimed from the 102-mile-long Morris Canal, which was completed in 1831 and retired in 1923 when overshadowed by the railroad. MCG, once all municipal trails are connected to the canal route, will stretch across six counties, creating a continuous 111-mile greenway; the 2018 MCG Corridor Study identifies 38 miles of existing trails. (For maps and more, see morriscanalgreenway.org.)

Follow the wall that runs between you and the cliffs, and go down stone steps onto a fairly flat dirt path with a few rocks. Many side trails lead to the right for fine views of Paterson and the same areas that are visible from Lambert Tower. Keep on MCG, skirting the huge parking lot to the left, suitable for buses and around 100 cars. Reach an open field and veer right to follow MCG. Far below to the right is I-80, and to the left is pretty Overlook Meadow. MCG goes downhill and merges with paved White Trail (rectangular white marker) at another parking lot.

Turn right (0.5 mile) to follow White Trail around the far edge of the parking lot for some more fine views. Check out the scenery with the 25-cent observation binoculars. Descend the steps to the right, following the stone wall, to stay on White Trail. The paved path ends, and picnic tables and benches are conveniently located on your left. Head downhill into the woods, where white birches buffer the traffic noise. Keep going down on a well-maintained path through a section that is beautiful in fall. A ravine is to the right.

White Trail rises past huge boulders, perhaps remnants of the rock quarries (primarily brownstone and traprock, including amethyst and prehnite) that thrived in this area for more than 150 years. At the junction with Yellow Trail (1.0 mile), go left to stay on White Trail (also known as Bridle Path). Keep left on White Trail to a gravel parking lot and basketball court. Cross the parking lot and road to stay on White Trail, heading toward Rocky Hollow Picnic Grove (green sign). The dirt-and-gravel path widens in this pleasant patch of woods. (Stay alert. Unmarked trails dot this section.)

Veer left to stay on White Trail, and pass more big rocks on the right. Turn right at the first junction to follow White Trail (1.2 miles); a concrete picnic table is on the right. The path widens at the second junction; turn right there and at the third junction to stay on White Trail. At the fourth junction, veer left to remain on White Trail, and take a few minutes to notice the fantastic tree shapes, the smells in the air, and the curious rock formations.

White Trail ends at a gravel path, and Yellow Trail (yellow rectangle) picks up; turn left on Yellow Trail (1.9 miles)—do not go straight. As you head down toward the equestrian center, you may see deer and other critters.

Exit the woods, cross paved Benson Drive, and turn right in front of the attractive stone gates to stay on Yellow Trail. The road is on your right, a startling reminder of this reservation's urban location. Weave through three small boulders, enter a beautiful, delicate woods, and head uphill to a house on the right. Brush through tall, wheat-colored, whispery grasses and autumn wildflowers. You are now on a very pretty hill, with the equestrian center on the left (2.2 miles). Turn left at a bend at the far end of the equestrian center. Follow Yellow Trail between some rocks before it veers to the right into open grasses. Walk over some unusual black rocks, the color highlighted by bright yellow blazes, and head uphill for an excellent view of New York City to the right (2.6 miles), this one more secluded than the earlier views. Sounds of gunfire may drift up from the private police shooting range below. Lambert Tower ahead marks the end of

This urban hike features stunning views of the New York City skyline.

the hike. Go downhill and cross the road to your car. If taking public transportation, reach MCG from Lambert Tower, descend 0.15 mile to Lambert Castle, go down the castle's driveway, and walk one block west (away from Paterson Avenue) toward the bus stop at the intersection of Valley Road, Mountain Park Road, and Fenner Avenue.

DID YOU KNOW?

Three ridges (called First, Second, and Third Watchung Mountain) make up the Watchung Mountains. Garret Mountain Reservation covers the northernmost part of First Watchung Mountain, sometimes called Orange Mountain. Second Watchung is also called Preakness Mountain, and Third Watchung is known as Hook Mountain. Volcanic magma formed the ridges nearly 200 million years ago.

OTHER ACTIVITIES

Visit Thomas Edison National Historical Park (Edison's home and lab) in West Orange. See the dramatic 77-foot-high falls at Paterson Great Falls National Historical Park and the newly renovated Hinchliffe Stadium, one of the few remaining stadiums that hosted a large number of Negro League baseball games; professional games resumed in 2023 and a Negro Leagues museum is planned (hinchliffestadium.com). Visit the Paterson Museum in the Thomas Rogers Building and stop by the American Labor Museum/Botto House in Haledon.

MORE INFORMATION

Open dawn to dusk. The Garret Mountain Reservation complex also has basketball courts, an equestrian center, multipurpose fields, pavilions, and picnic areas for a full day of family fun.

15 PALISADES INTERSTATE PARK: STATE LINE LOOKOUT TO PEANUT LEAP CASCADE

Enjoy Hudson River vistas, rocky cliffs, steep hills, the ruins of an Italian garden, and a rocky beach with a waterfall nearby.

Features

Location Alpine, NJ

Rating Moderate

Distance 3 miles round-trip

Elevation Gain 600 feet

Estimated Time 1.5–2 hours

Maps USGS Yonkers; njpalisades.org/pdfs/hikeStateline.pdf

GPS Coordinates 40° 59.327′ N, 73° 54.428′ W

Contact Palisades Interstate Park Commission, P.O. Box 155, Alpine, NJ 07620; 201-768-1360; njpalisades.org

DIRECTIONS

Driving: Head north on the Palisades Interstate Parkway. After Exit 2, go 1.8 miles to a well-marked blue sign for the State Line Lookout exit. Follow signs to State Line Lookout parking (room for around 50 cars).

Public Transportation: Take Coach USA/Rockland Coaches Route 9 bus, which departs from the Port Authority's George Washington Bridge Terminal in New York City (175th Street station on the A express subway line) or from the Port Authority Bus Terminal (42nd Street), with stops at Bridge Plaza in Fort Lee. The bus then travels north up US 9W to the state line by the entrance to Lamont-Doherty Earth Observatory. Leave the bus at this point and follow the concrete roadway of Old US 9W (closed to traffic) to State Line Lookout. The total distance is about 1.5 miles. The old roadway climbs an uphill grade going to State Line Lookout. Allow about 45 minutes for each direction, up and back down.

For additional schedule information for the Route 9 bus, visit Coach USA/Rockland Coaches (web.coachusa.com/rockland) or call 201-263-1254 (main office) or 212-279-6526 (New York City Office). For connecting bus information, also check NJ Transit, njtransit.com.

TRAIL DESCRIPTION

Prepare for a short but dramatic hike from atop the 520-foot Palisades Cliffs overlooking the Hudson River to the rocky beach at river's edge. The high cliffs provide a superb vantage point for observing birds and butterflies. In autumn, look for sharp-shinned hawks, ospreys, broad-winged hawks, peregrine falcons, and monarch butterflies. Bald eagles and ducks spend winter on the cliffs, and the park includes more than 5 miles of cross-country skiing trails. Spring brings great blue herons and swallows. In summer, watch double-crested cormorants dry their wings, red-tailed hawks soar, and tiger swallowtail butterflies float.

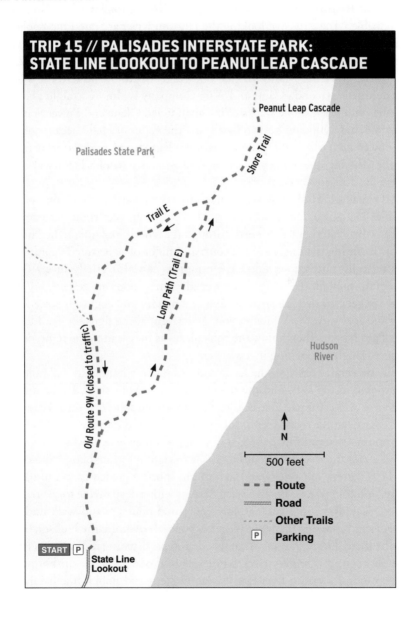

TRIP 15 // PALISADES INTERSTATE PARK:
STATE LINE LOOKOUT TO PEANUT LEAP CASCADE

It's no wonder the U.S. Department of the Interior and the National Park Service designated Palisades Interstate Park a National Historic Landmark in 1965. The 2,500-acre New Jersey side is about 12 miles long and a half-mile wide. The New Jersey and New York sides combined span 42 miles, from the George Washington Bridge in Fort Lee, New Jersey, to the Bear Mountain Bridge in Bear Mountain State Park, New York. This hike takes you on Long Path, which leads to rocky Shore Trail and Peanut Leap Cascade. Wear sturdy hiking boots because many sections are rocky and steep and can be slippery when wet, icy, or leaf covered.

Start at the cozy, charming Franklin Roosevelt–era State Line Café for food, drink, guidebooks, and bathrooms. (Franklin Roosevelt's Work Projects Administration made the café possible.) The cliffs overlooking the Hudson River at State Line Lookout are a birder's paradise and great for fall hawk-watching and leaf-peeping. Use the observation binoculars or your personal pair to pick out some landmarks. The Tappan Zee Bridge (technically the Governor Mario M. Cuomo Bridge) lies to the far left; the water tower from the defunct Anaconda Cable and Wire Company is almost straight ahead. To its right are the twin brick smokestacks of the abandoned Glenwood Power Station, built between 1904 and 1906 and known locally as "the Gates of Hell" because of its use in zombie movies and, allegedly, gang initiations. Rumors of renovation plans surface periodically. The big blue cube you see in Yonkers was part of a factory and is now a soundstage for film production.

Facing the majestic Hudson River, turn left (north) toward marker 1 on a paved path. Picnic tables are conveniently on your right. Very soon, veer right onto aqua-blazed Long Path, a dirt trail that heads north through the woods (0.2 mile). The Hudson is to your right. In spring, you may see the courtship flight of peregrine falcons: a series of dives, barrel rolls, and somersaults. These raptors can also briefly invert (fly upside down) to grasp prey on the wing. On a weekday, the woods are serene and quiet, but weekends can get crowded. The path widens and flattens and begins to descend, becoming rooty and rocky. At the Y intersection, go straight at the signs for Trail E (ski trail) and Long Path North. Then follow the aqua blazes as they lead to the right, down some stone steps through an opening in a wire fence.

Carefully descend, following the fence and using it as a handhold (0.7 mile) because you are exposed to the cliffs and the river far below on your right. In the distance is a stunning view of the Tappan Zee Bridge. The very steep steps end on a flat, rocky path that goes away from the river. Technically, you have crossed into New York; a 6-foot-tall state line boundary monument, erected in 1882, is somewhere nearby.

Descend across three wooden footbridges. Turn right on white-blazed Shore Trail (1.1 miles), which flattens out briefly and in autumn sports a golden carpet of oak, maple, sweet gum, and tulip leaves. Begin a steep descent with a deep ravine to the right.

Pick your way over some fascinatingly contoured boulders and walk under a large fallen tree. Keep following the white blazes to your left. Admire the Hudson below; you will soon be there. Descend some steep wooden steps, listening to the waves lapping on the rocky shores of this mighty river, 3 miles wide at one point. At the bottom of your descent (1.3 miles) awaits a fairy-tale warren of steps and hobbit-like habitats on the

Hikers ascend from the Hudson River and garden ruins at Peanut Leap Cascade.

banks of the Hudson. Capricious stonework, downed columns, a maze of stone walls and ramps, brick archways, and plunging stone steps are the remains of an Italian garden designed by the artist Mary Lawrence-Tonetti around 1900. She and her family entertained lavishly in the garden. After her death, the family donated the land to the park commission.

Linger on a lopsided bench jutting from tree roots, or stand on the rocky beach and dip your toes in the Hudson River; it's a pleasant spot for lunch or a rest. To the right, admire the Palisades sill (an outstanding example of igneous rock intruded between sediment layers), noting the scarred areas where quarries in the 1800s produced diabase traprock for paving stones and blocks. (Mining stopped in 1900 when the park commission took over.) Smell the brackish scent: the Hudson River is part salt water and part fresh water. Imagine immense quantities of shad ascending to the headwater to spawn in late March and early April.

Go back the same way. Before you leave, visit Peanut Leap Cascade, a waterfall to the left of the ruins. In some seasons, the cascade merely trickles.

To ease your return, skip the three wooden footbridges by going straight on rooty and rocky aqua-blazed Long Path (2.0 miles). Keep the stream on your left.

At the Y intersection, turn left toward State Line Lookout (sign) on an unblazed trail. Hike upward over roots and rocks. In summer, look for stalks of turtleheads and black-eyed Susans; fall brings white snakeroots, foxgloves, and asters. Go through the gate at the wire fence and turn left onto the paved road. A gentle ascent leads straight to the café, where you might spot soaring ravens. If you have time, take a short walk to the interesting Women's Federation Monument (see "Other Activities").

DID YOU KNOW?

Palisades Park has its own song, a tribute to its days as an amusement park. "Palisades Park" was written by Chuck Barris in 1962 and has been recorded by Freddy Cannon, Gary Lewis and the Playboys, the Beach Boys, and the Ramones, among others.

OTHER ACTIVITIES

For a challenging hike, turn right (south) at the Peanut Leap Cascade area to follow the talus-ridden shoreline of the Hudson and climb the difficult Giant Stairs. (The Giant Stairs are not suitable for dogs or young children and involve a scramble over a mile-long boulder field before ascending a steep trail.) For an easier hike, face the river at State Line Café and follow the clear signage for unblazed Women's Federation Monument Trail, a charming 0.6-mile walk to a miniature castle honoring the role of the New Jersey State Federation of Women's Clubs in shutting down the quarries and preserving the Palisades. Visit Kearney House, a home illuminating two centuries of family life on the Hudson River (open most weekends May through October), and Fort Lee Historic Park, an American Revolution encampment atop a 33-acre cliff (visitor center open Wednesday through Sunday; njpalisades.org/fortlee.html).

MORE INFORMATION

Open during daylight hours, 30 minutes before sunrise and 30 minutes after sunset. Restaurant and gift shop on premises.

16 WATCHUNG RESERVATION: WHITE TRAIL TO FELTVILLE

Discover hidden history deep in the woods as you explore an abandoned village and an eighteenth-century graveyard.

Features

Location Scotch Plains, NJ

Rating Easy

Distance 3.9-mile loop

Elevation Gain 550 feet

Estimated Time 2.5 hours

Maps USGS Chatham; ucnj.org/parks-recreation/paths-trails-greenways /watchung-reservation

GPS Coordinates 40° 40.211′ N, 74° 23.593′ W

Contact Department of Parks and Recreation, County of Union, 10 Elizabethtown Plaza, Elizabethtown, NJ 07202; 908-527-4900; ucnj.org/parks-recreation

DIRECTIONS

Take I-95 to NJ 18 North toward New Brunswick. After 4.33 miles, take the Metlars Lane ramp and keep left at the fork. Then stay straight to follow County Route 609. In 0.58 mile, turn left to stay on County Route 609 and follow it for 1.02 miles; then stay straight to go onto South Washington Avenue/County Route 665. In 1.32 miles, turn left onto County Route 529/Stelton Road and follow it for 3.42 miles before turning right onto US 22 East. In 6.67 miles, turn right onto Glenside Avenue (County Route 527). At a T intersection, turn left onto Sky Top Drive. In less than 0.5 mile, parking is on both sides of street. Watch for a picnic pavilion.

TRAIL DESCRIPTION

This historical, charming loop follows White Trail through the Deserted Village of Feltville and Glenside Park to purple-blazed History Trail, to blue-blazed Blue Trail, and back to white-blazed White Trail.

About 47 miles of trails are in 2,142-acre Watchung Reservation, the largest of Union County's 36 parks. The Union County Parks system was designed by the Olmsted brothers. The site is on both the New Jersey and National Registers of Historic Places. Since 1600, the property has hosted a copper mine, a printing business, a recreational resort, a sawmill, and a Boy Scout camp. Situated between First and Second Watchung mountains and divided by Blue Brook Valley, the reservation includes wetlands, ponds, rivers, hardwood swamps, forests, and meadows and is an important link in the Union County greenway. Migratory birds rest and refuel here. Other animals include red foxes, wood-chucks, red-shouldered hawks, great horned owls, and bats. Trees include American beeches, oaks, dogwoods, and tulip poplars, making beautiful fall and spring palettes.

At the kiosk in the parking lot nearest the picnic pavilion, pick up a map and self-guided tour of the Deserted Village of Feltville and Glenside Park (cell phone QR codes are on maps). Chemical toilets are available seasonally. The route starts at the Sky Top Picnic Area (sign). Turn left at the picnic area onto White Trail. Cross a stream and veer right at the fork, following white blazes. In winter, pine trees provide greenery. The broad, rooty, and rutted dirt treadway soon descends. Turn right at a wide road and then imme-diately turn left to stay on White Trail and head down the gravelly, rocky path.

Go up steps and cross a wooden bridge, noting the incredible shapes of downed trees. At the Drake Farm sign (0.6 mile), observe the stone foundations of a farmhouse and

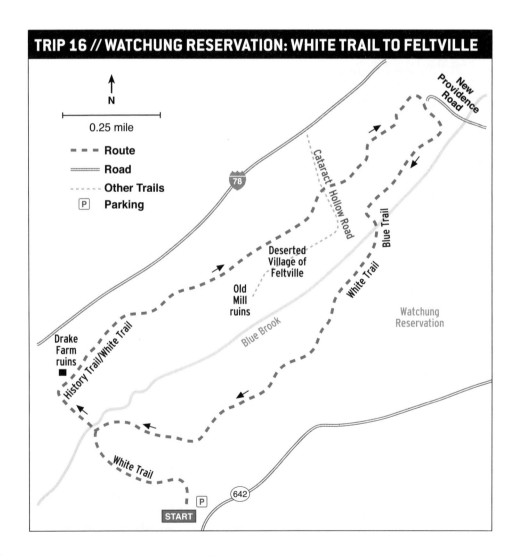

barn. The farm originally provided food for the residents of Feltville. The property was also used for grazing cattle and later converted to the summer resort of Glenside Park.

You are now on purple-blazed History Trail, which merges with White Trail. Turn right after the farmhouse, then right again, staying on History Trail. The trail narrows and becomes dirt before crossing a bridge over a stream. Descend and cross a streambed (dry in winter); the high banks make the path cozy. Veer left at the Y intersection. Note deep erosion to the right caused by a microburst (intense thunderstorm with strong bursts of wind). The trail widens and becomes less rooty as it winds pleasantly through a clearing.

Enter a large, paved road (where History Trail and White Trail temporarily join) and enjoy Masker's Barn on the right—a restored and heated barn that holds 150 people and can be rented for parties (1.4 miles). Built in 1882, Masker's Barn held horses and carriages that transported businessmen to the train station at Murray Hill. Their families stayed behind at Glenside Park to enjoy golf, tennis, croquet, baseball, fishing, and horseback riding at the resort.

Take time to explore the remaining buildings in the Deserted Village of Feltville and Glenside Park. (*Note*: Some are occupied today.) In about 1736, Peter Willcocks built a sawmill along Blue Brook to produce lumber. The sawmill operation cleared hundreds of acres of forest. In 1845, David Felt bought 760 acres of Willcocks's land. Visit the house of David Felt, founder of Feltville, who lived here with his family from 1845 to 1860. Felt ran a stationery business in New York City. He built a paper mill here along Blue Brook and then built an entire town to support the operation. The self-guided tour booklet contains some interesting details about his life.

Go behind the Felt house (which has an indoor bathroom) and down a path with handrails. Turn left at the Y intersection and head uphill to a 1700s cemetery. Linger a while, paying homage to Phebe Badgley Willcocks and others buried here. It's believed that the cemetery holds about two dozen family members. Purple-blazed History Trail ends here.

Continue straight on what is now just White Trail, noting the steep ravine to the right. At the Y intersection, turn left and keep bearing left onto a narrow, smooth dirt path. At the T intersection, go right, still on the white-blazed trail, down a wider dirt path with eerie, windblown trees. Turn right at the Y intersection, crossing over a drainage pipe, and go down a wide dirt path. Traverse a charming dirt bridge with brick railings and go right at the Y intersection.

Turn sharply right onto a dirt boardwalk onto Blue Trail (2.4 miles). Go over a bridge, ascend a narrow dirt path, and turn left at the Y intersection to stay on the blue-blazed trail. The terrain is a bit rugged with roots and rocks; a stream is to the right. Cross the stream. In winter, you'll hear the bare trees creak.

You are now back on White Trail. Go left at the white blaze on a steep, rooty path. Stay left to keep on White Trail, which merges with a pink-blazed trail temporarily (2.6 miles). Turn right at the junction to stay on White Trail as it goes up and down a muddy path (wetlands). Almost immediately, the trail turns left. Cross a ravine and climb a steep, rocky incline to a ridge (about 2.9 miles). Turn right at the Y intersection to stay on White Trail. Private homes are ahead on the left. Go straight at the next intersection and head downhill over a streambed, which can be wet in spring and

The cemetery holds about two dozen people, although only one headstone is original.

bone-dry in winter but is always rooty and rocky. At the road, stay to your left to remain on the white-blazed trail. Go up some timber steps to your left, traipsing through a forest of toothpick-thin trees and up a muddy trail. Suddenly you are back at the picnic area, where you can stop for lunch or return to the parking lot.

DID YOU KNOW?

Feltville was deserted—three times. The first time was by Feltville's creator, David "King David" Felt, who built this quasi-utopian mill town from 1845 to 1847. For fifteen years, it thrived under his benevolent leadership, fueled by his Unitarian ideals to provide a better lifestyle for urban industrial workers, and boasted 175 residents in 1850. In August of 1860, for reasons unknown, Felt sold the business and property to Amasa Foster and supposedly said, "Well, King David is dead, and the village will go to hell."

His prediction seemed to come true as ownership of the property changed hands six times over the next twenty years, and all business initiatives failed. For a while, the town may have been completely abandoned, earning its first reputation as a deserted village. In 1882, Warren Ackerman purchased Feltville at public auction—for the bargain price of $11,450—and built the summer resort of Glenside Park. In 1916, automobiles rendered proximity to the local train station less important, and the village became almost deserted for the second time.

In the 1920s, the Union County Park Commission purchased the property and incorporated it into Watchung Reservation; the park commission rented the houses to full occupancy until the 1960s. Again, for reasons unknown, Feltville was virtually deserted by 1984, although a few people still live there today, and there is a long waiting list for residency. See the online magazine *Weird N.J.* for entertaining rumors of ghosts and satanic rituals (weirdnj.com).

OTHER ACTIVITIES

Be sure to stop at the amazing Trailside Nature & Science Center (ucnj.org/trailside -nature-and-science-center). It has an ATM and a Wi-Fi lounge upstairs. One highlight is an enclosed exhibit called *Into the Night*, where visitors mingle with owls, raccoons, and other nocturnal creatures. Diners galore dot the area around the reservation. Kids will enjoy Bowcraft Amusement Park and Ponderosa Park in Scotch Plains. The nearby charming, upscale town of Westfield is worth a visit.

MORE INFORMATION

Open dawn to dusk. Dogs should be leashed, and bicycles are not allowed. The reservation includes barbecue pits for grilling.

BRANCH BROOK PARK

Enjoy the largest urban collection of cherry trees in the United States and hike Lenape Trail, which ends in Newark.

Features

Location Newark, NJ

Rating Easy

Distance 4.5-mile loop

Elevation Gain 160 feet

Estimated Time 2 hours

Maps USGS Orange; essexcountyparks.org/parks/branch-brook-park/about

GPS Coordinates 40° 46.691' N, 74° 10.447' W

Contact Essex County Department of Parks, Recreation and Cultural Affairs, 155 Prospect Avenue, Suite 100, West Orange, NJ 07052; 973-268-3500; essexcountyparks.org/parks/branch-brook-park. Branch Brook Park Alliance, 115 Clifton Avenue, Newark, NJ 07104; 973-969-1189; branchbrookpark.org/index.html

DIRECTIONS

Driving: Take I-95 to Garden State Parkway North. After 20 miles, take Exit 148 toward County Route 506 (Bloomfield Avenue). In 0.4 mile, merge onto John F. Kennedy Drive North. Follow it for 0.3 mile and then turn right onto Franklin Street (County Route 509). After 1.25 miles, Franklin Street becomes Heller Parkway. Street parking is available on Heller Parkway just past Sixth Street, at the intersection of Heller and Franklin streets. (The Cherry Blossom Welcome Center is a few blocks north on First Street, with parking for about 100 cars, but the lot fills up quickly during cherry blossom season.) *GPS coordinates*: 40° 46.691' N, 74° 10.447' W.

Public Transportation: Take Newark Light Rail to the Branch Brook Park stop. Walk left, under the overpass and away from the tennis courts. For more information, see njtransit.com.

TRAIL DESCRIPTION

This gorgeous, well-groomed park sprawls in the North Ward of Newark among the neighborhoods of Forest Hill, Roseville, and Belleville. It has the largest collection of cherry trees in the United States—more than 5,000 trees of more than 20 varieties (larger than even Washington, DC's display). It's best to get there mid-April to mid-May, although nature is capricious, and blooms have been known to pop as early as March.

When you arrive, head straight to the Cherry Blossom Welcome Center for a free map (the online map is rather small) to traverse this 360-acre, 4-mile-long public park.

Technically, the area is separated into the Northern, Middle, and Southern divisions and the Northern Extension. You must cross paved roads to stay on the park's footpaths, but it's simple to do. This guide suggests one possible route, but any path in the park will be easy to follow back. Ponds, streams, and lakes link the divisions, and nineteen art deco bridges cross the waters.

As in many sprawling urban parks, you can start your hike from anywhere in Branch Brook Park, but in spring, start in the Northern Extension, which has the heaviest concentration of cherry trees. Park along Heller Parkway, just past Sixth Street, by the Althea Gibson Tennis Center, away from the crowds at the Cherry Blossom Welcome Center. Note the sign for Forest Hill, a pre–World War II neighborhood known for its uniquely designed homes, including Beaux-Arts, Victorian, Colonial Revival, Gothic Revival, and

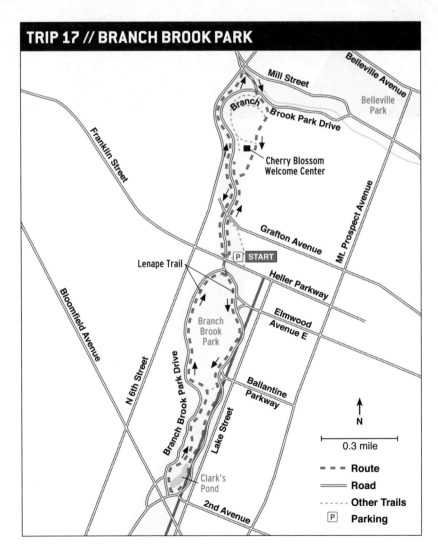

TRIP 17 // BRANCH BROOK PARK

Boasting more cherry trees than Washington, D.C., Branch Brook Park is best hiked mid-April to May for optimal bloom.

Spanish Revival. Walk toward the tennis center and a large Branch Brook Park sign, cross the street to the Patricia A. Chambers Cherry Tree Grove sign, and turn right. The Branch Brook Park train station is on your left, and tennis courts are across the road. As you stroll down the paved path admiring the blooms, take advantage of the self-guided cell phone tour via the QR bar codes posted periodically through the park. To participate in the QR tour, you must first download a QR code reader from your smartphone's app store.

Soon walk under an art deco bridge. Cross Branch Brook Park Drive to the parking lot, wander under the pink cloud of cherry blossoms to the unnamed paved path, and walk to the welcome center (0.5 mile). Get a map, enjoy the exhibits, and use the facilities, if necessary. Or plan your hike in the covered pavilion outside.

Walk past the baseball fields on your left. At the double yellow trail blaze, take the right fork. The unnamed path crosses a parkway (Branch Brook Park Drive, 0.7 mile). Turn left and follow the path up a steep hill, noting the many types and varieties of cherry trees. Pause to sit on a park bench and admire the scenery across the road and down the hill. Then continue straight on this lovely tree-lined path.

When you reach another art deco bridge, cross Branch Brook Park Drive again and walk under the ancient blooming cherry trees through the parking lot. If you'd like, use your map and wander the blossom-laden Northern Extension a bit more. To get in some mileage, head south to paved Lenape Trail.

Walk under the first art deco bridge again, following the path beneath it. Stay on the path toward the 2-mile loop of Lenape Trail (from Heller Parkway to Bloomfield Avenue). Cross Grafton Avenue (1.9 miles). The train station is to the right, the tennis courts to the left. Walk over Heller Parkway, scoot across the edge of the park, and cross Elmwood Avenue toward the paved walking path. The path's surface is springy because it's made from Porous Pave XL, a rubber chip, aggregate, and binder material. Turn left on the path (2.2 miles), admiring the beautiful green grass on your right. Time your walk with the concrete markers every 0.25 mile.

A pond and some stunning cattails appear on your right. A stone bridge spans the pond. (Attractive stone bridges dot the park, as do workout stations and benches.) Tangled woods and another bridge pop up on the right. Watch for two fountains that suddenly spout from the pond. Old city homes are to the left. Stay on the path as it circles to the right.

Enjoy the spectacular views of the pond and stone bridges as you circle around on the path. In April, across the road to your left, yellow trout lilies sprout, and white and pink wildflowers and clover coat the field like candy floss. Walk over two bridges, noting the high-rise apartment buildings to the left. Stop at the Lenape Trail sign at the end of the 2-mile loop and consider a plan to explore the entire 36-mile Lenape Trail another day. Established in 1982, it links a dozen county and municipal parks and was a joint undertaking of the Sierra Club and the Essex County Department of Parks, Recreation and Cultural Affairs. The trail starts in Millburn and ends in Newark (see "We Love Lenape Trail and Al Kent" on page 94).

Head to the right, back toward the tennis courts, and make your way to the Branch Brook Park sign and your car.

DID YOU KNOW?

Conceived by Frederick Law Olmsted in 1867, Branch Brook Park was America's first public county park. It is on the New Jersey and National Registers of Historic Places. Branch Brook is a tributary of the Passaic River, and the original park encompassed the Branch Brook valley, hence the name.

OTHER ACTIVITIES

Strap on roller skates or grab a tennis racket, basketball, or softball. A roller-skating rink, playing courts, and a ball field are in the park. Explore the Cathedral of the Sacred Heart, one of the largest Gothic-style churches in the country, in the park's Southern Division. Just minutes away, visit the Newark Museum and Newark Public Library or take in an event at the New Jersey Performing Arts Center or the Prudential Arena. Bloomfield and Forest Hill have many shops and restaurants.

MORE INFORMATION

Open dawn to 10 P.M. Check the park's website for summer events, including performances by the New Jersey Symphony and fireworks. The park complex includes playgrounds, a horseshoe pit, basketball courts, a roller rink, and other recreational amenities.

WE LOVE LENAPE TRAIL AND AL KENT

Almost 1 million people live within 5 miles of Lenape Trail, but relatively few know it exists. This rare urban trail in densely populated Essex County was established in 1982 and runs from Millburn to Newark, linking a dozen county and municipal parks, including Branch Brook Park (Trip 17), Mills Reservation (Trip 20), Eagle Rock Reservation, and South Mountain Reservation. About 30 percent of the 36-mile trail is on-street, winding through municipalities such as West Orange, Montclair, and Belleville. Distinctive yellow trail markers on trees and telephone poles (first painted in 1979) and a variety of other signage mark Lenape Trail.

The trail was a joint undertaking of the Sierra Club and the Essex County Department of Parks, Recreation and Cultural Affairs. But it was the brainchild of Albert "Al" Kent, who worked as a trail coordinator for the Morris County park system after retiring from the fuel oil industry. Kent wanted to create a trail through urban and rural areas that everyone could enjoy. His passion for this was so great that he planned and helped establish the 156-mile Liberty–Water Gap Trail, which runs across the entire state of New Jersey, from Liberty State Park in the east to the Delaware Water Gap National Recreation Area in the west (and includes Lenape Trail). In 2010, at age 84, he walked the entire Liberty–Water Gap Trail to publicize it. His daughter, Susan Bennett (who took

A Lenape Trail marker shows the signature yellow markers, first painted in 1979.

the photo shown in Trip 4), remembers hiking with him as a child and says that even in his 90s, he managed daily walks. He passed away in 2018 at age 92.

Lenape Trail connects eighteen parks and eleven municipalities in Essex County and offers much to explore. Visit the Nutley Museum, featuring fine art and items owned by the sharpshooter Annie Oakley, who moved to Nutley in 1892 and lived there for more than ten years. In Montclair, tiny (11.5 acres) Yantacaw Brook Park has a tranquil pond. Presby Memorial Iris Gardens (the Rainbow on the Hill) in Upper Montclair features more than 14,000 irises of approximately 3,000 varieties, with at least 100,000 blooms over the course of the season. Hike Lenape Trail to the 9/11 Memorial at Eagle Rock Reservation. Here, on the Watchung Mountains' ridgeline, a statue of a soaring bronze eagle faces midtown Manhattan. Other tributes include a wall of remembrance and World Trade Center artifacts that encourage visitors to linger in silence.

Hike the trail on your own from Branch Brook Park through Belleville Park, Booth Park, Yanticaw Park, Clark's Pond Preserve, Brookdale Park, Yantacaw Brook Park, Tuers Park, Presby Memorial Iris Gardens, Mills Reservation, Cedar Grove Reservoir, Cedar Grove Community Park, Cedar Grove Park, Hilltop Reservation, Verona Park, Eagle Rock Reservation, Degnan Park, O'Connor Park, and South Mountain Reservation.

Lenape Trail also serves to raise awareness of the Lenni-Lenape. When European settlers arrived, the Lenni-Lenape were living in the regions that are now New Jersey, Delaware, southern New York, and eastern Pennsylvania. Among many Algonkian people along the East Coast, the Lenni-Lenape were considered "grandfathers" or "ancient ones" from whom other tribes originated. One of the first groups to encounter European colonization, they were pushed north and west in the eighteenth century. Tribal communities now live in Oklahoma, Kansas, and Wisconsin in the United States, and in Ontario, Canada. People can learn more about the group's 10,000-year-old heritage by attending the Nanticoke Lenni-Lenape Annual Powwow in June at the Salem County Fairgrounds in Woodstown, New Jersey.

For a varied walk rich with history and natural delights, take Lenape Trail for an urban and rural adventure through Essex County, one of the most densely populated counties in the United States, and thank Al Kent for his long-ago vision to bring the outdoors to everyone.

Lenape Trail is maintained by the New York–New Jersey Trail Conference, in partnership with local park conservancies and the Essex County Department of Parks, Recreation and Cultural Affairs. See maps of the trail at nynjtc.org/content/Lenape-trail-guide.

NORVIN GREEN STATE FOREST (SOUTH)

Scramble up, down, and over boulders in this rigorous workout. Your reward? Excellent 360-degree vistas of New York City and Wanaque Reservoir.

Features

Location Ringwood, NJ

Rating Strenuous

Distance 5.4-mile loop

Elevation Gain 1,800 feet

Estimated Time 4–5 hours

Maps USGS Wanaque; nj.gov/dep/parksandforests/maps/norvingreen-area.pdf; nynjtc.org/sites/default/files/NYNJTC_NorvinGreen-South2017-WebsiteMap.pdf

GPS Coordinates 47° 04.191′ N, 74° 19.297′ W

Contact Mailing address: Norvin Green State Forest, c/o Ringwood State Park, 1304 Sloatsburg Road, Ringwood, NJ 07456; 973-962-7031; nj.gov/dep /parksandforests/parks/norvingreenstateforest.html

DIRECTIONS

Take I-287 to Exit 55 toward Wanaque (Ringwood Avenue/County Route 511). Go 4.0 miles north on Ringwood Avenue (becomes Greenwood Lake Turnpike) and turn left onto Westbrook Road. In 2.0 miles, turn left onto Snake Den Road, and in 0.31 mile, take the first left to stay on Snake Den Road. In 0.45 mile, arrive at 150 Snake Den Road (New Weis Center for Education, Arts & Recreation). A parking area has room for 50 to 60 cars.

TRAIL DESCRIPTION

The 5,416-acre Norvin Green State Forest offers some of the most rugged hiking in New Jersey through an undisturbed forest and over old logging and mining roads. Hiking maps divide the park into two sections, one north of West Brook Road and one south of West Brook Road. This trip covers the southern section, which has about 30 miles of crisscrossing trails. The northern section has about 24 miles of trails, including the very difficult but worthwhile 10-mile Stonetown Circular Trail, with about 2,500 feet of elevation gain. The forest is made up of mainly deciduous trees, including American chestnuts, with pitch pines and eastern red cedars at higher elevations. In the many wet areas, look for toads and red efts (a juvenile newt, or salamander). Black bears have been seen, perhaps drawn by the blueberry bushes. Fall, spring, and summer are good times to hike. Winter can be tricky because of the rocks and water (ice). Enjoy excellent 360-degree views of New York City and Wanaque Reservoir from Wyanokie High Point and Carris Hill (no bathroom facilities at this park).

On this hike, take green-blazed Otter Hole Trail to blue-blazed Hewitt-Butler Trail to yellow-blazed Carris Hill Trail. Then return on Lower and Mine trails (blazed white and yellow-on-white dots, respectively) to Hewitt-Butler and Otter Hole trails for a rigorous workout with maximized views. Trail markers overlap, so stay focused on the primary markings.

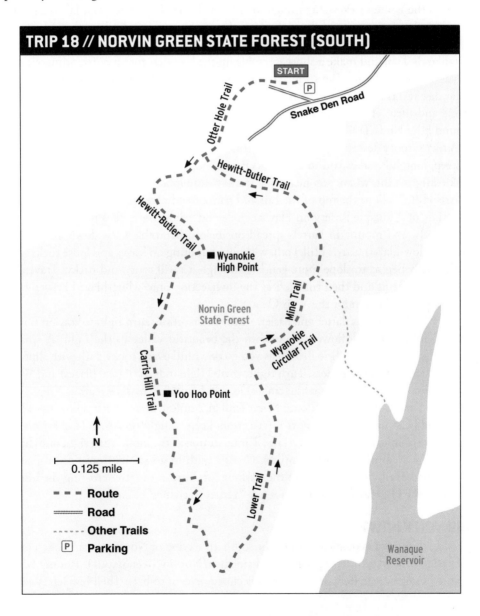

Head toward the sign for the New Weis Center for Education, Arts & Recreation. Walk down a paved road, which soon turns into a packed-dirt path that leads to a sign reading "To All Trails." In spring, note the beautiful blooming forsythia on the right in the field with picnic tables.

Go straight at the trailhead and turn left at the Y intersection onto rooty, rocky, green-blazed Otter Hole Trail. A lovely waterfall and brook are on the left. The steep path includes some impressively large boulders.

Turn left onto a bridge. At the intersection and Richard Warner Trail kiosk (0.5 mile), go straight onto blue-blazed Hewitt-Butler Trail. Carefully hike up and across a boulder field. At the Y intersection, stay straight on Hewitt-Butler Trail. Find your favorite glacial erratic rock among many to choose from, and enjoy amazing views along the way.

At about 1.1 miles, take a tiny detour to the left onto turquoise-diamond-blazed Highlands Trail and make a short scramble up the boulders for an outstanding view at Wyanokie High Point. The scenic panorama includes the New York City skyline on a clear day and the winding expanse of Wanaque Reservoir. Go back down the way you came and turn left to continue on blue-blazed Hewitt-Butler Trail, shared by southbound Highlands Trail.

A rocky, rooty descent through a beautiful valley and streams, followed by a climb up a steep, long hill, takes you to Yoo Hoo Point. Stop and turn around to gaze at Wyanokie High Point, where you just came from, before following the yellow markings to Carris Hill. Walk to the top of the hill and pause to admire another 360-degree vista, this time of Wanaque Reservoir. Hawks circle and yellow butterflies flit. Wild azaleas, dogwoods, and mountain laurels spread out below. Scramble back down and follow steep, yellow-blazed Carris Hill Trail, with tough footing on leaves and loose rocks. The path finally begins to slope more gently, although it's still rooty and rocky. Traverse a couple of streams and then turn left at the intersection onto white-blazed Lower Trail (2.8 miles), at the sign for the Weis Center.

The hike briefly gets flatter and easier. At the intersection, turn right to stay on Lower Trail. Violets and wildflowers abound in the beautiful valley to the right. A stream gurgles (probably Blue Mine Brook) as you go downhill over a rocky path with slippery leaves. Watch for salamanders. Turn right where Highlands Trail (teal blazes) and Wyanokie Circular Trail (red on white circles) join (4.1 miles). Cross a stream.

At the Y intersection, go left onto Mine Trail (4.2 miles), blazed with yellow-on-white dots, and head uphill. At the next intersection, keep straight on Mine Trail for one of those end-of-hike killer inclines. At the T intersection at the kiosk, turn right onto blue-blazed Hewitt-Butler Trail (4.9 miles). Cross a path to go straight onto green-blazed Otter Hole Trail, heading back to the parking lot. Turn right after crossing the bridge and pass the Highlands Natural Pool (see "Other Activities").

DID YOU KNOW?

Take a self-guided geological tour of the southern section of Norvin Green State Forest (see page 8 of nj.gov/dep/njgs/enviroed/freedwn/NorvinGreenSF.pdf). Roomy Mine (named for surveyor Benjamin Roome) is closed, except to bats. The New Jersey Field

Wanaque Reservoir as seen from Wyanokie High Point.

Office of the U.S. Fish and Wildlife Service designates this site a bat hibernaculum for hibernation and breeding. (See "Did You Know?" in Trips 4 and 13.) To learn more about bats, investigate the nonprofit New Jersey Bat Sanctuary in Milford (njbats.org). A few miles north in West Milford lies Long Pond Ironworks State Park; the ironworks was a source of iron during the American Revolution and the Civil War.

OTHER ACTIVITIES

Visit the New Weis Center for Education, Arts & Recreation at 150 Snake Den Road on the grounds of the state forest. Call 973-835-2160 for hours and programs. The center is privately owned and operated by the Highlands Nature Friends Inc. (highlandsnaturefriends .org/home.html).

Get a day pass for the Highlands Natural Pool, a stream-fed freshwater swimming pool at the start of Otter Trail (973-835-4299). Visit Ringwood's 96-acre New Jersey Botanical Garden, and explore the historical estate and grounds at Ringwood Manor.

MORE INFORMATION

Open 8 A.M. to 8 P.M. Fishing is permitted in designated areas. Pets must be leashed. No bathroom facilities are available, so please plan accordingly.

19 PLAINSBORO PRESERVE

Soothe your soul with a secluded woods hike to a peaceful 50-acre lake; the nature center is a must for children.

Features 👫 ⛺

Location Cranbury, NJ

Rating Easy

Distance 4.9-mile loop

Elevation Gain 200 feet

Estimated Time 2.5 hours

Maps USGS Highstown; njaudubon.org/places-to-visit/plainsboro-preserve

GPS Coordinates 40° 20.972' N, 74° 33.584' W

Contact 80 Scotts Corner Road, Cranbury, NJ 08512; 609-799-4013; plainsboronj.com/250/Plainsboro-Preserve

DIRECTIONS

Follow US 1 north or south to the Scudders Mill Road exit in Plainsboro Township. Take the Scudders Mill Road exit and follow the road to the traffic light at the intersection of Scudders Mill Road and Dey Road (County Route 614). Turn left onto Dey Road. At the first light, turn left onto Scotts Corner Road. The preserve's entrance is 1.0 mile up on the left. A gravel parking lot holds 50 to 60 cars. Two parking spots are universally accessible to the Rush Holt Environmental Education Center.

TRAIL DESCRIPTION

If you seek peaceful, easy walks, head to the 630-acre natural area of the Plainsboro Preserve. Quiet waters, warblers, deer, flowers, soothing greens, and quiet fields will revive your spirits. More than 5 miles of marked trails wander through wet meadows and mature beech woods and around the 50-acre human-made McCormack Lake.

A cooperative project among Middlesex County, Plainsboro Township, and New Jersey Audubon, the preserve boasts the excellent Rush Holt Environmental Education Center, with a reference library, gift shop, and bathrooms. Inside are exhibits on turtles, snakes, and frogs. (*Note:* When the center is closed, no bathroom facilities are available at the preserve.)

In spring, the preserve teems with wildflowers and mating birds. Monarch butterflies flit in summer, but so do mosquitoes (wear repellent). Fall brings a canopy of color. Flat trails make winter walks possible, and the wide water grows blossoms of ice.

Start on White Trail, and stroll trails blazed from yellow to red to green to blue before returning on White Trail. Walk through an upland forest, across a stream and a wet area, through scrublands, and along a lake. The markings can be a little confusing, but with only about 5 miles of trails, plus a lake to anchor you, don't worry about getting lost.

From the parking lot, head left to the trailhead sign (the environmental center is on your right) and take White Trail, a wide gravel path that gives way to dirt with fields on either side, to head toward Yellow Trail. Ignore Orange Trail, almost immediately to your right, which leads to a nature trail that you can visit on the way back to the parking area.

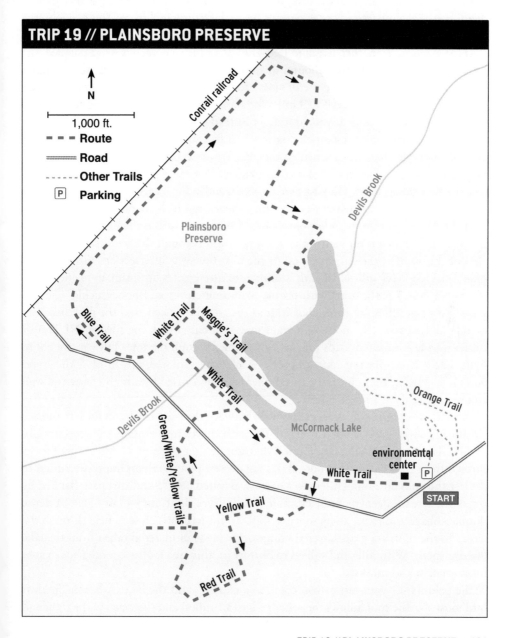

Keep going straight on White Trail, glimpsing McCormack Lake on the right through the trees. Walk past adorable birdhouses and informative nature signs. The lake is lined with bayberry shrubs. Sit on a bench and admire this body of water, created by sand mining, which shaped much of the preserve. The lake is alive with fish, reptiles, amphibians, waterfowl, and plants. Look closely in the shrubbery to your right for a concrete structure, once part of a sand-mining operation.

Continue on White Trail past many numbered birdhouses. At birdhouse 48, the trail splits; turn left toward Yellow Trail (0.3 mile). Pass a grassy field (still farmed), enter the woods at the trail sign, and go straight onto Yellow Trail. The wide, flat dirt path is shady and cool, courtesy of the American beech forest microclimate. You may observe some of the salamanders that live here near logs and rocks.

At the Y intersection, turn left onto Red Trail (0.5 mile): a gorgeous, sand-dappled dirt path lined by logs. Bird songs abound in spring. It's a little rooty—wear sturdy hiking boots. Ferns, downed trees, and pretty moss adorn this peaceful sanctuary. At the T intersection, go left on Yellow Trail (0.9 mile) for about 50 yards before veering to the right toward Green Trail. (*Note*: If you go straight instead of right, you will reach a "No Trespassing" sign.) The trail is essentially narrow and flat, rooty, and a bit wet—mosquitoes may be a nuisance here in summer. At the next Y intersection, near the bench, turn left toward the green, white, and yellow trail markers (1.3 miles). The shaded, grassy path narrows to dirt and roots. Go past two rings of wooden log "seats" to your right. Yellow Trail curves prettily into denser woods, with a sheltering dirt bank on the left.

At the T intersection, turn left onto a broad path toward Blue Trail via White Trail (1.5 miles). The lake is on your right, shining bright through the trees. Enjoy an open view of the water at the culvert pipes. At the next four-way intersection, turn left onto Blue Trail loop (1.7 miles). In early summer, nature creates an intimate tunnel along this wide, grassy path, lined with purple-blooming clover and honeysuckle. Cattails wave and dragonflies sail through the air as the woods thicken, and the path becomes muddy and narrow. The noise of a train may suddenly break the silence: NJ Transit tracks are a few hundred yards to your left, visible through the trees. But you are out of sight, like a child playing hide-and-seek. A black-tea-colored stream of acidic water flows to the right; the color is a natural phenomenon caused by a high content of iron and vegetative dyes, such as tannin.

The path morphs to soft moss as you walk between the train tracks on the left and the stream and sloping woods on the right. The path curves to the right, but keep straight on Blue Trail, admiring the fern forest. Old train ties line the way, as well as small rocks thrown from the tracks. The route skirts big culvert pipes with an impressive ditch to the left and goes up a small hill onto a narrow, elevated pebble-and-dirt path flanked by trees. The stream deepens to black. Blue Trail curves right, into a fairy glen of dense skunk cabbage and ferns, along rooty terrain. To the left you can see a field through the trees. To the right are grass-covered hummocks, made of material taken from the lake (dredge spoil). With hills and valleys to burrow in, this area is also a good place to spot foxes, snakes, and minks.

The field flanks your left as you come to a clearing and the lake. A bench sits near birdhouse 77. The trail follows the water's edge (3.1 miles) and then cuts to the right and

A memorial bench on McCormack Lake peninsula offers quiet contemplation.

heads into the woods. (You can continue straight here and walk a short path along the lake to a little peninsula where you may see turtles. Then simply double back.) In the woods, walk a narrow path among dirt hummocks. Cross two small footbridges, still on Blue Trail, which has some ups and downs. Deer are common here—if you encounter one, just keep walking; it will likely bound away. Walk through a clearing and then the trail splits.

Go left to head back on White Trail. At the T intersection, segue left onto Maggie's Trail at the sign (3.5 miles), a narrow peninsula jutting into the lake. You'll think you're at the Jersey Shore, given the sand (from mining) and the coastal vegetation. Watch for moths, dragonflies, turtles, and frogs, and try to spot a river otter. The path ends at a stone memorial bench, with beautiful views of the lake on three sides. Backtrack and go left onto White Trail at the Y intersection (4.1 miles) at the wooden footbridge. At the next three intersections, keep on White Trail back to the parking lot. (Consider a quick side trip on Orange Trail on the left before the parking lot, which leads to a nature trail. Steps lead down and then up a steep gully to a pretty view of the lake.)

DID YOU KNOW?

Bayberry shrubs have blue-gray nutlets, which provide food for tree swallows and yellow-rumped warblers. In the preserve's American beech forest microclimate, the trees trap air and moisture, causing temperatures to be warmer in winter and cooler in summer. McCormack Lake hosts rare water milfoil, mudwort, and sandplain flax.

OTHER ACTIVITIES

The preserve is adjacent to the Scotts Corner Conservation Area, a prime spot for hiking and bird-watching. Visit the nearby Cranbury Museum at 4 Park Place East. Hike on the Delaware and Raritan Canal in Princeton. While in Princeton, visit the Princeton University Art Museum in McCormick Hall (closed for construction when this book went to press, slated to reopen in spring 2025), and stop by Carnegie Lake and watch the university rowing teams practice. Many eateries are on County Route 614 (Cranbury) and in Plainsboro and Princeton.

MORE INFORMATION

Trails are open dawn to dusk. The Rush Holt Environmental Education Center usually is open Tuesday through Saturday, 9 A.M. to 6 P.M.; Sunday, noon to 5 P.M.; closed Mondays and holidays. Winter hours starting in November usually are Tuesday through Saturday, 9 A.M. to 4 P.M.; Sunday, noon to 4 P.M.

20 MILLS RESERVATION

Score dramatic views of New York City on this rocky hike through woods and along the edges of an exposed quarry.

Features 🏃 🐕 🔍 ☀️

Location Cedar Grove, NJ

Rating Easy to Moderate

Distance 2.5-mile loop

Elevation Gain 300 feet

Estimated Time 1.5 hours

Maps USGS Orange; essexcountyparks.org/parks/mills-reservation/about

GPS Coordinates 40° 51.295' N, 74° 12.526' W

Contact Essex County Department of Parks, Recreation and Cultural Affairs, 155 Prospect Avenue, Suite 100, West Orange, NJ 07052; 973-268-3500; essexcountyparks.org/parks/mills-reservation

DIRECTIONS

From Garden State Parkway, take Exit 154 (Clifton). Bear left after the toll booths, following the sign to US 46, and travel west on US 46. In 0.9 mile, take the Valley Road exit. At the bottom of the ramp, bear right onto Valley Road north, but immediately turn left, following the sign for Montclair. Bear left again at the sign "U-Turn, Montclair." Proceed south along Valley Road for 1.0 mile and turn right onto Normal Avenue. Cross the railroad tracks, continue uphill for another 0.3 mile, and turn left into the parking area for Mills Reservation at the top of the hill. The gravel lot has space for about twenty cars, and it can fill up quickly.

TRAIL DESCRIPTION

The parking lot is not well marked. It sits about 50 yards past the intersection of Normal Avenue and Granite Drive. If you go past the fenced-in body of water (Cedar Grove Reservoir), you have overshot. Seven trails totaling 6.1 miles (with a lot of overlap if you want to add length) wind through this woodland and wetland delight, part of First Watchung Mountain. Trail blazes are inconsistent in this 157-acre reservation, so take a moment to walk down wide, graveled, white-blazed Mills Loop Trail to look at the map and trails kiosk on the left. (No bathrooms are available.) You might want to snap a photo for reference, although be aware that the park has several unblazed trails that are not on the map and that the map is oriented with south facing up! Even though some blazes and intersections are a bit confusing, and the posted map does not show all intersections and trails, don't be afraid to explore. You can always follow the white blazes of Mills Loop Trail—a perimeter path—back to the parking lot.

The trip described here largely loops around the outside of the park, which allows visitors to enjoy excellent views of New York City at Quarry Point, to admire the steep dropoffs along old quarries and to see the original park entrance. The highlights here are the views, so visit during a leafless season: late fall, winter, or early spring.

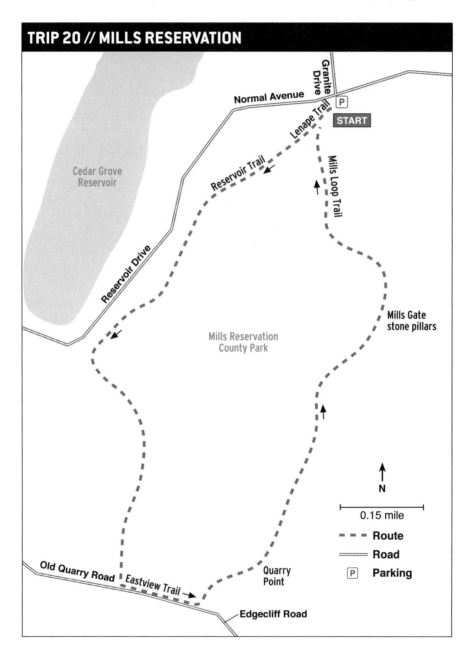

Mills Loop Trail is the most popular route (many people and dogs), but you'll start on a quieter one: head for the black-dot-on-yellow Lenape Link Trail marker on the west side of the parking lot, which connects with yellow-blazed Lenape Trail. The grassy, narrow path invites you into the woods. In season, raspberries greet you on the left. Turn left to follow yellow-blazed Lenape Trail south. The treadway quickly becomes packed dirt and stone with tricky footing as it curves south.

In just a few hundred yards, veer right where Lenape Trail overlaps with red-blazed Reservoir Trail and follow the red and yellow blazes. At the next Y intersection, the two trails split from each other. Veer right again to stay on red-blazed Reservoir Trail. (You will follow the red blazes until you reach the southern end of the preserve.) Head downhill on the shady but quite rooty path. When it veers to the right, keep straight to remain on the red-blazed trail. At about 0.33 mile, cross a plank footbridge, after which the red markers show a turn to the right. Note the person-sized flat rocks as you cross them. Reservoir Trail quickly veers south again, paralleling the western edge of the preserve and the road. The shady path becomes rockier, with uneven footing over gentle ups and downs. Cross a dry creek bed over more of those eerie flat stones—part of the basalt that forms the Watchung Mountains. Basalt is created when molten lava extruded from Earth's surface cools rapidly.

The trail splits to follow unblazed side paths several times over the next stretch—stay with the bright red blazes of Reservoir Trail. On the right, you can see Cedar Grove Reservoir behind a tall, green fence. Mosses and ferns brighten the forest as you parallel the road and cross a few small streams gurgling their way down to the reservoir. Where Reservoir Trail just about meets Reservoir Drive (a short connector goes out to the road), turn sharply left to stay on red-blazed Reservoir Trail, heading away from the reservoir (0.8 mile). Cross a footbridge and go slightly up into the woods, following the route within sight of a line of houses. In 1,000 feet, the red blazes turn south once again, passing behind another line of houses. A large log with carved steps lends a whimsical feel to this part of the hike.

The trail curves to the left one final time and ends at an old road at 1.2 miles, now the wide, yellow-blazed Lenape Trail. Check out the informational sign with some history of the quarries, reservoir, and the town of Cedar Grove. Unfortunately, the map on the sign is outdated, but head south along the wide former road toward a second parking lot (room for eight cars). Turn left onto blue-blazed Eastview Trail and climb a short, steep basalt hill just before you reach the lot. Take an interesting walk along an exposed rocky ledge, with the parking lot below. (*Note*: Make sure to keep close any small children or easily distracted birders who may be with you.) At the Y intersection, keep right to stay on Eastview Trail. Watch your footing on the rocks as you enjoy a high ledge-walk around an old quarry. Go a short distance downhill to an intersection, and take the far-right path (still blue) to continue along the bluff. Look below for old quarry formations.

Going uphill is rocky and the footing is tricky, but you are rewarded at the clearing with excellent views of the abandoned quarry and New York City. A few steps farther is Quarry Point (1.5 miles), a spacious area with a bench where you can sit and look out at New York City over the remains of a concrete platform where antiaircraft guns were

Two stone pillars mark the original 1954 entrance into Mills Reservation.

installed during World War II. New Jersey Audubon hosts its spring hawk count here. You may hear a train whistle mournfully in the distance.

When you are finished lingering, walk in front of the bench and turn left to go downhill into the woods. At the bottom of the short slope, you can follow the blue blazes, but it's best to move slightly south onto an unblazed but well-traveled trail along the edge of the bluff. A small clearing on the right offers the best view yet of New York City, but tread carefully as you gaze—it's a long way down. The path is rocky but flat, with a protective wire fence on the right along stretches. The scenery is spectacular on clear, leafless days and includes the colorful houses below in the town of Montclair.

Work your way back to blue-blazed Eastview Trail, which proceeds uphill, following the ledge/bluff, and continues to be very rocky. Descend to a five-way intersection with a kiosk (1.8 miles). Take the middle-right trail (blazed blue) that follows a wide former road. Within 100 feet, the blue blazes leave this wide path, so abandon the blazes and keep right to stay with the wide path (marked orange on maps, but actually unblazed). The flat dirt path loops between the stone pillars of the original Mills Reservation Park and then widens, with a gully to the left, heading toward two unmarked Y intersections. At the first Y intersection, go straight. The cinder path slopes gently downhill. Lovely houses stand on posted property to the right. At the second Y intersection, keep straight on the cinder path. Then, at a T intersection, turn right onto a gravel path, which is white-blazed Mills Loop Trail (2.1 miles), and you are almost at the parking lot.

DID YOU KNOW?

The Lenape word watchung means "high hill." Cedar Grove resident Arthur Wynne invented the first modern crossword puzzle (called "word-cross") in 1913. Famous residents of Montclair include musician/songwriter Joe Walsh, astronaut Buzz Aldrin, late-night host and comedian Stephen Colbert, and makeup artist Bobbi Brown.

OTHER ACTIVITIES

Hike the easy-to-challenging trails of Cedar Grove's Hilltop Reservation, a 284-acre preserve with a high point of 284 feet. Spend a weekend in Montclair (designated a Climate Showcase Community by the EPA) exploring the art museum and art galleries, live theater, the Yogi Berra Museum & Learning Center (Berra lived in Montclair for more than 50 years), the 12-acre Van Vleck House & Gardens, and the King Memorial Garden (honoring Martin Luther King Jr.). History buffs will enjoy the 33-building walking tour through the Historic District.

MORE INFORMATION

Mills Reservation is one of eighteen parks connected by Lenape Trail. Use this link to discover the reservation's place in Lenape Trail: nynjtc.org/content/lenape-overview.

21 WAWAYANDA STATE PARK

Large rocks, a beautiful lake, and shady trails make for a pleasant loop hike.

Features 👤🐕💧🍃🎿🏊🏞️💲🚜

Location Hewitt, NJ

Rating Easy

Distance 6-mile loop

Elevation Gain 425 feet

Estimated Time 3.5 hours

Maps USGS Wawayanda; nj.gov/dep/parksandforests/maps/wawayanda-trails.pdf

GPS Coordinates 41° 11.414′ N, 074° 25.709′ W

Contact Wawayanda State Park, 885 Warwick Turnpike, Hewitt, NJ 07421; 973-853-4462; nj.gov/dep/parksandforests/parks/wawayandastatepark.html

DIRECTIONS

Take I-287 to Exit 55. Turn right onto County Route 511 Alt/Ringwood Avenue. After 14.0 miles, take the right split onto the Warwick Turnpike. After 4.6 miles, reach a left turn to enter Wawayanda State Park. Pass the visitor center and follow signs for the Wawayanda Lake Day Use Area, which is a left turn 2.2 miles from the park entrance. A large lot offers more than 100 parking spots, although it may fill up when the swimming area of the lake is open. Be careful—Global Positioning System (GPS) units may send you to the Auxiliary Entrance Gate, which is only open part of the year.

TRAIL DESCRIPTION

Wawayanda State Park is just a few miles from New York State. It's most famous for having about 20 miles of the Appalachian Trail (AT) run through it, but the park has more than 50,000 acres with more than 60 miles of trails! It's also home to a large concentration of black bears (as someone once joked, "Black bears are almost like squirrels up here"), so take the proper precautions.

Grab a trail map when you come through the entrance booth into the park. This hike, Wawayanda Lake Loop Trail, was put together in 2021 by the New York–New Jersey Trail Conference and combines four or five other trails into one continuous orange-blazed trail. Drive 2.2 miles from the entrance booth, following the signs for Wawayanda Lake. Park in the large lot.

Once parked, enjoy a lovely view of the Wawayanda Lake swimming area right in front of you. Don't let the scenery distract you from starting your hike though, as this orange-blazed trail runs across the open area at the edge of the parking lot between you and the lake. Step off the asphalt, turn right, and follow the plastic posts with orange blazes down toward the ramp. Go past the ramp, along the first section of wooden fence, and turn left through the gap in that fence. (A sign here may still label this as Pump House Trail, one of the routes used to create Wawayanda Lake Loop Trail.) After a few dozen feet, the trail curves to the right and enters the woods.

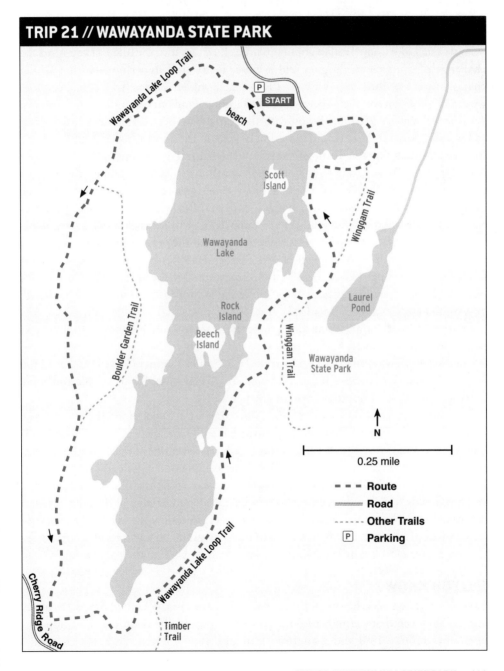

TRIP 21 // WAWAYANDA STATE PARK

Wawayanda Lake Loop Trail

P
START

beach

Scott Island

Wawayanda Lake

Winggam Trail

Rock Island

Laurel Pond

Beech Island

Boulder Garden Trail

Winggam Trail

Wawayanda State Park

N

0.25 mile

- - - Route
=== Road
---- Other Trails
P Parking

Wawayanda Lake Loop Trail

Cherry Ridge Road

Timber Trail

The first stretch is more of a wide, gravel-strewn service road that does double duty as a trail. Stroll 0.1 mile up this road. It continues straight, but follow the orange blazes and turn left to begin to head southwest along the west side of the lake.

This next segment of trail is randomly strewn with large rocks that vary from the size of baseballs to the size of cars or small buildings, remnants of the departing glaciers at the end of the Wisconsin glacial period. Wawayanda Lake itself is also a remnant of that glacial period, although the lake was later expanded through the use of dams.

At 0.8 mile into the hike, the trail intersects with blue-blazed Boulder Garden Trail, which is a little more than a half-mile long and meets back up with orange-blazed Wawayanda Lake Loop Trail in about 0.6 mile (1.4 miles into the hike). If you want the challenge of some elevation gain and a loose, rocky trail underfoot—with a strong chance of wet feet thrown in for extra fun—take Boulder Garden Trail here. For those who aren't keen on wet feet, Wawayanda Lake Loop Trail curves to the right, crosses a stream, and reaches a T intersection with that same blue-blazed Boulder Garden Trail at 1.4 miles. Turn right at this intersection to stay on the orange-blazed trail (if rejoining from Boulder Garden Trail, go straight at this same T intersection).

At 2.4 miles, Wawayanda Lake Loop Trail continues in two directions. The way *not* to go is to follow it slightly to the right across a sometimes dry, sometimes wet drainage area onto Cherry Ridge Road, where it will dead-end. Instead, turn very sharply left to stay on the other part of Wawayanda Lake Loop Trail. This is easy to miss, so pay attention! Within 0.1 mile, the trail turns right to stay with the orange blazes.

At 2.8 miles into the hike, green-blazed Timber Trail heads off to the right. Go left to stay with the orange blazes. At 3.0 miles, cross a small rocky area. Take a dozen steps down to the lake here for a pleasant view of the water. Stop and scan the lake for wildlife or wave to kayakers as they float by.

Continuing on the trail, climb along some short, rocky stretches; be careful how you place your feet! In winter, find pleasant views to the left of the lake. At 3.3 miles, turn left to stay on Wawayanda Lake Loop Trail. In 0.2 mile, a series of large boulders to the left offers an attractive scene of the lake from a bit of elevation. Sit for a while and enjoy a snack, being careful not to share with any bears.

The trail drops back down at 4.1 miles, affording a clear spot along the lake to take in another view. At 4.5 miles, the trail turns left and overlaps for a short while with blue-blazed Wingdam Trail. Together, these trails pass over one of the dams that creates the larger version of Wawayanda Lake. The water passing under your feet is heading for Laurel Pond. At 4.9 miles, the orange blazes turn left while the blue blazes continue straight. Follow the orange blazes as the trail loops along the edge of the lake, offering additional views of the water. At 5.4 miles, turn left to follow the lake's edge, curving past a small picnic area. The final stretch of trail passes the boat launch and boathouse, the picnic area, and finally the swimming area, leading back to the parking lot.

DID YOU KNOW?

Lake Wawayanda was the site of the first YMCA camp in the United States. This was also possibly the first permanent boys' summer camp in the country. The camp was open from 1886 to 1891 and again from 1901 to 1919.

An impressive glacial erratic stands near the intersection of Boulder Garden Trail and Wawayanda Lake Loop Trail.

OTHER ACTIVITIES

Wawayanda State Park is home to 19.6 miles of the Appalachian Trail, including scenic Pinwheel Vista. Swimming may be available at the lake during summer. The park also offers snowshoeing (rentals available at the park office), off-road biking, cross-country skiing, horseback riding (no rental facilities), boating, canoeing, kayaking, group campsites, fishing, and ice fishing.

MORE INFORMATION

Seasonal entrance fees may apply from Memorial Day to Labor Day—check the park's website to see if fees are currently in effect before you go. The gates are open from April 1 to October 31 between 8 A.M. and 8 P.M. and from November 1 to March 31 from 8 A.M. to 6 P.M. Hours of the Auxiliary Entrance Gate may vary.

FOLLOW THE SUPER GREEN ROAD:
THE EAST COAST GREENWAY

The East Coast Greenway (ECG) links 450 communities and 15 states along the eastern seaboard, between Calais, Maine, and Key West, Florida. The ECG's spine is 3,000 miles long, accompanied by approximately 1,050 miles of off-road, protected, multiuse paths. As an urban, shared-use trail, the ECG is right at home in New Jersey, the most densely populated state in the United States.

The New Jersey route is bound on either side by rivers and stretches 96 miles between Pennsylvania and New York. At the northern end in Jersey City, a ferry carries you across the Hudson River to New York City. At the southern end in Trenton, the pedestrian-friendly Calhoun Street Bridge deposits you in Morrisville, Pennsylvania. The rest of the ECG in New Jersey passes through the state's two largest cities, Newark and Jersey City, as well as through Trenton, New Brunswick, and a surprising variety of rural landscapes. In fact, nearly 100 miles of protected greenway exist in New Jersey, including the Delaware and Raritan Canal (see "From Mules to Multiuse: Today's Delaware and Raritan Canal State Park" on page 40). The canal intersects the ECG for 36 miles and is the greenway's longest completed trail.

Other designated ECG trails in New Jersey include portions of the Hudson River Waterfront Walkway in Jersey City (see Trip 24), Newark Riverfront Trail, Roosevelt Park in Edison, Middlesex Greenway in Middlesex County, and Johnson Park Path in Piscataway.

The ECG, spearheaded by the North Carolina–based East Coast Greenway Alliance, is a testament to collaboration, shared vision, and cooperation among volunteers and officials at the local, state, and national levels. In 1991, eight cyclists met in a room in New York City to plot the vision. In summer 1992, ten dedicated cyclists took a month to explore the route from Boston, Massachusetts, to Washington, DC, garnering media attention and endorsements from local and state officials. In 1995, the East Coast Greenway name and logo were trademarked. (Consistent signage is still being placed today.) In 1997, the Delaware and Raritan Canal in New Jersey became the first local trail segment to be mapped for public use. In 2000, the East Coast Greenway Alliance partnered with Amtrak. (Because the route generally follows the Amtrak East Coast corridor, many trailheads can be reached by public transportation. In New Jersey, contact NJ Transit for details, njtransit.com; and Amtrak, amtrak.com/bike.) In 2005, cyclists Jenny and Wil Hylton traveled the entire ECG without sponsorship, which garnered tremendous national publicity

for the greenway. The project steamrolled, and more funding, partners, and segments were added. Today, tens of millions of dollars in state and federal funds go toward closing key gaps in the ECG.

In New Jersey alone, many volunteers and more than 30 partners support the trail, including the Outdoor Club of South Jersey, the Adirondack Mountain Club (North Jersey Chapter), Bike New Jersey, the Canal Society of New Jersey, Recreational Equipment, Inc. (REI), and the New Jersey Transportation Planning Authority, New Jersey Conservation Foundation, and the New Jersey departments of environmental protection and transportation. Honor their efforts and hike the ECG today.

The East Coast Greenway Alliance in Durham, North Carolina, heads the project with partners at the local, state, and national levels. Check greenway.org to find updates, maps, and directions for navigating the ECG.

22 CHEESEQUAKE STATE PARK

Visit the excellent interpretive center. Hike through a hardwood forest and the Pine Barrens and over freshwater streams. Cross an Atlantic white cedar swamp on boardwalks.

Features 🚶🐕💧📍⛷️△🏕️$

Location Matawan, NJ

Rating Moderate

Distance 3.3-mile loop

Elevation Gain 370 feet

Estimated Time 2 hours

Maps USGS South Amboy; nj.gov/dep/parksandforests/maps/trailguides /comprehensive-cheesequake-trails.pdf

GPS Coordinates 40° 26.200′ N, 74° 15.926′ W

Contact Cheesequake State Park, 300 Gordon Road, Matawan, NJ 07747; 732-566-2161; nj.gov/dep/parksandforests/parks/cheesequakestatepark.html

DIRECTIONS

From north or south, take Garden State Parkway to Exit 120 and turn right at the end of the exit ramp onto Matawan Road. Follow Matawan Road to the first traffic light and turn right onto Morristown Road. At the next light, turn right onto Gordon Road. The parking lot on the left holds 30-plus cars.

TRAIL DESCRIPTION

Cheesequake State Park comprises 363 acres of varied hiking environments, from a coastal salt marsh habitat to upland forests, and it is just minutes from Garden State Parkway. You'll see vegetation representative of both southern and northern New Jersey. Cheesequake typifies the charm of so many of the state's parks, quickly winding from urban to suburban to rural.

Because of the well-marked trails, this is a good beginner's hike, with one caution: the route has lots of steps. (Fortunately, it also has lots of benches.) Follow Green Trail to the park's highlight: an Atlantic white cedar swamp, where great horned owls live. Look for nature markers near sweet bay magnolias, swamp azaleas, and sphagnum moss. Every season brings visual delights, but avoid hot weather when the bugs thrive (generally May to October).

The park office, to the right of the admissions tollbooth, provides flush toilets and maps. Cheesequake is part of the New Jersey Coastal Heritage Trail (see "The Ultimate

Multiuse Trail: New Jersey Coastal Heritage Trail" on page 164). Turn right from the parking lot, and almost immediately the paved trailhead lot appears on your left. All five color-coded trails leave from here; you can even string together different loops for a longer hike. A water fountain is on one side of the lot, and a talking kiosk is on the other.

Walk beneath the trailhead arch, and head toward the Green Trail marker on the wide, shaded dirt path, which is sure to contain a dog or two. Right away the trail forks; turn left to follow the green blazes. A dramatic stepped boardwalk leads down through oak, sassafras, and sweet pepperbush. Turn left at the bottom, toward the shared Red, Green, and Blue trails, ignoring the Yellow Trail entrance to the right. You are on the way to the not-to-be-missed interpretive center (listed as "Nature Center" on the map). Cross a bridge over freshwater wetlands and climb wooden steps on a long and rooty dirt path. At the top of the hill to your left are dozens of birdhouses. This is the interpretive center's backyard. Inside the center, find live turtles, taxidermy, bones, and wonderful wall displays that explain cedar swamps, freshwater and saltwater wetlands, second-growth forests, and more. An auditorium hosts educational programs for grades K–12.

At the interpretive center, turn right on the combination Blue, Green, and Red trails, following the split rail fence. Read the educational signs about plants and trees. The dirt path is rooty but flat and winds charmingly through the forest, with a sloping hill to

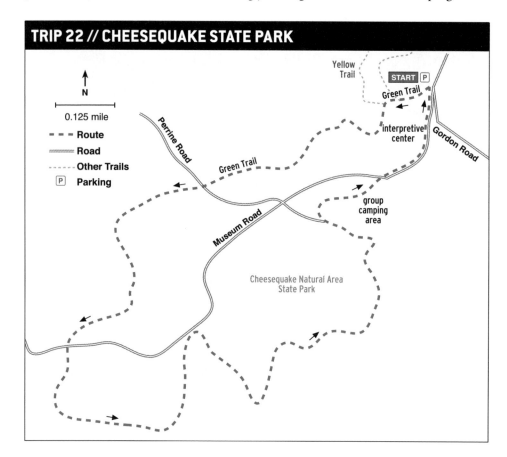

TRIP 22 // CHEESEQUAKE STATE PARK

N

0.125 mile

- - - Route
===== Road
······ Other Trails
P Parking

Yellow Trail

START P

Green Trail

interpretive center

Perrine Road

Green Trail

Gordon Road

Museum Road

group camping area

Cheesequake Natural Area State Park

your right. At about 0.2 mile, descend slightly through a lovely fern-filled hollow. Walk along a slight ridge, with gentle ups and downs, surrounded by sheep laurel shrubs that bloom in June and July. (*Caution:* Sheep laurel is toxic if eaten.) The trail opens up to a meadow vista, which you can appreciate from the cool, secluded woods. Turn left to go downhill (no trail markers here), over steps and a long boardwalk that covers a seasonally wet area. Sit on one of the three benches to admire the deep green views.

At 0.3 mile, enjoy 42 steps up a hill to an intersection where you turn left onto Green Trail. Walk among slender young trees on a path that winds like a circling cat. At the next intersection, veer right to stay on Green Trail, gazing into the huge gully on your left (at the 0.5-mile marker). Descend steps and observe the pitch pines at the nature marker. These trees, a hallmark of the Pine Barrens, are precisely evolved. Intense heat is necessary for the cones to open and release their seeds, and the trees' thick bark protects them during forest fires. Cross a wooden bridge over a stream, and then trek up and down rooty hills surrounded by blueberry bushes. Walk in the shade, up steps, past a beautifully shaped sassafras tree with a nature marker at 0.6 mile. Cross gravel Perrine Road and turn right on tree-lined Green Trail. Watch out for poison ivy as you admire the lovely hollow and field visible through the woods to the right.

You are traveling through what was once a thriving Atlantic white cedar swamp. The swamp has transitioned into wetlands with red maple, birch, and sweet pepperbush. After ascending a slight hill, turn left to stay on Green Trail at the fork (follow the arrow). Down the hill, a field opens up to the right before more steps down to a long boardwalk. Walk slowly through an immense cedar swamp, noting the copper waters gleaming against the emerald-green grasses and ferns. Easily the trail's highlight, the swamp hosts many varieties of flowers, goldenrods, red-berried American hollies, and eastern red cedars. Rest on a bench and meditate on the artistic, gigantic root balls of overturned trees. (Hurricane Sandy in October 2012 closed this section for a year.) You'll wonder where the dinosaurs are in this Jurassic Park–like setting. The boardwalk zigzags, interspersed with small areas of rooty ground, until finally a dirt path leads uphill and then down.

At 1.3 miles, go under a trail arch and cross wide dirt Museum Road (turn left on Museum Road if you want to head back). Veer left onto Green Trail. Enjoy the flat dirt treadway with no roots as you walk through a forest of eastern white pines. (White sand occasionally replaces the dirt.) The narrow path takes you up a hill and steps. At 1.6 miles, traverse a series of three bridges, watching for darting chipmunks and butterflies. The path is flat and wide and then slopes downhill, banked by green moss and ghost pipe. At 2.1 miles, bear right to stay on Green Trail, with a park road to your left. Note the verdant marsh and ferns. Quite soon, turn right at a fork. The area is sometimes muddy, but well-placed logs allow for safe crossing. Quickly reach a 100-year-old oak felled by Hurricane Sandy, with hillocks on the right adding drama. Traverse a boardwalk and bridge. At the 2.4-mile marker, turn left to stay on Green Trail. The hillocks and marsh render the tiny, winding path secluded yet oddly comforting. An observation platform juts over the water. Linger here to watch dragonflies, hear frogs, and appreciate the river birches.

Continue on the boardwalk, climbing steep steps at about 2.6 miles. Then head downhill to a large broken tree and a charming copper-colored stream to the left. Fluffy green grass flanks the path, which goes over steps and a bridge. Note the smooth brown pebbles on the sandbar. Pass a stand of American beeches, and then go under a trail arch to arrive at Group Campsite East, part of the Gordon Field Group Campgrounds, where you can use the flush toilets and the picnic tables (2.7 miles). Turn left onto the paved campground road. Just past the campsite, turn right as Green and Red trails rise onto a rooty path into the woods. A series of ups and downs ends at another trail arch, where you turn right onto paved Museum Road (3.1 miles). Note the black birch tree at the nature marker before following Museum Road back to the parking lot.

DID YOU KNOW?

Migratory hawks and waterfowl, including snowy egrets, black ducks, and northern harriers, flock here in fall. In spring and summer, ospreys live on the park's nesting platforms. Perrine Pond on Blue Trail has a bird blind for viewing.

OTHER ACTIVITIES

Canoeists and kayakers will enjoy Cheesequake Creek's self-guided water trail; more water-related activities can be found at Old Bridge Waterfront Park. Dining options are available on Routes 34 and 516, as well as in the tiny town of Old Bridge Township. Drive a race car at Raceway Park, a fabled American drag strip in Englishtown. Search for the foundations of a Cold War Nike missile site in a pine forest on Jake Brown Road, heading west off US 9 South.

Dozens of birdhouses behind the interpretive center invite many species, from cardinals to goldfinch.

MORE INFORMATION

Open 8 A.M. to 6 P.M. Seasonal entrance fees may apply from Memorial Day to Labor Day—check the park's website to see if fees are currently in effect before you go. Swimming in designated areas is permitted when lifeguards are on duty. Group picnics and camping sites are by reservation. Biking is allowed on multiuse White Trail. Recreational facilities are partially accessible for persons with disabilities; for more information, please contact the park office at 732-566-2161.

23 | RAMAPO MOUNTAIN STATE FOREST

More than 20 miles of trails web this 4,269-acre park, providing something for everyone: giant boulders, lakes, castle ruins, and views of New York City.

Features 🎿🚵🥾🐕🔍⛷️☀️🚌

Location Oakland, NJ

Rating Strenuous

Distance 5.4 miles round-trip

Elevation Gain 650 feet

Estimated Time 3 hours

Maps USGS Wanaque; nj.gov/dep/parksandforests/maps/ramapo-trail.pdf; nynjtc.org/map/ramapo-mountain-state-forest-map

GPS Coordinates 41° 01.951′ N, 74° 15.119′ W

Contact Mailing address: Ramapo Mountain State Forest, c/o Ringwood State Park, 1304 Sloatsburg Road, Ringwood, NJ 07456; 973-962-7031; state.nj.us/dep /parksandforests/parks/ramapo.html

DIRECTIONS
Driving: Take Exit 57 off I-287. At the light, turn left off the exit onto West Oakland Avenue. Go 0.5 mile on West Oakland Avenue (which becomes Skyline Drive, passing under I-287) and quickly turn left into a gravel parking lot at the brown wooden park sign. The lot has room for 30 to 40 cars.

Public Transportation: From the Port Authority Bus Terminal in Manhattan (operated by the Port Authority of New York and New Jersey), take NJ Transit bus 197 to Ringwood Avenue at Burnside Place in Wanaque. Walk to Back Beach Park, traveling east on Burnside Place, and then to Decker Road and to Fourth Avenue (15 minutes, 0.8 mile).

TRAIL DESCRIPTION
Where to start with this delicious 4,269-acre hunk of woods that borders Ramapo Mountain Reservation? A flat 3-mile stroll around sparkling, island-dotted Ramapo Lake? A rugged trek on red-blazed Cannonball Trail to cross the footbridge over I-287? A short journey to the "balanced boulder" on purple-blazed Tamarack Trail? Those are all great options, but on this hike, you'll take blue-blazed MacEvoy Trail to white-blazed Castle Point Trail, discovering dramatic views of rocky lakes and mountains and exploring the romantic ruins of Van Slyke Castle. Autumn brings fiery color to the

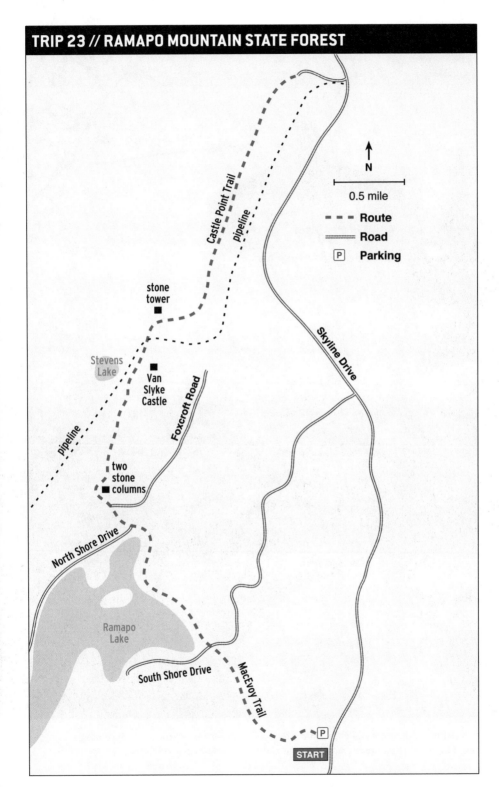

N

0.5 mile

- - - Route
——— Road
P   Parking

Castle Point Trail

pipeline

stone tower ■

Stevens Lake

Van Slyke Castle ■

Foxcroft Road

pipeline

two stone columns ■

North Shore Drive

Skyline Drive

Ramapo Lake

South Shore Drive

MacEvoy Trail

P

START

The water tower on the Van Slyke Castle grounds. Large portions of the castle, including a swimming pool, chimney, furnace, and crumbling stone walls, can still be explored today.

leaves; spring astonishes with flowers. Winter makes footing tricky on the rocks, but the unobstructed views are spectacular. Cool woods refresh in summer.

From the gravel parking lot, head toward the two chemical toilets and a trail kiosk, where blue-blazed MacEvoy Trail starts. The trail goes between two pretty rock walls and forks immediately. Take the right fork uphill; do not turn left because that dead-ends at a creek. Enjoy a brief boulder scramble. Take time to look into the valley on your left, noting the gorgeous outlines of an off-trail boulder field.

The path levels out as your feet pound over rock face. Follow the wide, rocky route uphill, keeping on the blue-blazed trail until it intersects a paved road at Ramapo Lake, a 120-acre human-made body of water (0.7 mile). Turn left on paved South Shore Drive to walk out onto the dam and admire the lake. (For an easier alternative, just take the 3-mile stroll around the lake.) Turn around, retrace your steps, and turn left onto paved North Shore Drive, which follows the lovely lake, with many viewing spots. To the right are interesting rock gardens. Pass a large private estate on your right and a dry, boulder-filled streambed. In 1.1 mile, go right at the Y intersection, toward two stone columns. Pass between them on a gravel road (technically, MacEvoy Trail, but it's not blazed here) and ignore the first trail on the left as the road begins to curve. In about 50 yards, at the next Y intersection, look for a big brown-and-white sign on the left for white-blazed Castle Point Trail. Turn left here, noticing the enormous boulders to the right of the sign (1.2 miles).

You are now on the steep and rocky, but short, white-blazed Castle Point Trail to the Van Slyke Castle ruins. After a brief level patch, the trail veers left through a rugged climb to a narrow dirt path hemmed in by shrubs and trees. At a huge pile of rocks, veer left and scramble up. Take one more hop to the right onto the rock outcropping for a rewarding look at the forest. Two rock outcroppings on your left provide beautiful views of the lakes and woods. Get back on Castle Point Trail, go left around a boulder, and hoist yourself over a rock wall, flush with the ground behind it. Turn around and sit on the wall, drinking in the scenery, spectacular in autumn.

Back on the trail, climb atop the boulders on the left for an excellent panorama of Ramapo Lake and Stephens Lake. Continue up the trail to the castle site (1.4 miles) and take time to explore the old fireplaces and mantels. The former "castle," now an eerie ruin that springs up amid the trails, has a complicated history. As you walk among the dilapidated remains, imagine what life in the early 1900s must have been like in this mansion built by Wall Street tycoon William Porter, who named it Foxcroft. Porter died in a traffic accident in 1911. His widow, Ruth A. Coles, then married Manhattan attorney Warren Van Slyke, who later died from complications following a gallstone operation in 1925. Ruth Coles remained in the house until her death in 1940. She left the home to her family, who promptly sold it. A couple bought it in 1942 but then abandoned the property during a bitter divorce. Vandals burned the long-vacant building in 1959, before the state of New Jersey bought the property from the estate of Clifford F. MacEvoy.

Resuming the hike, keep to the left of the ruins, and at the Y intersection, go left on white-blazed Castle Point Trail. Pass a concrete structure that was once a swimming pool. As the trail levels out, note the rock outcropping on the left with gorgeous views of the lake. Climb uphill now, over rocks and through a boulder field, to a stone tower (1.7 miles) that once held the mansion's water cistern; metal pipes still lead from it. Walk around the tower and peer in before heading back to Castle Point Trail and going north.

The uphill trek north on Castle Point Trail is rocky. Climb the outcropping to the left for attractive views of the forest and lake, and then go down a rugged hill. The trail intersects with a mowed public utility path at 2.7 miles.

This hike ends at the public utility path. (*Note*: With a detailed topographic map, you can explore the area further.) Turn around and go back the way you came, past the tower and castle and over the stone wall, following white-blazed Castle Point Trail all the way. Once down, turn right onto the gravel path at the intersection, pass between the stone pillars, and then turn left onto North Shore Drive. At the intersection of North Shore and South Shore drives, go left and then quickly turn right onto blue-blazed MacEvoy Trail. At the Y intersection, go right to stay on the blue-blazed trail back to the parking lot.

DID YOU KNOW?

The Ramapough Mountain Indians are descended from the Lenni-Lenape. Several thousand still live in New Jersey. The Ramapough Lenape Nation was recognized in 1980 by the state of New Jersey but has never been federally recognized. Two movies have been made about the Ramapough: *Mann v. Ford* (2011), which documents the tribe's lawsuit against Ford Motor Company for creating a toxic waste landfill near affordable housing for tribal members, and *American Native* (2013), which details the Ramapough Lenape Nation's efforts to gain federal recognition.

OTHER ACTIVITIES

Go south (turn right out of the parking lot) on Skyline Drive (Lakeside Avenue) to Pompton Lakes for both ice cream and food at the Ice Cream Station and Deli. About 5 miles away are Ringwood State Park (visit Ringwood Manor) and New Jersey Botanical Garden in Ringwood. Within 10 miles are the 107-acre freshwater wetlands at Celery Farm in Allendale, administered by the Fyke Nature Association, and the 81-acre wildlife sanctuary at J. A. McFaul Environmental Center in Wyckoff.

MORE INFORMATION

Open sunrise to sunset. The park allows fishing and horseback riding. Biking is fine on multiuse trails. Hunting is permitted except on Sundays. The park is partially universally accessible; call the park office for details at 973-962-7031.

24 LIBERTY STATE PARK

Enjoy an easy-to-reach trail with trees, flowers, birds, green grass, and the immense Hudson River, all in the lap of New York City.

Features 👥🐕♿💧🔎⛷️🎯⛺🚌

Location Jersey City, NJ

Rating Easy

Distance 5.2-mile loop

Elevation Gain 20 feet

Estimated Time 2 hours

Maps USGS Jersey City; nj.gov/dep/parksandforests/maps/libertystatepark.html

GPS Coordinates 40° 41.673′ N, 74° 03.528′ W

Contact Liberty State Park office, 200 Morris Pesin Drive, Jersey City, NJ 07305; 201-915-3400, ext. 101; nj.gov/dep/parksandforests/parks/libertystatepark.html

DIRECTIONS
Driving: Take the New Jersey Turnpike to Exit 14B toward Liberty State Park/Jersey City. Bear left toward Liberty State Park and Science Center/Port Liberte. In about 100 feet, turn left onto Bayview Avenue, travel 0.25 mile, enter a roundabout, and take the first exit of the roundabout to Morris Pesin Drive. Park at the end of the road in the clearly signed lot on the right, with space for about 100 cars.

By rail: NJ Transit's Hudson-Bergen Light Rail stops at Liberty State Park Station near the Liberty Science Center, which is on the north end of the park (park office is on the south end). Walk 5 minutes to the Liberty Science Center, go through the parking lot, and turn left onto Phillips Street toward the water and path.

By water: From North Cove Marina, directly in front of the World Financial Center in New York City, take the Liberty Landing Ferry to Liberty Landing Marina. Walk east, away from the marina, toward the Central Railroad of New Jersey Terminal, and proceed to any section of the waterfront to get on the Hudson River Waterfront Walkway.

TRAIL DESCRIPTION
Start in the park office at 200 Morris Pesin Drive and pick up a map and other information, such as ferry schedules for Ellis and Liberty islands, Battery Park, and Manhattan. (A map is not strictly necessary for directions but lets you know which landmarks you're observing.) On this hike, follow the red-hexagonal-tiled path of the Hudson River Waterfront Walkway toward the Statue of Liberty, turn left at Liberty Landing Marina, and make your way back along any of the footpaths that cut through the green.

Liberty State Park is a verdant, flower-and-tree-filled, 1,212-acre space, surrounded by water on three sides. This south-to-north route passes Liberty Island, Ellis Island, the Central Railroad of New Jersey (CRRNJ) Terminal, the 9/11 memorial, Liberty Landing Marina, the Grove of Remembrance, Christopher Columbus Plaza, and the Liberty State Park Nature Interpretive Center. Visit the center (hudsonreporter.com/2021/06/24/liberty-state-park-nature-interpretive-center-reopens) and enjoy the nature walk, tidal marsh, and pier—all surprisingly peaceful and pleasant in this urban setting. You can turn around at any time for a shorter stroll.

In spring, the park is alive with cultivated flowers and blooming trees. Summer brings crowds, concessions, festivals, fireworks, and activity. Fall slows and moves into a quiet and serene winter, with many varieties of ducks and birds.

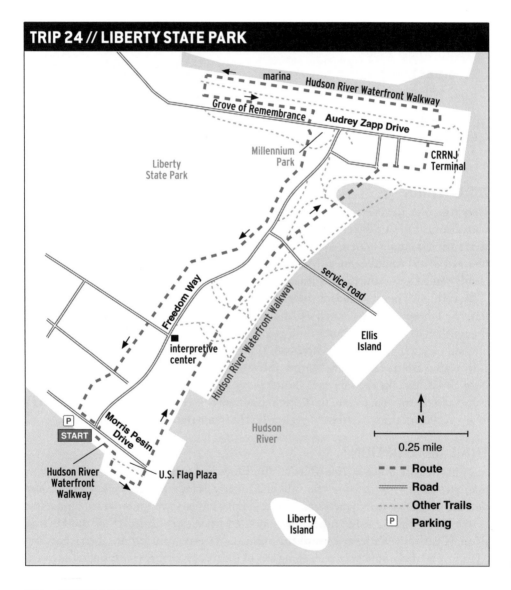

TRIP 24 // LIBERTY STATE PARK

marina
Hudson River Waterfront Walkway
Grove of Remembrance
Audrey Zapp Drive
Liberty State Park
Millennium Park
CRRNJ Terminal
Freedom Way
service road
interpretive center
Ellis Island
Hudson River Waterfront Walkway
P
START
Morris Pesin Drive
Hudson River
Hudson River Waterfront Walkway
U.S. Flag Plaza
N
0.25 mile
Liberty Island
- - - Route
——— Road
······· Other Trails
P Parking

From the park office, make your way through U.S. Flag Plaza to the path along the water (New York Harbor and the Hudson River), and head north (away from the park office) for an up-close-and-personal sighting of the Statue of Liberty. This 2-mile promenade is beautiful, with excellent city views. Walk toward New York City, with Lady Liberty on your right, perched atop Liberty Island. (You can take a ferry to Liberty and Ellis islands from the CRRNJ Terminal.) Look closely at the rocks along the water; you may spot a sunning harbor seal. The Verrazzano-Narrows Bridge, which connects Staten Island and Brooklyn, shines in the distance.

A park sign provides information about Morris Pesin. Frustrated with a 3-hour trip from Jersey City by car and ferry to visit Liberty Island, Pesin made a well-publicized 8-minute canoe trip from Jersey City to Liberty Island in 1958. This trip sparked Pesin's eighteen-year crusade to create an urban state park that offered easier access to the Statue of Liberty. On June 14, 1976, his dream came true.

Admire the grandeur of the next famous sight: the Renaissance revivalist immigration station perched atop 27-acre Ellis Island in the harbor. Twelve million immigrants passed through Ellis Island. Two-thirds of them landed at the CRRNJ Terminal, where trains took them to their destiny. Ferries to Ellis Island run daily, except for December 25. For a pleasant view of Ellis Island, pause at the bridge that runs to the island (1.3 miles). You can't hike the bridge, which is only for authorized personnel, but you can always ride the ferry. Interestingly, 90 percent of the island is in New Jersey; the other 10 percent belongs to New York, as ruled by the U.S. Supreme Court in 1998. As 100 percent is federal property, state ownership is merely a point of pride. When you visit, try to discover which state "owns" which part.

Sightseeing and news helicopters buzz through the sky as you enjoy the spring tulips and daffodils; nascent tree blossoms soften the horizon. Head to the Victorian-style CRRNJ Terminal and enter through the wide doors. Here, you can buy ferry tickets to the Statue of Liberty and Ellis Island. Bathrooms and snack shops are available, as well as information on the terminal's history. Use peaked in 1929 (21 million passengers), but times changed, and the terminal ceased railroad operations on April 30, 1967.

The "Empty Sky" 9/11 monument is next on the walkway (2.2 miles). This is New Jersey's official memorial to honor the 749 state residents who died in the attacks on September 11, 2001. The two 30-foot-tall, 210-foot-long structures are stunning. Walk the 12-foot-long alley of bluestone with the names of the deceased etched in its walls. Visitors are allowed to take a rubbing with pencil and paper.

Pass the water fountain on the left and you are at Liberty Landing Marina (2.6 miles), with its gorgeous boats and views of terraced apartments across the water in Jersey City. Several restaurants are near the marina. In spring, the cherry trees are beautiful. Pass the Marine Center building on the left; the path changes to black asphalt and then ends. Go left and walk through the parking lot for vehicles with boats, cross the cobblestone road, and turn left onto the paved path (3.1 miles). Stroll through greenery back toward the park office.

Explore the landscaped Grove of Remembrance on your right (watch out for cyclists). Turn right on the path with the one-way sign, across from the Marine Center building. Then turn left and go through circular Millennium Park. Cross two paved roads and turn right on the second path after the two roads. In spring, the pine trees are yellow with pollen. Go left at the Y intersection toward Christopher Columbus Plaza. Playgrounds and restrooms appear. Go right at the next Y intersection, carefully cross a road that is open to traffic, and pass the bridge to Ellis Island (4.0 miles). This lovely, verdant section of the park is called the "Green Ring" (4.4 miles). Flags from many nations line Freedom Way to the right. Bear left toward a fitness station and climb the hill to the right for benches if you need a rest.

Don't miss the interpretive center on the left (4.6 miles), with its lovely nature walk. Stroll on the dock stretching across the tidal pond; hear the *konk-a-ree* of the red-winged blackbird and the "trickling" song of the marsh wren. Lady Liberty peeks through the reeds.

When you leave, note the Daily News building to the right as you head toward the Verrazzano-Narrows Bridge and the park office.

DID YOU KNOW?

The waterfront path is part of a longer route: the official Hudson River Waterfront Walkway. When complete, the walkway will cover 40 miles (18.5 as the crow flies) and span nine New Jersey municipalities, from the George Washington Bridge in Fort Lee to the Bayonne Bridge in Bayonne. For updates and access points, visit hudsonriverwaterfront.org.

OTHER ACTIVITIES

Take a 2-hour kayak ecotour of the Hudson River Estuary from June through September with Liberty State Park Kayak Eco-Tour; call Liberty State Park at 201-459-2070 for

Liberty State Park in spring brings daffodils, tulips, and stunning views of the New York City skyline.

details (visithudson.org/hcgrouptours/liberty-state-park-kayaki-eco-tour/). Explore the Liberty Science Center at the north end of the park, where you can enjoy films, laser shows, the biggest planetarium in the Western Hemisphere, and much more. Dine at the upscale Liberty House Restaurant. Visit Boxwood Hall, an American Revolution site, in nearby Elizabeth (908-282-7617). And don't forget the ferry into Manhattan.

MORE INFORMATION
Open 6 A.M. to 10 P.M. The park is partially ADA accessible. Call the park office for details.

3 // JERSEY SHORE

The Jersey Shore region, part of the Atlantic Coastal Plain, is home to pinelands, beaches, and marshes. Also known as the Outer Coastal Plain, here the soils are nutrient-poor compared with the fertile, loamy earth of the Inner Coastal Plain, which earns New Jersey its nickname of the Garden State. But the Shore's sandy soil supports many rare plant species, such as yellow-flowered bog asphodel, white milkweed, seaside buttercup, and sphagnum moss, and also provides mineral riches. The pure quartz sand was once heavily used for glassmaking and the finer silica sand for producing cosmetics and silica gel. Visitors will see remnants of industrial factories while wandering the lowlands and rolling hills.

This region has four major coastal rivers: Manasquan, Shark, Navesink, and Shrewsbury. You'll get an overview of Navesink and Shrewsbury rivers at Hartshorne Woods Park (Trip 27), as well as an education on World War II coastal defenses as you explore the old bunkers. The Jersey Shore's beaches (see Trips 29 and 30) are crowded with vacationers in summer, but in the off-season hiking is rewarding, peaceful, and beautiful. Lighthouses, seaside towns joined by sandy beaches, county parks, state parks, and wildlife management areas round out "the Shore" experience.

The hikes in this section cover a good sampling of the region. Get ready to walk in the woods, wander the Pine Barrens (see Trip 26), roam along rivers, pound the sands and boardwalks along the ocean, and enjoy learning some history.

Facing page: A ship's outline seen offshore from Ocean Grove.

25 CLAYTON PARK

Spring flowers, cozy trails, and mountain laurels make this park a wonderful refuge—physically close to the madding crowd yet spiritually far from it.

Features

Location Imlaystown, NJ

Rating Easy

Distance 4.2-mile loop

Elevation Gain 490 feet

Estimated Time 2 hours

Maps USGS Allentown, USGS Roosevelt; co.monmouth.nj.us/documents/130/Clayton-Park-ADA-Final-2021.pdf

GPS Coordinates 40° 09.362' N, 74° 30.286' W

Contact Monmouth County Park System, 805 Newman Springs Road, Lincroft, NJ 07738; 732-842-4000; monmouthcountyparks.com

DIRECTIONS

From I-195, traveling east or west, take Exit 11 (Imlaystown/Cox's Corner). If eastbound, turn right. If westbound, turn left. Get on County Route 43 (Imlaystown/Hightstown Road). At the first intersection, turn left onto County Route 526 and then immediately turn right to continue on County Route 43 (Davis Station Road). Follow for 1.0 mile. Turn left onto Emley's Hill Road and proceed to the park on the left. A Global Positioning System (GPS) device may show Cream Ridge, New Jersey. The gravel parking lot holds about 30 cars.

TRAIL DESCRIPTION

Clayton Park is a bit off the beaten path, but the road signs to get there are clear, and you'll enjoy the drive past rolling farmlands, tree farms, and horse farms. You'd never know that Six Flags Great Adventure is less than 10 miles to the west, off I-195. Such are the contrasts of rural and urban in the great state of New Jersey.

The 450-acre park is known for its wildflowers in spring. In April and May, discover jack-in-the-pulpit, trout lily, spring beauty, purple hepatica, wild geranium, trillium, and wild ginger. Trees include large American beech, black oak, and the tulip poplar, with its orange-centered blooms. Ferns line many sections of the trail, layered beneath spicebush and viburnum. Lyme ticks are also prevalent in season, so take precautions.

The 7-mile network has signposts at intersections but can still be a bit confusing because the colors on three separate trails are similar or the same. Dark blue square blazes mark two trails (Bridges Trail and Old Forge Trail), and a somewhat lighter blue square blaze marks a third (Doctor's Creek Trail)! But don't let that keep you from this enchanting adventure. The park is small, so it's hard to be lost for long, especially if you remember where you came from. Additionally, the kiosk at the parking lot has a posted map as well as printed maps you can stick in your pocket. (The parking lot also has a chemical toilet and picnic tables.) This hike uses four routes: green-blazed Glen Trail to dark-blue-blazed Bridges Trail to light-blue-blazed Doctor's Creek Trail and then to dark-blue-blazed Old Forge Trail. (*Note*: Trails can be slippery in wet conditions and are also popular with mountain bikers and horseback riders.)

Start on green-blazed Glen Trail, a packed-dirt path. At the intersection, where a chemical toilet is conveniently located, veer left to continue on Glen Trail. Within 50 yards, veer right onto dark-blue-blazed Bridges Trail (0.1 mile), which is level but can be leaf-strewn and slippery. Head downhill and note the two small trees growing in the middle of the path, which becomes rooty and flattens out as the valley slopes to the left. The trail widens and gets smoother as it curves sharply on red dirt. Cross a wooden bridge over a deeply rutted ravine (0.5 mile). At the junction just past the bridge, veer right, still on dark-blue-blazed Bridges Trail (Bridges Trail also goes to the left). The path ascends slightly and may be muddy.

Keep straight, ignoring the two unmarked trails to the right at the "Caution" fences. The dirt path descends. Stay straight, ignoring two more unmarked trails, this time to the left. At the intersection, turn right onto light-blue-blazed Doctor's Creek Trail at a double-trunked tree. Go downhill, where the path levels out, and veer right on Doctor's Creek Trail (0.9 mile), which also goes left. Note the "Restricted Area" sign to the left.

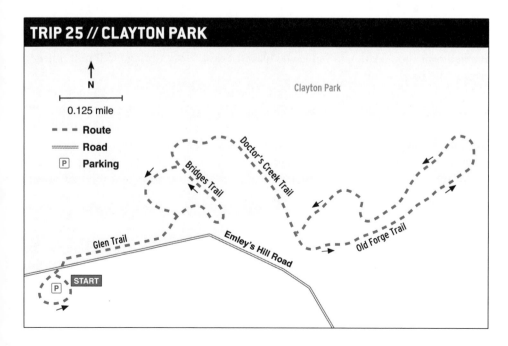

TRIP 25 // CLAYTON PARK

Take a rooty downhill trek to a beautiful stream. The dirt path widens; a house is on the left. Cross a wooden bridge over a stream and admire the phalanx of skunk cabbages (1.0 mile).

At the Y intersection, turn right onto dark-blue-blazed Old Forge Trail (Doctor's Creek Trail goes to the left, 1.1 miles). The narrow, muddy trail is at first flanked by high banks, but as they diminish, the bare tree shapes become more fancifully shaped. Look for "the lovers" tree: two trees entwined in an embrace. The banks reappear as the trail ascends steeply and becomes worn and uneven. The reward is a spreading green meadow behind a slatted wooden fence, with a valley sloping dramatically to the right. The path is sandy here and tracks the curve of the meadow.

At the Y intersection, go right on dark-blue-blazed Old Forge Trail (1.4 miles), which also goes to the left. Head uphill, following the fence on your right. Then start downhill on a hard dirt path—go straight to continue on Old Forge Trail, ignoring an unmarked trail to the right. The path levels, and hills slope to the left. Continue straight, ignoring an unmarked trail to the left. The fence ends, and the woods path descends. Water shines from an unnamed pond to the right. Head down a steep bank, where you can see geese and ducks in the water. (*Caution*: The footing is uneven here.) Mountain laurels line the way, and hundreds of skunk cabbages proliferate in the watery valley to the right.

The route gradually ascends, following the valley to the right. Admire the magnificent swelling land contours as you wander up and down past wildflowers.

At a three-way intersection, turn left to continue on Old Forge Trail toward the white parking lot sign (2.4 miles). (You aren't very near the parking lot yet, but "P" signs appear.) The meadow is ahead. Turn right at the next "P" sign. Enjoy the wildflowers, butterflies, and the field and valley to the left. As the path winds, a field, a road, and a house appear on the right, and a valley and hills on the left. At the Y intersection, turn left toward parking lot signs, still on dark-blue-blazed Old Forge Trail, which eventually merges with Doctor's Creek Trail. Detour to the right toward the house for a view of the water and perhaps some amphibians and soaring red-tailed hawks. Once on the marked trail (both dark and light blue blazes) again, cross a bridge (3.0 miles) over a stream and head uphill.

At the Y intersection, turn left on dark-blue-blazed Bridges Trail (3.1 miles) toward the white parking lot sign. At the next few junctions, continue following the white "P" signs. Go over a bridge and a steep hill. At the bottom of the hill, head toward the "P" sign and take green-blazed Glen Trail (3.8 miles) back to the parking lot.

On the drive out, stop at the educational Clayton Park Activity Center on Davis Road. Just beyond, admire the beautiful stained glass windows of a restored private home that was formerly a Baptist church.

DID YOU KNOW?

In 1720, the great-great-grandparents of Abraham Lincoln donated land where the Old Yellow Meeting House was built (72 Yellow Meeting House Road, Imlaystown). This private land and old cemetery are open during the day. Tours upon request: Friends of OYMH, P.O. Box 23, Cream Ridge, NJ 08514; oymh.org.

Skunk cabbage abounds in wet areas throughout Clayton Park.

OTHER ACTIVITIES

Visit the Imlaystown Historic District. Hike 1,500-acre Crosswicks Creek Park in Allentown. Explore Colliers Mills Wildlife Management Area, a National Audubon Society Important Bird Area, in New Egypt. No blazed trails exist in the wildlife area, but see the online topographic map at the New Jersey Division of Fish and Wildlife website: nj.gov/dep/fgw/pdf/wmamaps/colliers_mills.pdf. In Jackson, stroll easy paths at Bunker Hill Bogs. Robbinsville, to the north, is the geographic center of New Jersey and home to the 6,300-acre Assunpink Wildlife Management Area.

MORE INFORMATION

Open 7 A.M. to dusk. Fishing allowed with proper permits. Pets must be leashed.

26 WELLS MILLS COUNTY PARK

Well-maintained trails, bogs, hills, and an excellent nature center make this a scenic Pine Barrens primer and a good workout in cooler, bug-free months.

Features

Location Waretown, NJ

Rating Moderate

Distance 8.3-mile loop

Elevation Gain 750 feet

Estimated Time 4 hours

Maps USGS Brookville; co.ocean.nj.us/WebContentFiles//4ad91c49-a29e-4f34-93b1-4b915cbc94e0.pdf

GPS Coordinates 39° 47.761′ N, 74° 16.589′ W

Contact Wells Mills County Park, 905 Wells Mills Road, Waretown, NJ 08758; 609-971-3085. Administered by Ocean County Department of Parks and Recreation, 1198 Bandon Road, Toms River, NJ 08753; 877-627-2757; oceancountyparks.org.

DIRECTIONS

From Garden State Parkway southbound or northbound, take Exit 69 (Waretown) and turn left (west) onto Wells Mills Road (County Route 532). Proceed approximately 2.5 miles to the park entrance on the left. A large parking lot holds at least 50 cars.

TRAIL DESCRIPTION

With more than 900 acres, Wells Mills County Park is the largest park in Ocean County and is part of the Pine Barrens (see "Get Away from the Crowds in the Pine Barrens and the Pinelands" on page 143). Pine and oak forests predominate on 16 miles of hiking trails. Habitats include Atlantic white cedar and maple-gum swamps, a freshwater lake, streams, and bogs. Blueberry bushes abound, as well as curly grass ferns, pitcher plants, sundews, turkey beards, and large swaths of sphagnum moss. Wildlife includes deer, foxes, Fowler's toads, and eastern box turtles. The well-marked trails roll up and down over dirt and sand, with boardwalks over marshes. This trip uses only white-blazed Macri Trail (also called Penn's Hill Trail), which makes a big circle through the park. Several trails connect, making it easy to design longer or shorter routes. It's best to hike during cooler weather to avoid the bugs; Lyme ticks are also prevalent, so use precautions. The boardwalks, bridges, and steps can be icy in winter, and they may be slippery in wet conditions. In fall, beautiful tundra swans float on Wells Mills Lake.

Make your way to the three-story Wells Mills Nature Center, which has indoor toilets. Look around at the exhibits, grab a map, and climb to the third-floor observation deck for a pleasant view of Wells Mills Lake. Sign in at the trailhead to the right of the

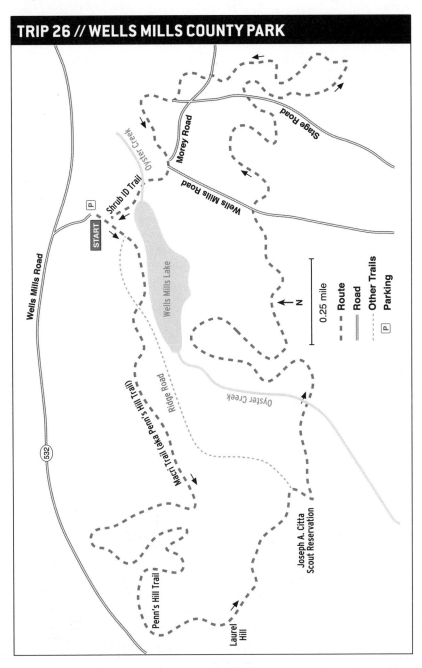

TRIP 26 // WELLS MILLS COUNTY PARK

Oyster Creek

Morey Road

Stage Road

Shrub ID Trail

P

START

Wells Mills Road

Wells Mills Lake

Wells Mills Road

0.25 mile

N

- - - Route
— Road
········· Other Trails
P Parking

Wells Mills Road

532

Macri Trail (aka Penn's Hill Trail)

Ridge Road

Oyster Creek

Penn's Hill Trail

Laurel Hill

Joseph A. Citta Scout Reservation

nature center at the edge of the lake. Then start your journey on white-blazed Macri Trail, where you'll see a green "7" sign. All elevation gain, such as it is, occurs at the beginning of the hike.

Walk past pretty, human-made Wells Mills Lake—no natural lakes exist in the Pine Barrens. The path is rooty here, but after traversing a wooden boardwalk, it softens with pine needles, and pine trees line the way. Stay on white-blazed Macri Trail (blue-blazed Conrad Trail goes to the right).

Walk through a small swamp with coppery, tannic cedar water. The soft dirt path leads through narrow trees. Pause on one of the many picturesque bridges or inviting benches to admire the islands in the lake. Continue straight on white-blazed Macri Trail at the Estlow Trail/All Terrain Bike Trail junction, heading downhill. Go straight over a dirt road and then uphill on a pine straw–strewn path that muffles your footfalls. The texture and color of the tree bark is extraordinary: thick brown slabs like floating islands, rimmed with green lichens and dusted with colorful fungi. Feel the trees' skin and marvel at the myriad colors. Cross a dirt ditch and keep following Macri Trail. Logs block some side paths—a sign to stay off them. Short bushes line the trail as it winds through black-barked trees. Traverse a long, serpentine boardwalk, head up a slight hill (1.0 mile), and then descend through the pines.

Hike uphill (the white-blazed trail is now called Penn's Hill Trail) and cross a ditch on flat terrain before the path begins to roll. Spring-green bushes lighten the woods. As you walk on a ledge with a dropoff below, some bare hardwoods on the right observe your passage (2.0 miles). Go across an unmarked trail and down a hill; cross a wooden bridge

Plank bridges span the swampy areas of Wells Mills County Park; use caution.

at the bottom. Admire the mountain laurels as you climb 126-foot Penn's Hill. The trail winds to the left and reaches sandy Laurel Hill at a lofty elevation of 130 feet (2.8 miles).

Descend and cross a footbridge; the path begins to level out. Note the expanse of sphagnum moss. After another footbridge, the path rises, and you are rewarded by a boardwalk spanning mossy water. The bank slopes to the left of the pine straw–covered path, which heads toward a grove of mountain laurels. Walk up and down some fun wooden steps. The forest thickens, and the path becomes rooty and wet from the Wells Mills Lake tributaries. More boardwalks and upward steps lead to a fence. Step over the bottom rail and turn right onto a wide path to continue on the white-blazed trail, again called Macri Trail, passing briefly through Joseph A. Citta Scout Reservation (3.4 miles). At a "Do Not Enter" sign on a gate, turn sharply left, staying on Macri Trail.

Walk on a bridge over Oyster Creek (3.8 miles), and go uphill. At a big intersection with a dirt road, an all-terrain bike trail, and a green-blazed trail, go left (3.9 miles), following white blazes onto a wide, sandy path (get out your beach ball). At the sign for Ocean County Park, turn left onto Macri Trail, blanketed with pine straw. Admire the tunnels of mountain laurels, enjoy a long boardwalk, and look for toads before heading uphill. Enter a field of miniature trees covered with ghostly white lichens. From here on out, the trail is flat. At 5.7 miles, cross a dirt road, Morey Road, for the first time.

A long boardwalk and a bridge cross the muddy, watery bogs of Oyster Creek (6.4 miles). Tread an angled boardwalk that leads to a beach of white sand, pine straw, and sphagnum moss. Cedar chips on the path give way to a fairy-tale-like narrow, sandy ribbon lined with moss. At a road (which is probably a firebreak, a gap in vegetation to slow or stop the progress of a fire), go straight to continue on the white-blazed trail. Enter a controlled-burn area with a huge firebreak trench to the right.

The winding route traverses several unnamed dirt roads and all-terrain bike trails; follow the white blazes. Enjoy another boardwalk. Go straight across Morey Road, which has a gate to the right (7.3 miles). A pretty valley with a sometimes-dry stream-bed is to your right on this wide white sand treadway. At the next road, turn right to stay on Macri Trail, which becomes a cinder path. Cross another bridge and watch for amphibians. To your right is pink-blazed, 0.7-mile Shrub ID Trail (8.1 miles), which you can explore if you want. Otherwise, keep straight and then turn left at the Y inter-section, continuing to follow white blazes. The lake is on your left now, and benches are available here if you need a rest. Return to the nature center and parking lot, remem-bering to sign out at the trailhead before you leave.

DID YOU KNOW?

Every October, Wells Mills County Park hosts the annual Pine Barrens Jamboree, a day of music, hiking, food, and crafts. The short Visually Impaired Persons' (VIP) Trail starts near the nature center. VIP Trail has a guide rope and a tape player that indicates special objects to be heard, felt, or smelled.

OTHER ACTIVITIES

Go northeast on Wells Mills Road to Bryant Road and visit the Candace McKee Ashmun Preserve, a 4,000-acre semi-wilderness in the Forked River Mountain Wildlife Management Area. Check out folk, blues, and country music on Saturday nights at the nonprofit, volunteer-run Albert Music Hall on Wells Mills Road. Operated by the Pinelands Cultural Society, it's one of the best deals around: $6 for adults and $1 for children 11 and younger; 609-971-1593; alberthall.org.

MORE INFORMATION

Open 7 A.M. to dusk. Picnic areas must be reserved. Fishing is permitted. Some areas are handicapped accessible. The nature center's Elizabeth Meirs Morgan Observation Deck is named for this very active naturalist and conservationist in Ocean County.

GET AWAY FROM THE CROWDS IN THE PINE BARRENS AND THE PINELANDS

What's the difference between the Pine Barrens and the Pinelands? Quite simply, New Jersey's Pinelands is a political area, and the Pine Barrens is a geographic region within the Pinelands. A pine barrens is any area of sandy, acidic soil where pines, oaks, cedars, blueberries, cranberries, and other acid-loving plants predominate. Early settlers called places with this nutrient-poor soil "barren" because traditional crops did not grow well there.

John McPhee's 1967 best-selling book *The Pine Barrens* (Farrar, Straus and Giroux) ignited the public campaign to save the Pinelands. His accounts of the Pinelands' natural resources and the effects of water and fire on this region hold true today.

The New Jersey Pinelands National Reserve (PNR) was created by Congress in 1978 with the passage of the National Parks and Recreation Act; it was the first national reserve in the country. The PNR is huge: it includes 1.1 million acres and covers portions of 7 counties and all or part of 56 municipalities in central and southern New Jersey. To help protect the Pinelands from development and to manage growth, the New Jersey Pinelands Commission was created in 1979. The commission includes representatives from state, county, and federal agencies. Today, the Pinelands Commission, the National Park Service, the New Jersey Department of Environmental Protection, New Jersey Division of Parks and Forestry, and nonprofit groups work together to protect the PNR.

The water of the shallow, slow-moving surface streams in the Pine Barrens is filtered by sandy underground layers of earth. Within these layers, separated by silt and clay, lies a huge natural reservoir: the Kirkwood-Cohansey aquifer system, which extends more than 3,000 square miles. The contents, an estimated 17 trillion gallons of water, could cover the entire state of New Jersey in a lake 10 feet deep. This aquifer is the Pinelands region's primary source of drinking water and provides approximately 90 percent of all the water to streams, wetlands, and rivers in the Pinelands. The brewed-tea color of the surface water stems from a high iron content and natural vegetative dyes, such as tannin. The water's high acidity helps produce some of the distinctive flora of the Pinelands, such as carnivorous sundews and pitcher plants, orchids, and Pine Barrens gentians.

Water helped support New Jersey's industries as far back as the 1700s, including shipbuilding, paper mills, sawmills, charcoal kilns, bog iron smelters, and glassmaking. Once-thriving villages and factories are now ghost towns that fascinate visitors today. Ghost towns in the Pine Barrens include Martha, Ong's Hat, and Harrisville, all in Burlington County. Other deserted villages in the Pine Barrens are Estell Manor (Trip 32) and Atsion (Trip 42). (See *Ghost Towns and Other Quirky Places in the New Jersey Pine Barrens*, by Barbara Solem-Stull [Plexus Publishing, 2005]. Read *Idiot!* by Christopher Klim [Hopewell Publications, 2007] for a quirky novel set in the Pine Barrens.) Also curious are the countless perfectly round 20- to 30-foot-wide circles sprinkled throughout the pine forests; these are remnants of charcoal kilns and are especially striking beneath a thin coating of snow. Abandoned sand quarries hold pristine lakes and ponds, with beaches of quartz sand and miles of surrounding sugar-sand trails. In fact, water—be it wetlands, bogs, streams, or cedar swamps—covers 35 percent of the PNR. And despite the PNR's immense acreage, fewer than 100,000 people live there—a virtually uninhabited region by New Jersey standards!

Despite all that water, wildfires are common in the Pinelands due to the seasonally dry ecosystem. Fires have shaped the PNR's ecology over the centuries. Prescribed burning began in the late 1930s to manage tree-stand composition and wildlife habitat. Today's controlled burns help prevent wildfires, but fire is actually a friend to pine tree survival. The intense heat causes the pinecones to "pop," allowing the seeds to sprout and new trees to grow. The Forest Resource Education Center in Jackson holds a public burn every October. Scientists predict that wildfire suppression over the next several decades will eventually encourage oaks to grow in place of pines. Whether caused by fires wild or controlled, the acres of blackened trunks in the Pinelands lend a surreal quality to the landscape.

Native cranberries and blueberries have continued to adapt to the Pine Barrens' conditions and are a major component of New Jersey's agricultural industry. In fact, the blueberry was first cultivated by a Pine Barrens resident, Elizabeth White, in 1916. Educational cranberry tours are available today (see Trip 50). Flooded cranberry bogs bring a watery beauty to the Pine Barrens and provide homes for tundra swans and many varieties of amphibians. In fact, the Pine Barrens tree frog, a state endangered species, needs the acidic waters of the Pine Barrens' swamps and bogs to survive, and its range is primarily restricted to this area.

Whether called the Pinelands or the Pine Barrens, this wide expanse of natural beauty and preternatural quiet remains an extraordinary region that must be experienced to be believed. Follow the footsteps of John McPhee.

> *I was in the pines because I found it hard to believe that so much unbroken forest could still exist so near the big Eastern cities, and I wanted to see it while it was still there.*
>
> John McPhee, *The Pine Barrens*, 1967

For more information about the Pinelands, contact:

State of New Jersey Pinelands Commission and Pinelands National Reserve, 15 Springfield Road, P.O. Box 359, New Lisbon, NJ 08064; 609-894-7300; nj.gov/pinelands.

New Jersey Department of Environmental Protection, P.O. Box 420, Trenton, NJ 08625; 609-777-3373; dep.nj.gov.

Pinelands Preservation Alliance, 17 Pemberton Road, Southampton, NJ 08088; 609-859-8860; pinelandsalliance.org.

27 HARTSHORNE WOODS PARK

Water, woods, and history meet in 794 acres of hills, deep forests, beaches, and World War II heavy artillery bunkers.

Features 🏃🐕💧🎣🔍⛷️💦🏕️🔦🏇🚴

Location Locust, NJ

Rating Strenuous

Distance 9.3-mile loop

Elevation Gain 1,600 feet

Estimated Time 5 hours

Maps USGS Sandy Hook East, USGS Sandy Hook West; co.monmouth.nj.us /documents/130/Hartshorne-Woods-Brochure-web2022.pdf

GPS Coordinates 40° 24.014′ N, 74° 00.803′ W

Contact Monmouth County Park System, 805 Newman Springs Road, Lincroft, NJ 07738; 732-842-4000; monmouthcountyparks.com

DIRECTIONS

From Garden State Parkway, take Exit 109 toward Red Bank/Lincroft. After 0.23 mile, merge onto Half Mile Road. After 0.54 mile, turn right onto West Front Street. In 1.12 miles, turn left onto County Route 13 and follow it for 0.12 mile before turning left onto NJ 35. Continue for 0.47 mile and then turn right onto Navesink River Road, which becomes Locust Point Road. After about 1 mile, turn right onto Hartshorne Road. In about 0.5 mile, Hartshorne Woods Park is on the left (Buttermilk Valley Entrance). The paved parking lot holds about twenty cars.

TRAIL DESCRIPTION

Hartshorne Woods was a former coastal defense site and now has 15 miles of trails over 794 acres, with three main hiking sections. The Buttermilk Valley section goes through a beautiful forest of oaks, mountain laurels, and wildflowers. The Monmouth Hills section becomes more rugged and uneven as you venture deeper into the forest. The Rocky Point section (Navesink Military Reservation Historic District) is hilly, exposed to sun, and has a mix of paved and dirt paths. Here are two World War II bunkers, a Cold War radar surveillance site, and fantastic views of Navesink River and the towns of Sea Bright (on a barrier peninsula) and Rumson.

Many turnaround points can shorten this hike, which starts at the Buttermilk Valley Entrance and rounds the perimeter of the park on Laurel Ridge, Grand Tour, Rocky Point, Bunker Loop, and Cuesta Ridge trails. (Square blue blazes mark Laurel Ridge,

Bunker Loop, and Cuesta Ridge trails, so you must read the trail names to distinguish among them.) Look for egrets, barred owls, woodpeckers (both red-bellied and downy), and hummingbirds. The twisted branches and triple-trunked trees are fantastic. In summer, the area is gorgeous with phlox and blueberries. In fall, the trees glow, and goldenrods and berries shimmer.

Pick up a map from the parking lot kiosk to the left of the chemical toilets; a water fountain is here as well. Face the woods and go to the very far right of the parking lot for blue-square-blazed Laurel Ridge Trail, which starts in the woods on a wide dirt path. Go uphill over water bars and past mountain laurels galore. Step carefully around big rocks and roots on the rolling path and pass a ranger residence before heading into a wooded valley. Walk slowly to admire the fabulous tree bark. At 0.4 mile, a path on the right leads down to Hartshorne Road, but go left to stay on Laurel Ridge Trail.

The trail bends charmingly at a wooden fence on the right. At the intersection, go straight as Laurel Ridge Trail winds up and down, with a valley to your right. Get ready for a steep downhill with tricky footing. Look out for mountain bikers in this part. Descend into deep woods and, in summer, a forest of ferns. An uphill section of sand and dirt leads to a wooden "Hopes and Dreams" box (handmade by an 8-year-old girl named Charlie) where you can leave a note about a hope or dream and read others' notes as well.

Watch for a wooden fence to the left just before Laurel Ridge Trail meets challenging black-diamond-blazed Grand Tour Trail. Turn sharply right (1.9 miles) onto Grand

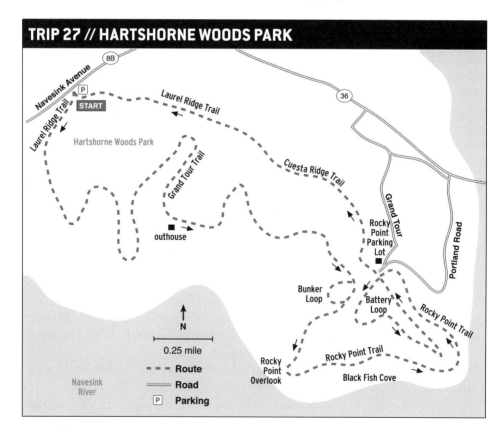

TRIP 27 // HARTSHORNE WOODS PARK

Tour Trail (shared briefly with blue-square-blazed Laurel Ridge Trail; if you want to head back, turn left on Laurel Ridge Trail here). Walk past laurels and fern forests. Veer left toward the fence (ignore a rogue path to the right that leads to a house). At the maintenance sign, turn left. (If you need to use the facilities, turn right down a narrow 50-yard path to a chemical toilet.) Smell the honeysuckle as Navesink River comes into view on the right. The river is a tidal estuary flowing into Shrewsbury River at Sea Bright, continuing into Sandy Hook Bay and ultimately the Atlantic Ocean.

At 3.1 miles, you are at the midpoint connector of Grand Tour Trail's figure-eight loop. Turn right at this intersection and head downhill into a sunny, rocky area where phlox, goldenrods, and blackberry bushes bloom in summer. (For a shorter hike, turn left and take the blue-square-blazed Cuesta Ridge Trail back to the parking lot.) The path widens as you reenter the shady woods.

At the next junction, go left, away from the sign for Hartshorne Road. Traverse another rugged open area with flowering bushes and plants before the woods begin again. At 3.6 miles, turn right at the next black-diamond-blazed junction. Note the "triplet" tree on the left before the wide trail heads slightly up past a fern garden to the right.

Arrive at an intersection with a paved road and two stone pillars on the right. Go across the road into black-diamond-blazed Rocky Point Trail's wooded area (trash can on right of trail entrance). The steep downhill is a mountain biker's delight, so be alert. A rocky ascent leads to a chain-link fence on the left. Carefully step down onto a cute footbridge.

Go right at the paved path onto blue-blazed Bunker Loop Trail (marked on the park's trail map but not on the actual trail, 4.0 miles). The huge hill to your left is the back of a World War II bunker. Explore this bunker and another bunker here; then return to where you started and turn right into the woods to continue on Rocky Point Trail. Wind and weather have twisted the laurels into an enchanted forest.

Don't miss the Rocky Point Overlook side trail loop, marked as such, for a worth-while detour. Turn right onto the side trail at 4.7 miles, and keep to your right for a loop-around view (better in leafless seasons) of Navesink River (4.9 miles). Continue the circle and arrive back at the intersection to proceed on Rocky Point Trail. Turn right where the path soon splits.

At 5.7 miles, reach a paved road. Turn right onto it to reach Black Fish Cove, with a pier, picnic table, and chemical toilet. Linger to enjoy a spectacular view of Navesink River.

Return via the paved road and quickly turn right onto a dirt path at a tree with a metal black-diamond marker for Rocky Point Trail. In the woods, watch for a wooden fence on your right. Stay on this narrow trail; do not take side paths. Look to your right to see the town of Sea Bright, on a barrier peninsula, bordered to the west by the con-vergence of Navesink and Shrewsbury rivers and to the east by the Atlantic Ocean, which you can see and smell. Cross a paved road to stay on Rocky Point Trail. Go over a bridge in the woods and enjoy a cardio workout uphill.

At about 7.4 miles, reach another paved road and the Rocky Point parking lot. Turn left to walk blue-square-blazed Battery Loop Trail (and visit one of the chemical toilets if needed), keeping the parking lot on your right. At the junction, turn left and come to two big bunkers, one with a huge gun; a sign explains the gun's construction, use, and significance.

The fishing pier at Black Fish Cove on the tidal Navesink River.

Between these bunkers is a gravel road that heads to the right—take it to climb a big hill (actually the top of one of the bunkers) and sit on the bench for a spectacular water view. Explore further or head back down toward the Rocky Point parking lot.

With the Rocky Point parking lot on your left, cross the road, heading toward two stone pillars with an "Authorized Vehicles Only" sign. A water tower is on your right. Go between the pillars onto a paved road, keeping straight. In a few hundred yards, you'll see blue-blazed Cuesta Ridge Trail on your right. Take this dirt road into the woods, straight to the Buttermilk Valley parking lot. Don't turn left or right on any side paths. Cuesta Ridge Trail becomes Laurel Ridge Trail. It's a pretty woods walk, mainly flat but with some rocky, rutty areas. Go straight at the "Dismount Area" sign and head toward the water fountain, kiosk, and chemical toilets.

DID YOU KNOW?

Water views and hills appealed to many nineteenth-century artists. A simple online search of Hartshorne Woods Park art history reveals nineteenth-century paintings that prove true the novelist James Fenimore Cooper's statement that this is one of the most beautiful combinations of land and water in America.

OTHER ACTIVITIES

Less than 1 mile north, off NJ 36, view the New York City skyline from Mount Mitchill Scenic Overlook and Monmouth County's 9/11 memorial. Keep going southeast to the nonoperational Twin Lights Lighthouse, a unique structure built in 1862 with two nonidentical towers linked by keepers' quarters and storage rooms; one beacon flashed and the other remained fixed (call 732-872-1814 for hours and fee). Five minutes farther is Sandy Hook, a popular beach for swimming and hiking, which is linked to history with Fort Hancock and is home to the oldest continuously operating lighthouse in the United States. To the south, find 8 miles of trails and river views at Huber Woods Park in Locust.

MORE INFORMATION
Open 7 A.M. to dusk. Limited bunker tours are offered from 10 A.M. to 4 P.M. on Saturdays and Sundays, May 27 through October 15, 2023; contact the park for more details. Invasive plant management may periodically close some portions of Grand Tour Trail. Group cabin camping is by reservation.

28 ALLAIRE STATE PARK

Enjoy myriad activities on this nature walk, with a railroad past and present (working steam railroad) that leads to historic Allaire Village.

Features 🚶 🐕 💧 ⛺ 🚻 $ ✎

Location Wall Township, NJ

Rating Easy

Distance 5.2-mile loop

Elevation Gain 250 feet

Estimated Time 3 hours

Maps USGS Farmingdale and Asbury; nj.gov/dep/parksandforests/maps/allaire -trail.pdf

GPS Coordinates 40° 09.530′ N, 74° 07.845′ W

Contact Allaire State Park, 4265 Atlantic Avenue, Farmingdale, NJ 07727; 732-938-2371; nj.gov/dep/parksandforests/parks/allairestatepark.html

DIRECTIONS

From I-195, take Exit 31B. Merge onto Lakewood-Farmingdale Road and immediately turn right at the light onto Allaire Road. Drive 1.0 mile (passing the Allaire Family Campground) and turn right at the sign for Allaire State Park/Allaire Village. Continue until that road dead-ends in the main parking lot for Allaire, which fits approximately 400 vehicles.

TRAIL DESCRIPTION

Allaire State Park (3,000 acres) was created from the woods surrounding an old iron-works. Iron was first produced here in the 1760s but reached its peak with the Howell Works, founded by James Allaire, which operated from 1822 to 1850. The property was later used as a scout camp and was in private hands until the 1940s, when it was given to the state of New Jersey. Today, the park offers a wide variety of activities for outdoor enthusiasts—hiking, road biking, mountain biking, camping, horseback riding, and disc golf. It also includes the restored historic village, a small museum, a nature center, and even a working steam railroad. If that isn't enough, special activities throughout the year range from flea markets to old-time baseball games.

You will, of course, be starting with the hiking. The park contains more than 22 miles of blazed, multiuse trails, plus many miles of unblazed trails. This trip explores the northern portion of the park by creating a loop of the purple, yellow, green, and red trails.

Begin at the paved trail at the back of the parking lot, labeled on the map in purple as Capital-to-Coast Trail, which when completed will stretch 55 miles from end to end—but your journey is considerably shorter. The trail parallels the entrance road before swinging east to parallel Atlantic Avenue. If you hear a train whistle, you aren't stuck in an old country song—that's the Pine Creek Railroad in the park, which gives rides along a half-mile oval on weekends from April to December, with special excursion rides during Easter, Halloween, and Christmas. (Check njmt.org for pricing and details.) A gap in the fence appears on your left; walk through it to leave Capital-to-Coast Trail, crossing Atlantic Avenue at the crosswalk. Turn left and walk along the shoulder of the road for 50 feet toward the car gate. A gap in the rail fence allows hikers to pass through and walk down wide, grassy, and gravelly yellow-blazed Upper Squankum Trail. This long, straight segment follows the right of way and the bed of the now-defunct Freehold and Jamesburg

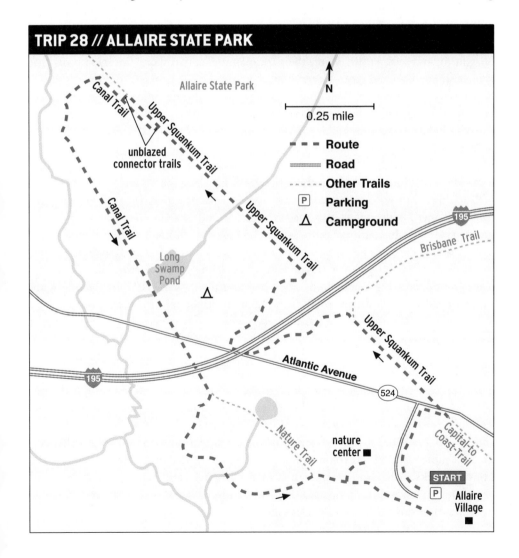

Agricultural Railroad, which ran from 1872 to 1965. (Watch out for flying Frisbees from the disc golf course that crosses this path in several places.)

Just before the old railway road cut dead-ends at a guardrail by I-195, Upper Squankum Trail turns left and enters a swampy stretch of woods. The trail can be muddy here, so watch your step. As the trail reaches paved Atlantic Avenue, watch for a fence. Turn right and stay to the inside of the fence. Run the gauntlet of this green tunnel, passing under a pair of highway bridges before going through a tall fence. Here, at 1.3 miles, the trail turns sharply right and begins to climb. In warmer months you'll hear the campers as you pass Allaire Family Campground. Two forks will appear; stay to the right for each of them, as the left forks quickly disappear. Finish the climb by turning left onto a familiar-looking gravel-and-grass road, which is the other side of the rail bed that you left east of I-195. Head northwest along the road/yellow-blazed trail. Keep an eye out for deer, although you might be pleasantly distracted if you are fortunate enough to hike here in fall when the leaves have changed.

At 2.5 miles into your journey, you'll be paralleling green-blazed Canal Trail, just out of sight to your left. At this point, the park map marks two short, unblazed trails that connect the yellow- and green-blazed trails. Choose one and turn left to reach the green-blazed trail. When you get there, turn right to continue in the same northwesterly direction that you have been heading. A water-filled ditch to your left is what remains of a canal built during the iron-working period to move water from local streams to Mill Run to increase the power of that creek. Canal Trail makes a wide loop, so you are now heading southeast in the direction of Allaire Village. Today, the variety of trees here make for some of the best bird-watching in the park, which sits along the Atlantic Flyway.

Reaching a four-way intersection, pause to take your bearings. The trail to your right leads to a small parking lot. The ones to your left and straight ahead are each blazed green; go straight to continue southeast. At 3.5 miles, reach Long Swamp Pond, a great place to have a snack and to observe waterfowl and water creatures, such as herons, frogs, and turtles. After your rest, continue down Canal Trail, skirting the edge of the campground, crossing a field, and very, very carefully crossing Atlantic Avenue again (no crosswalk here). Walk under I-195 and then turn right onto red-blazed Nature Trail at 4.0 miles. This stretch of the nature trail is wide and flat. Vernal pools exist here in spring, important for many species that live part of their lives in water and part on land.

Nature Trail passes a peat bog and then meets back up with green-blazed Canal Trail. Turn right to stay on the red- and green-blazed trails, but turn left within a few hundred feet to cross the bridge and walk up to the nature center, open in season (call 732-938-2371 for days and hours). Backtrack across the bridge, and turn left onto Canal Trail once more to proceed to Allaire Village. End your hike at 5.2 miles at the "Welcome to Allaire Village" sign near the parking lot. It's strongly recommended that you do a bit more walking to explore Allaire Village, site of the village of Howell and the Howell Works. A bakery, general store, mansion house, and blacksmith shop are all here, but the gem is the iron furnace that still stands, which you can visit on a short side path that runs downhill from the blacksmith shop.

DID YOU KNOW?

In late 2019, large dinosaurs began to mysteriously appear in the woods at Allaire State Park. Constructed largely of downed wood and wire, a T-rex, a triceratops, a pterodactyl and her baby, and a stegosaurus rose from the forest floor near the group campground. The public soon began to flock to the woods to take in the magic of the Allaire dinosaurs. The creator eventually came to light, a woman named Robin Ruggiero. Sadly, a vandal or vandals used wire snips in October 2022 to destroy many of the creations (exploringallaire.com/visit/dinos-in-allaire).

OTHER ACTIVITIES

In summer, see the Jersey Shore BlueClaws, the Minor League Baseball team of the South Atlantic League and the High-A affiliate of the Philadelphia Phillies, in nearby Lakewood. The InfoAge Science & History Museums (infoage.org) are a dozen museums sharing one small area. The series of buildings grew from the Marconi wireless telegraph station.

MORE INFORMATION

Open 8 a.m. to 4:30 p.m. Seasonal entrance fees may apply from Memorial Day to Labor Day—check the park's website to see if fees are currently in effect before you go. Camping is available from April 1 to December 15 (njportal.com/DEP/NJOutdoors).

Looking for birds at Long Swamp Pond along Canal Trail on a bright fall day.

29 MANASQUAN TO ASBURY PARK

Hike 10 miles of boardwalk traversing eight northern New Jersey beaches. Sand dunes, surf, seabirds, and shells make this trip a winner.

Features 🚶🐕♿💧🎣🏊🚌🚴

Location Manasquan, NJ

Rating Moderate

Distance 9.8 miles one way

Elevation Gain 50 feet

Estimated Time 4 hours

Maps USGS Asbury Park; *DeLorme New Jersey Atlas & Gazetteer*

GSP Coordinates 40° 07.001′ N, 74° 02.435′ W

Contact New Jersey Department of State, Division of Travel and Tourism, P.O. Box 460, Trenton, NJ 08625; 800-VISITNJ (847-4865) for free publications. For other inquiries, call 609-599-6540; visitnj.org/nj/beaches/boardwalks.

DIRECTIONS

Driving: To Manasquan train station: Take NJ 34 South heading toward Sea Girt/ Manasquan. Turn right onto County Route 524 Spur (Atlantic Avenue). From there, drive a short distance to the train station: turn right onto North Main Street. Turn right after the 7-Eleven on the left. The Manasquan train station is on the left. Buy a ticket ($3.50) at the self-service terminal and enjoy the short one-way ride to Asbury Park, the fourth stop. Trains run about every hour.

Public Transportation: If leaving from New York's Penn Station or New Jersey terminals, take the North Jersey Coast Line train to Asbury Park and back. See njtransit.com for more information.

TRAIL DESCRIPTION

In this unique hike, you'll start at the Manasquan train station, ride the rails to Asbury Park, and then tread the boardwalks and beaches along the Atlantic Ocean back to Manasquan. It's a brilliant way to get the most out of eight fabulous beach towns in one day without arranging a car shuttle at either end of the hike. At any point, you can leave the oceanfront and explore the towns of Asbury Park, Ocean Grove, Bradley Beach, Avon, Belmar, Spring Lake, Sea Girt, and Manasquan. You can even cut the hike short and take a train from Bradley Beach, Belmar, or Spring Lake back to Manasquan. (*Note*: You'll be on boardwalks and sand and probably in the water, so don versatile footwear.) If you plan to stay and swim, you must buy a beach badge. These range from

$5 to $10 a day and are usually discounted for seniors and members of the military; they are often free for children 11 and younger. (See nj.com/news/2023/05/jersey-shore-beach-badge-tag-prices-for-every-town-in-2023-from-free-to-150.html for details.)

The beaches are fine in any season. Crunch frozen sea-foam in winter; enjoy the calm in early spring before the crowds arrive; walk respectfully past sea turtle eggs in summer; and relish the scarlet Virginia creeper on the sands in fall.

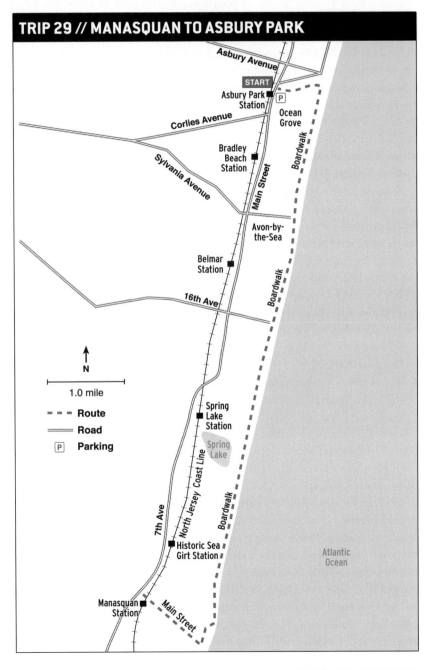

It's about three blocks from the Asbury Park train station to the beach. Walk to Spring-wood Avenue and go left (east) to the next intersection at Main Street (NJ 71). Cross Main Street to Lake Avenue (Springwood becomes Lake Avenue). Stay on Lake Avenue and pass Emory Street and Grand Avenue (both are on your left, Wesley Lake is on your right); pass the colorful Asbury Park paddleboats. At Heck Street (on your left) turn right onto a bridge (0.6 mile). Immediately after the bridge, turn left on a path through Founders Park. Wesley Lake is now on your left. After the park, the path goes along Beach Avenue and intersects the boardwalk. Turn right onto the boards, heading south (0.9 mile).

Asbury Park is one of New Jersey's northernmost beaches (only Deal, Sea Bright, and Sandy Hook are farther north) and perhaps most famous for the Stone Pony nightclub, where Bruce Springsteen performed in 1974. (The Stone Pony is still open, and Spring-steen still shows up once in a while.) It's best known as a destination for fun and sun. The 1-mile boardwalk was built shortly after the town was founded in 1871 by manu-facturer James Bradley. The Great Depression and the postwar years slammed this and other shore towns, but revitalization began in 2007, with restoration of the Paramount Theatre and Convention Hall. Dogs can enjoy Yappy Hour at the Wonder Bar. Asbury Park also has a thriving LGBTQ+ community.

Keep walking on the boards, smelling the salty air, maybe stopping for a cold drink, until you reach Ocean Grove (1.3 miles). Ornamental signs proclaim each town as you hike the boardwalk.

Ocean Grove, besides having a laid-back beach and an adorable main street, is a per-manent camp meeting site for the United Methodist Church. Since 1869, hundreds of tents (now attached to wooden structures, with ownership passed down through gener-ations) have housed worshippers from May through September. Churchgoers gather in the Great Auditorium, built in 1894. The acoustically acclaimed auditorium is used for worship and concerts and holds 10,000 people. Take a seat and a break from the sun in the large Boardwalk Pavilion. Then walk, noting the absence of parking meters, to Bradley Beach (1.8 miles).

It's said that the notorious pirate William Kidd anchored his ship at Bradley Beach back in 1679. His treasure is rumored to be buried between two large pines in the area that is now Brinley Avenue. Bradley Beach is known as a quiet, family-friendly shore town. Stroll the boardwalk made of honeycomb-patterned stone, and linger on the bright blue benches and watch the surfers; the beach between Third and Fifth avenues is reserved for these daredevils. Pause in the shady gazebo on Fifth Avenue and then proceed to Avon (2.5 miles).

Avon, or Avon-by-the-Sea, has a short boardwalk, about eight blocks long, but some swear it's the prettiest stretch of sand on the Jersey Shore. The Victorian homes are cer-tainly gorgeous and are visible from the oceanfront. You may want to stop and eat at the enclosed Avon Pavilion restaurant. Avon's boardwalk ends at the jetty, where the water is calmer and crabs scuttle at low tide.

Next, hoof it to Belmar (French for "beautiful sea"), where the 1.3-mile boardwalk is made of Trex, a wood alternative constructed from recycled materials. Belmar offers wheelchair and stroller access to the beach via Mobi-Mats, hard surface ramps. Play-grounds every few blocks, with filling stations for water bottles, make Belmar truly

A happy pair of bikes along the boardwalk.

child-friendly. Quench your thirst and satisfy your hunger at the Fifth Avenue Pavilion. Belmar has lovely sand dunes—but be careful not to walk on them! Dunes provide shore protection and habitat for plants and animals.

Watch seagulls dive as you enter Spring Lake (5.4 miles), which has a 2-mile stretch of Trex boardwalk and is a true rarity: it's noncommercial, so it has a great ocean view. Lack of boardwalk storefronts also allows you to admire the Victorian homes, left over from the 1800s when barons of industry vacationed here. Bed-and-breakfasts are abundant in this laid-back, upscale community. Natural springs feed into the town's largest lake, hence the name.

The next town, Sea Girt, is small, only 1 square mile, with 0.5 mile of Trex boardwalk. Windswept cedars from boardwalk to water give the place a wild, unexplored feel. Visit the 1896 lighthouse at the mouth of the boardwalk (Nine Ocean Avenue), which marks the inlet leading to Wreck Pond (6.7 miles). The picturesque Sea Girt Lighthouse that put an end to the wrecks is about a 15-minute drive away. It is open for tours a few days each week between April and November (seagirtlighthouse.com).

On to the finish line—Manasquan (8.2 miles). Elks Beach is devoted entirely to those with limited mobility, offering a platform and beach wheelchairs. The 1-mile asphalt boardwalk is also accessible. Walk over the Glimmer Glass Bridge, a drawbridge that spans the tidal inlet. The beach part of the hike ends here.

Visit the ice-cream shop on Ocean Avenue if you feel like rewarding yourself. Then make your way along Beach Front Road, which parallels the ocean until it intersects

Main Street (8.8 miles). Turn right on Main Street and stroll a pleasant mile through town to the Manasquan train station on the left.

DID YOU KNOW?

The sand dunes at Bradley Beach were constructed using snow fences and discarded Christmas trees. Inlet Beach at Manasquan has one of the finest surfing beaches on the East Coast. The knobbed whelk, found along the beaches, is the New Jersey state seashell. Italian restaurants at the Jersey Shore serve it under the name scungilli.

OTHER ACTIVITIES

Hike Manasquan Reservoir (Trip 31), a 1,204-acre expanse of woods, wetlands, and fields. An easy 5-mile perimeter trail showcases waterfowl. The reservoir's 1-mile Cove Trail leads to the educational Manasquan Reservoir Environmental Center (331 Georgia Tavern Road, Howell, NJ 07731; 732-751-9453).

On a rainy day, play pinball at the Silverball Retro Arcade in Asbury Park (1000 Ocean Avenue) or visit the Paranormal Museum (627 Cookman Avenue), displaying the alleged skull of the Jersey Devil (see "Have You Seen the Jersey Devil?" on page 180).

MORE INFORMATION

The boardwalks are open 24/7. Free beach and surf wheelchairs are available at Asbury Park. For details on ramp access to the boardwalks, see wonderswithinreach.com or contact the town of each beach described above.

30 ISLAND BEACH STATE PARK: JOHNNY ALLEN'S COVE TRAIL AND BARNEGAT INLET TRAIL

Choose between a short hike or a long one (or do both!) on a barrier reef that separates Barnegat Bay from the Atlantic Ocean. Experience green thickets of fauna, sugary dunes, towering osprey nests, and a beckoning lighthouse.

Features

Location Seaside Park, NJ

JOHNNY ALLEN'S COVE TRAIL
Rating Easy
Distance 1.2 miles round-trip
Elevation Gain 100 feet
Estimated Time 30 minutes

BARNEGAT INLET TRAIL
Rating Moderate
Distance 4.1-mile loop
Elevation Gain 200 feet
Estimated Time 3.5 hours

Maps USGS Seaside Park; nj.gov/dep/parksandforests/maps/islandbeachstatepark.html

GPS Coordinates 39° 45.968′ N, 74° 05.807′ W

Contact Mailing address: Island Beach State Park, P.O. Box 37, Seaside Park, NJ 08752; 732-793-0506; state.nj.us/dep/parksandforests/parks/island.html

DIRECTIONS
Take Garden State Parkway to Exit 82A. Go east on NJ 37 for about 6 miles to NJ 35. Turn right and follow signs on NJ 35 through town to the park, where you can pay at one of two kiosks (See "More Information" for rates). The most accurate address is at the intersection of NJ 35 South and 24th Avenue.

TRAIL DESCRIPTION
Johnny Allen's Cove Trail—parking lot 16
Island Beach State Park is a jewel in the crown of the Jersey Shore. With 3,000 acres of sand dunes, beaches, tidal marshes, freshwater wetlands, and maritime forests, this

10-mile-long, undeveloped barrier island is worth the entrance fee. The park is divided into three sections—northern, central, and southern—and this two-part hike explores the southern section, which includes Johnny Allen's Cove (a self-guided nature trail) and beach walks. The northern and central sections are worth exploring on your own for the pretty beaches, short nature trails, ocean swimming, and Fisherman's Walkway boardwalk. Beach wheelchairs are available for the swimming area and Fisherman's

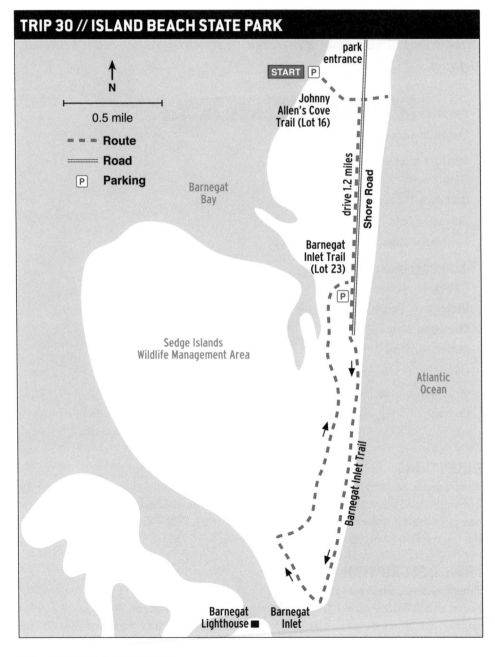

TRIP 30 // ISLAND BEACH STATE PARK

N

0.5 mile

- - - Route
=== Road
P Parking

park entrance

START P

Johnny Allen's Cove Trail (Lot 16)

drive 1.2 miles

Shore Road

Barnegat Bay

Barnegat Inlet Trail (Lot 23)

P

Sedge Islands Wildlife Management Area

Atlantic Ocean

Barnegat Inlet Trail

Barnegat Lighthouse ■

Barnegat Inlet

Walkway and for surf fishing; check at the pavilion at parking lot 7 during the season or call the park office in the off-season.

If possible, go on a fall day, free from big crowds and entrance fees. (Park officials restrict access when all of the almost 2,000 parking spots are full.) Part of the New Jersey Coastal Heritage Trail route (see "The Ultimate Multiuse Trail: New Jersey Coastal Heritage Trail" on page 164), Island Beach State Park has nine easy-to-moderate trails that show off dunes, beach plums, shadbush, bayberry, fiddler crabs, and osprey nesting platforms. (The park is home to the state's largest osprey colony.) In winter, red foxes are stunning against the stark landscape, along with harder-to-see snowy owls. In fall, surf anglers dot the shores. Spring brings festivals, flowers, and birds.

Pay the entrance fee (if necessary) at one of the two kiosks. The building attached to the kiosks has maps and flush toilets, so be sure to grab a map before setting out. The paved road bisects the barrier reef, with the Atlantic Ocean on the left and Barnegat Bay on the right. Common reeds, wind-twisted pines, and beach heather (a lovely golden color in May) border the road, along with "Turtle Xing" and "Do Not Feed Fox" signs (foxes love beach plums). In September, yellow goldenrods, red-budded prickly pear cacti, and silver-gray bayberries catch the eye.

Numbered parking lots sit along both sides of the road. Drive past lot 7, for Fisherman's Walkway Trail (the only universally accessible trail). For a sneak peek at the ocean, pull in at lot 9 and walk a narrow, sandy path that's shaded by dense sea shrubs before it opens onto a wood-railed boardwalk. Stroll past the blooming ocean goldenrod to the white sand and azure sea. You may see surf anglers, whose cars are parked legally if they have a Mobile Sport Fishing Vehicle Permit.

Return to your vehicle and drive past the canoe and kayak access point at lot 13 on the right. You'll soon reach the interpretive center and the nature center at lot 16 on the left, 7.0 miles from the park entrance. Staffed by volunteers from Friends of Island Beach State Park, the centers do not have regular hours; call 732-793-1315 (Island Beach Nature Programs) to find out hours of operation. But you can still stroll the grounds and admire Janet's Garden, a living herbarium. Flush toilets and water fountains are available. In late August or early September, sit on the blue benches between the two buildings and try to count the wind-pushed migrating monarch butterflies feeding in the flowerbed. Check out the pathways, painted with the outlines of turtles, squid, and seals. Head about 100 yards down the sand and crushed-shell path toward your first trail of the day: Johnny Allen's Cove Trail.

At the T intersection, the posted sign states that you can walk 0.3 mile left to Barnegat Bay on Johnny Allen's Cove Trail, or 0.2 mile right to the Atlantic Ocean. Turn left down the sandy path, stopping to read the many educational nature signs. Pass a lovely grove of cherry and holly trees. Blackbirds fly into an anchoring thicket of American holly, pitch pine, shadbush, black cherry, red cedar, and blueberry. The thicket "anchors" the sands of the barrier island and also provides food and cover for numerous birds. Look for the sassafras tree's slate-blue berries on stems that turn crimson in autumn.

Cross Ocean View Trail (0.2 mile), which is the paved road you drove in on (only one road exists on the barrier reef, so you can't get lost) and continue on the path to enter Johnny Allen's Cove Trail. Feel the cool bay breezes as you crunch along the narrow treadway of crushed shells that look like uncooked oatmeal, but don't kneel for a better look—the shells are sharp! The blueberries here bloom in spring; 8-foot-tall reeds with tiny purple flowers at their base stand guard. A carpet of yellow and purple asters leads to a dainty wooden bridge. Beyond are the salt marsh and Barnegat Bay (0.4 mile). In the distance, to the left, is an osprey nesting platform. Look for fiddler and horseshoe crab shells before turning around and heading back. Go straight at the sign for the Atlantic Ocean and Barnegat Bay (nature center on your right) and walk toward the ocean.

Hear the surf as you stroll down a sunny, sandy path, reading nature signs. Pass through a magnificent coastal thicket, which tapers off into fantastic windblown shapes that give way to white sand, crimson-leaved Virginia creeper, and green Japanese sedge grass. Follow the wooden fence to a bench, noting pointy bird tracks in the sand. (*Note:* Be sure to stay off the dunes.) Dip your toes in the ocean before returning to lot 16 and the parking area.

Barnegat Inlet Trail—parking lot 23
For this longer (4.1 miles) part of the hike, drive 1.2 miles south to lot 23 (space for 50 cars) at the literal end of the road. Walk toward the Barnegat Inlet Trail sign at the beginning of the parking lot. Travel a short footpath and turn right onto the beach (0.1 mile). You are approaching Barnegat Inlet. Keep moving, admiring the dunes and distant Barnegat Lighthouse to the right, watching the ocean and anglers to the left. Wet seashells shine; birds stalk the water for dinner. Walk until you reach the inlet, with a great view of the lighthouse (1.6 miles). Curve right around the inlet along the rock seawall (if you go straight, you'll be swimming in Barnegat Inlet). Watch for passing sailboats.

Barnegat Lighthouse, known as "Old Barney," is across the inlet on Long Beach Island.

The seawall path here has a different feel, quieter, as the waves lap the stones. Partially buried sandbags at the path's end are reminders of the ocean's force. Backtrack, turning left in about 300 yards to reach the circular sand parking lot and read the nature marker about birds. An unmarked trail leads from the circular sand parking lot; take it to the winter anchorage canoe and kayak access area (3.6 miles). The trail runs between dunes and passes houses and fishing shacks. Walk to the road (3.8 miles) and turn right to get back to your car. If possible, catch the sunset before you leave.

DID YOU KNOW?

The town of Seaside Park measures only 0.77 square mile and has a year-round population of about 2,200 residents. In 1945, scientists from Johns Hopkins University tested the world's first supersonic antiaircraft missile here as part of Operation Bumblebee.

OTHER ACTIVITIES

To the north, the borough of Seaside Heights offers amusement parks, arcades, rides, and a boardwalk. To the south is South Seaside Park. Less than 5 miles away are Barnegat Lighthouse State Park and the Barnegat Light Museum, Double Trouble State Park, and William J. Dudley Park. Lots of dining options are on NJ 35 and NJ 37. Red Fox Beach Bar & Grill is in Island Beach State Park.

MORE INFORMATION

Open 8 A.M. to sunset. Seasonal entrance fees may apply from Memorial Day to Labor Day—check the park's website to see if fees are currently in effect before you go. No fees are ever charged for bicycles or walk-ins. When all parking spots are full, no more vehicles are allowed in. Surf fishing is permitted by registering with the New Jersey Saltwater Recreational Registry Program dep.nj.gov/saltwaterregistry. Picnics are allowed, but no tables are available, so bring your own blanket.

THE ULTIMATE MULTIUSE TRAIL: NEW JERSEY COASTAL HERITAGE TRAIL

The 300-mile New Jersey Coastal Heritage Trail (NJCHT) joins areas of maritime heritage, coastal habitat, wildlife migration, relaxation and inspiration, and historic settlements. Congress authorized the NJCHT in October 1988 so the public could visit, understand, and enjoy the resources associated with coastal New Jersey. The trail links five regions along the Atlantic seaboard: Sandy Hook, Barnegat Bay, Absecon, Cape May, and Delsea. Even though it was originally designed for vehicular travel, the NJCHT does connect many walkable areas of interest to hikers. In fact, at least four hikes in this book follow parts of the NJCHT: Cheesequake State Park (Trip 22), Island Beach State Park (Trip 30), Belleplain State Forest (Trip 35), and Cape May Point State Park (Trip 37).

Put your hiking shoes or bicycle in the car and start at the top with the Sandy Hook Unit of the Gateway National Recreation Area. Stop in at the visitor center in the Lighthouse Keepers Quarters at the north end of the park. Visit the lighthouse and the lighthouse museum. (Call 732-872-5916 for hours; nps.gov/gate/learn/historyculture /sandy-hook-lighthouse.htm). Take a walking tour of Fort Hancock, a coastal defense fort from 1895 to 1974. Drive to and tour the nearby Nike Missile Radar Site at Horseshoe Cove, guided by Nike veterans. Drive south to visit the Barnegat Bay region, with its attractive ribbon of barrier islands. Walk Long Beach Island's 18 miles of sandy shore. Climb the 217-step Barnegat Lighthouse for an osprey's-eye view of the barrier island known as Island Beach State Park (Trip 30). Drive south on Garden State Parkway to County Route 539 and head toward Tuckerton and the Great Bay Boulevard Wildlife Management Area. A road to nowhere, this narrow, 4-mile spit of land is the best bird-watching area in Ocean County.

In the Absecon and Cape May regions, drive to North Wildwood and visit the 1874 Victorian-design Hereford Inlet Lighthouse (also called both Swiss Carpenter Gothic and Stick Style). Hike Corson's Inlet State Park in Ocean City and wander Cape May Point State Park (Trip 37).

Check out nearby Fort Mott State Park in Pennsville. Fort Mott was part of a postbellum three-fort defense system (see Trip 36). (The other two were Fort Delaware and Fort DuPont.) A welcome center provides more information about the ecosystem and Fort Mott's history. The easy Nature Interpretive Trail is universally accessible.

The New Jersey Coastal Heritage Trail is not just a hiking route: it's an environmental, cultural, historical, and educational journey.

Federal authorization for the NJCHT had expired in 2011, but in 2019, a bill signed by then-president Donald Trump restored federal support. The NJCHT is now eligible for federal dollars through 2025. For guides to the trail's five regions, see New Jersey Leisure Guide: new-jersey-leisure-guide.com/coastal-heritage-trail.html

31 MANASQUAN RESERVOIR

A loop hike rings a massive 770-acre reservoir that provides a habitat for 200 species of birds.

Features

Location Howell, NJ

Rating Moderate

Distance 6.6-mile loop

Elevation Gain 250 feet

Estimated Time 3 hours

Maps USGS Farmingdale; co.monmouth.nj.us/documents/130/Manasquan -Reservoir-Brochure-web-2022.pdf

GPS Coordinates 40° 10.230′ N, 74° 12.267′ W

Contact Manasquan Reservoir Visitor Center, 311 Windeler Road, Howell, NJ 07731; 732-919-0996; monmouthcountyparks.com/page.aspx?Id=2531

DIRECTIONS

From I-195, take Exit 28B for US 9 toward Freehold. Drive 0.2 mile down US 9 and turn right onto Georgia Tavern Road. In 0.4 mile, turn right onto Windeler Road. Continue for 1.5 miles and then turn left to enter Manasquan Reservoir. A large parking lot has room for more than 100 cars. Smaller lots are also available along the loop trail.

TRAIL DESCRIPTION

This 1,200-acre park is dominated by 770-acre Manasquan Reservoir, a massive water holding area of more than 4 billion gallons of water! The reservoir, 40 feet deep in places, is a very popular spot for outdoor enthusiasts of hiking, biking, bird-watching, fishing, and boating (boating requires a daily or seasonal launch pass). The most popular route is 5.1-mile Perimeter Trail, but the hike described here has been lengthened by including 1.1-mile Cove Trail and the short Bracken Trail.

Start at the visitor center parking lot by hiking clockwise around the reservoir, which will initially put you heading west on the trails. Perimeter Trail here is composed of crushed stone; it is more than 10 feet wide and shared by hikers, runners, and cyclists. This tends to be the most crowded stretch of trail, so take the short side path on the right at 0.2 mile to a small dock and your first notable view of the reservoir, where you'll likely encounter no one except an occasional angler. Scan the skies to look for bald eagles, which have frequented this part of the reservoir for many years.

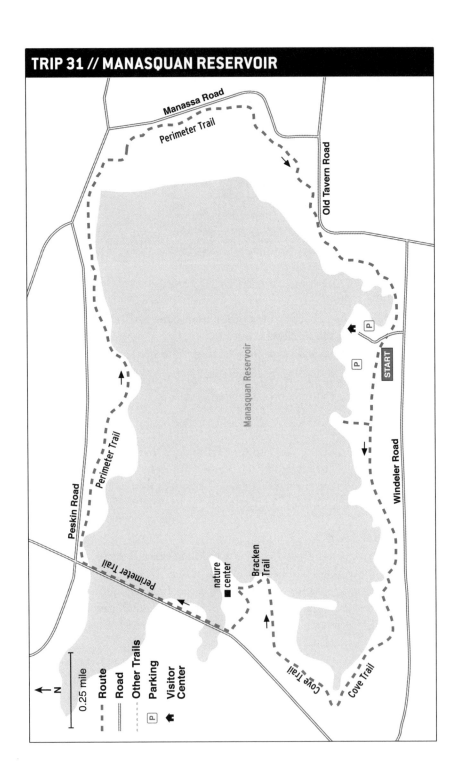

Back on the broad main pathway, travel until you cross a footbridge. Just after the bridge, turn left onto the pedestrian-only Cove Trail at 0.9 mile into the hike. This much narrower trail leaves the lake and heads into the swamps along Timber Swamp Brook, which will give you a break from the crowd of folks who are usually on the larger loop. Meander through the marshy terrain, traversing some small footbridges. Keep a sharp ear and eye out for frogs and toads that lurk in muddy spots, and, if you've timed your hike well, enjoy their springtime symphony of croaks and calls.

At 2.1 miles, Cove Trail reaches Perimeter Trail, which is so wide it's impossible to miss! Cross Perimeter Trail and head straight onto the unblazed, unnamed trail across the way. Once you enter the woods, stay straight at the next intersection for a pleasant view of the reservoir and another chance to peer into the skies. Then backtrack to the intersection you recently passed (if you get to Perimeter Trail, you've gone too far) and turn right onto another leg of the unnamed, unblazed trail. When you come to a paved walkway, turn right onto it and enter the nature center.

The nature center offers fantastic exhibits for children and adults alike, including fossils, the various habitat types at the reservoir, and even some live animals (helpful if the wild ones haven't been considerate enough to pose for you). Don't miss the light-up display that shows how the reservoir is filled. The center also provides a great chance to check in on recent animal sightings and—according to the park brochure—"seasonal listings of mammals, birds, reptiles, amphibians, and 'watchable insects,' such as butterflies and dragonflies."

The trail exits the back of the nature center. Curve to the right to enter Bracken Trail, which follows the border of this small peninsula. The nature trail gives you the opportunity to identify a range of plant life and to check for a variety of birds on the marshy edge of the reservoir. Watch for the ghostly tree stumps sticking out of the water from when the reservoir was filled; they are now a habitat for birds and fish.

Bracken Trail ends at the nature center parking lot. Follow the sidewalk, crossing the edge of the parking lot, and then take advantage of the crosswalk to head north on Perimeter Trail, which you will follow for almost the entire rest of the hike. At 2.8 miles, the trail curves north to parallel Georgia Tavern Road. This stretch offers the longest water views on the route, so watch for wading birds, such as great blue herons and snowy egrets. The segment also passes scenic Chestnut Point.

The water views disappear as the trail curves to the right to follow the north side of the reservoir. This delightfully shady stretch presents occasional views of the dam and offers a bird blind along the way.

Pass the access gate for the dam at 5.0 miles. A small, historical cemetery on the roadside is worth stopping at to pay your respects. The trail now curves south, revealing some admirable large trees.

At 6.4 miles, leave Perimeter Trail for the last time, taking a side path to the right for a final view of the reservoir. Cross a footbridge between the reservoir and a small pond before reaching the main parking lot and end of the hike.

Ghost trees line the edges of Manasquan Reservoir.

DID YOU KNOW?

The trails here are very popular—the park receives more than a million visitors each year! But the main purpose of the property is as a major water supply for Monmouth County, providing up to 30 million gallons of water each day. The reservoir is filled by the Manasquan River via a pumping system.

OTHER ACTIVITIES

The reservoir is popular for boating and offers kayak rentals (May 1 to October 31) and rowboat rentals (April 1 to October 31). A launch pass (fee), needed to get on the water, is available by the boat launch at the visitor center. Nearby is Monmouth Battlefield, the site of the last major northern battle of the American Revolution and the spot that made Molly Pitcher a legend. Monmouth Battlefield also hosts the annual Spirit of the Jerseys State History Fair each year.

MORE INFORMATION

No entrance fee. Park opens daily at 7 A.M. November 1–March 31 and at 6 A.M. April 1–October 31. Park closes at dusk. Parts of the main loop trail in either direction from the visitor center are wheelchair accessible.

Atlantic County is in the Atlantic Coastal Plain. A coastal plain is a flat, low-lying piece of land next to an ocean. The entire Atlantic Coastal Plain is the largest geographic area of New Jersey and covers more than half the state. Beaches, dunes, lagoons, meadows, tidal salt marshes, brackish bays, and river estuaries characterize the landscape.

The topography is mainly low and flat, with the highest elevation approximately 150 feet above sea level. Atlantic City, in the eastern portion, sits on Absecon Island, which is known as a "drumstick" barrier island: fatter in the updrift direction (the direction from which the sand comes), like the meaty end of a drumstick, and thinner on the other end (the direction in which the sand is going). Absecon Island is artificially stabilized with human-made seawalls, breakwater installations, and jetties.

Even so, at 8 P.M. on October 29, 2012, when Hurricane and Superstorm Sandy made landfall near Atlantic City, the effects were devastating. The storm had the widest gale diameter ever observed and hit during the highest tide of the month, creating a record storm surge. (The last similar surge was in 1821.) Wind and water damaged or destroyed oceanfront properties and homes and covered the roads with sand, making Hurricane Sandy one of the costliest storms in U.S. history. After the storm, many beaches were 30 to 40 feet narrower. Fortified beaches fared better, as did those with sand dunes. Still, the devastation was immense: 70 to 80 percent of the city was underwater.

Surprisingly, the salt and tidal marshes of the Atlantic Coastal Plain remained remarkably stable, proving much more resilient than the land mass. Recovery to vegetation, artificial bird nests (such as osprey platforms), and mammal population was unexpectedly quick. Experts conclude that for ecosystem resilience, large disturbances to wetland stability may be less important than long-term preservation strategies. In short, during Hurricane Sandy, the coastal marsh system functioned as nature designed. Visit the marshes at Edwin B. Forsythe National Wildlife Refuge (Trip 33) and see for yourself.

The Pinelands National Reserve absorbs several inland municipalities in Atlantic County (see "Get Away from the Crowds in the Pine Barrens and the Pinelands" on page 143). The Pinelands is known for sandy, acidic soil and a preponderance of pine trees, Atlantic cedar swamps, marshes, migratory birds, and water-filled cranberry bogs. It also contains mining pits (see Trip 34) and interesting industrial ruins (see Trip 32) and is considered the birthplace of the fabled Jersey Devil (see "Have You Seen the Jersey Devil?" on page 180; see also Trip 33).

All wildlife is important in the Atlantic Coastal Plain, but the New Jersey section provides habitat for sixteen species federally recognized as endangered or threatened, including the piping plover and the northeastern beach tiger beetle. Among state endangered species are the bald eagle, black skimmer, peregrine falcon, and short-eared owl. Regional protective priorities include the eastern box turtle and northern diamondback terrapin. The hikes in this section, especially at the Edwin B. Forsythe National Wildlife Refuge (see Trip 33), afford a first-rate education on the wildlife in this area.

32 ESTELL MANOR PARK

This hike includes a 1.8-mile boardwalk in a swamp, paths through the historic ruins of World War I munitions production facilities, and lookouts over the majestic South River.

Features

Location Mays Landing, NJ

Rating Easy

Distance 5.6-mile loop

Elevation Gain 150 feet

Estimated Time 2.5 hours

Maps USGS Dorothy, USGS Mays Landing; atlantic-county.org/parks/estell-manor
-parks-trails.asp

GPS Coordinates 39° 23.908′ N, 24° 44.547′ W

Contact Atlantic County Park System, 109 Boulevard Route 50, Mays Landing, NJ 08330; (609) 625-1897; atlantic-county.org/parks/estell-manor-park.asp

DIRECTIONS

From I-295 South, take Exit 60A toward Camden. In 24.0 miles, merge onto NJ 73 South via Exit 36A, toward Berlin. In 22.0 miles, keep left at the fork to go onto Mays Landing Road. In 6.0 miles, turn slightly right onto Eighth Street, go 0.08 mile, and turn left onto Black Horse Pike (US 322 East). Drive 5.0 miles and turn right onto Weymouth Road (County Route 559). After another 5.0 miles, turn right onto Old Harding Highway (County Route 606). In 0.5 mile, take the second left onto US 40 East (Harding Highway). Go 0.76 mile and take the first right onto Boulevard Route 50. In 1.75 miles, reach Estell Manor Park (109 Boulevard Route 50).

TRAIL DESCRIPTION

The informative Warren E. Fox Nature Center (with flush toilets) awaits in the Estell Manor Park parking lot (50-car capacity), resplendent with butter-yellow ginkgo trees in autumn. Enter the center and pick up trail maps and a nature trail guide, then explore the exhibits of live turtles and snakes, dioramas, impressive taxidermy, and historical artifacts. The knowledgeable rangers will probably recommend spending an extra hour to take the 2.2-mile driving tour on Purple Heart Drive before hoofing the easy and universally accessible Swamp Trail Boardwalk to Bethlehem Loading Company History Trail (BLCHT) and returning to the parking lot. Pick up a free guide to the eighteen stops along BLCHT and learn about this once-expansive World War I munitions plant and administration buildings.

It's better to drive (versus walk) the paved 2.2-mile loop. Pull over and exit your car to visit the ruins of the Estellville Glassworks, an early nineteenth-century glass factory. Next is the humbling Veterans Cemetery, with more than 5,000 interments. Walk the short, unnamed hiking trail on the right at the beginning of the cemetery to reach a platform with 180-degree views of Stephen's Creek. Drive to the next parking lot and get out of the car to visit a playground and a curious floating dock. At the far-right corner of the lot, near the water and a smoker's corner, is a paved walking path to the

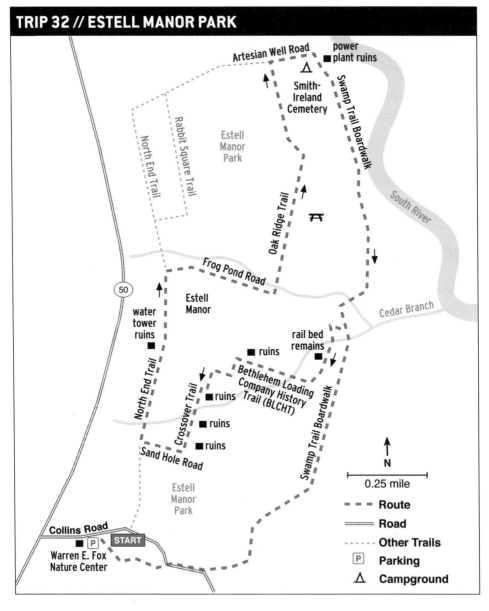

TRIP 32 // ESTELL MANOR PARK

right that leads to Steelman's Creek Burial Ground, a small 1700s cemetery that is worth a visit. Get back in the car and drive to the nature center parking lot.

Now strap on your hiking shoes, head to the back of the nature center, and follow the sign to Swamp Boardwalk Trail, listed simply as "boardwalk" on the sign. (*Note*: The trails in this park are marked, not blazed with a color.) The elevated, universally accessible 1.8-mile nature trail features streams, a cedar swamp, a coastal forest (a wild palette of color in autumn), ruins of the Bethlehem Loading Company, and two overlooks of the South River. The property boasts more than 27 miles of trails, so be sure to pick up a trail guide at the nature center.

The boardwalk begins with a tree ID game—use the handy map and pencil provided by the park and walk the short trail to the right to test your knowledge. Now proceed, crossing over the loop you just drove, stepping carefully on the sometimes-slippery leaf-covered boards. In 0.1 mile at the intersection, go right at the boardwalk sign (to the left is a sign for Greenbriar Trail). Red holly berries shine in the woods. At the T intersection (0.5 mile), turn left to stay on the boards (Mistletoe and Center trails are to the right). Veer right, ignoring Sand Hole Road to the left (0.7 mile). An army of cedar trees crowds the boardwalk. Soon a bench and swamp observation area appear on the right. At the next bench and a kiosk (1.2 miles), take the fork on the left, which puts you on Bethlehem Loading Company History Trail (BLCHT). Explore the ruins of the Bethlehem Loading Company, a World War I munitions plant where explosives were mixed and loaded into shells, mainly of the 155 mm variety.

Bold red arrows provide accurate guidance along this history trail, which consists of many crisscrossing dirt paths that can be uneven and wet as they wind through the woods. But the red arrows and posted maps make BLCHT easy to follow. Numbered signs at the eighteen stops explain the significance of each ruin. You'll visit five stops on this hike. Follow the red arrows to marker 14, and see part of the 30.5-mile railroad bed that delivered 75 carloads of building supplies daily. Go straight to traverse Crossover Trail (glance left at the beautiful clearing); trees and shrubs hem the path. Marker 15 stands at the remains of the large, two-story pouring/filling building. Turn left to follow the next red arrow. As you walk, note the concrete hole on your left, part of the footings for an elevated piped-steam heat system. Turn right at the next red arrow, passing a pretty field on the left. Follow the arrows to marker 16, admiring the lovely swamp to the right, and view the site of the receiving building, where components used to make 8-inch Howitzer shells were unloaded. Continue to marker 17 and see what's left of the buildings where the shells were poured. Heavy concrete walls that separated the extruding machines from each other still stand, eerily overgrown with vines and trees. Continue through the quiet woods to marker 18, the foundations of the shell-finishing building, where the 8-inch shells were packed with everything but the fuse—that operation was performed on the battlefield. (*Note*: Fifty percent of munitions workers were women.)

To exit BLCHT, turn right at the next red arrow onto dirt Sand Hole Road; a kiosk is on the right (1.9 miles). Sand Hole Road ends at a T intersection with North End Trail (2.0 miles). (If you want to head back now, turn left toward the nature center. If you have time, explore more of BLCHT.) Turn right onto wide North End Trail, watching for bicyclists, toward Artesian Well Road. Keep straight and ignore all side paths.

In operation from 1825 to 1877, Estellville Glassworks, the ruins of which you'll pass on this hike, was the first of its kind capable of producing both holloware (bottles) and window glass.

Ruins of the Bethlehem Loading Company water tower are on your left. Turn right at the kiosk (2.5 miles) onto Frog Pond Road. Swamp Boardwalk Trail appears at 2.8 miles; turn left away from the boardwalk to Oak Ridge Trail. Oak Ridge Trail becomes a very pretty, if a bit rooty, dirt path, moss-lined and shaded by trees.

Cross Eagle Bridge, and turn right on Artesian Well Road (3.5 miles), toward the chemical toilets and lovely Great Egg Harbor River/South River straight ahead. Ruins loom before you. Notice the water gurgling from the pipe in the front part of the ruins, the topmost point of an artesian well (undrinkable water). When you've had your fill of the sights (but not the water), head south along Swamp Trail Boardwalk. BLCHT marker 12 (ruins of the power plant) pops up at 3.6 miles, and the boardwalk soon splits. Turn right for a 30-second walk to the Smith-Ireland Cemetery, which is surrounded by an unlocked iron fence and is only 1.7 miles from the nature center.

Backtrack to the boardwalk and follow it all the way back to the nature center; ignore side paths. Walk through a small, pretty section of marshes along South River. Near dusk, each step flushes birds from the tall grasses edging the boardwalk, their wings rustling like silk sheets. Continue to enjoy the magic at the South River lookout, admiring the broad, cloud-reflecting ribbon that curls toward civilization. The boardwalk ends at a paved path that leads to the nature center.

DID YOU KNOW?

This is headquarters for Atlantic County's parks and recreation division. In winter, vultures roost near the park entrance, a primordial sight when they spread their wings in the thin sun. Rebecca Estell Bourgeois Winston of Estell Manor was the first female mayor elected in the state of New Jersey. Her house is now the veterans museum listed in "Other Activities."

OTHER ACTIVITIES

Visit the Atlantic County Veterans Museum (adjacent to the park and Veterans Cemetery), featuring military artifacts from the American Revolution through today. Visit Weymouth Furnace on County Route 559, north of US 322 (Black Horse Pike), a former iron furnace and paper mill on Great Egg Harbor River. Here, see interesting paper-mill ruins and a canoe/kayak landing. Park at Weymouth Furnace and cross the street to hike the unmarked trails of John's Woods Preserve, a property of New Jersey Natural Lands Trust (southjerseytrails.org/2017/02/14/johns-woods-preserve-and-weymouth-county -park-mays-landing-nj). Paddle Great Egg Harbor River from Weymouth Furnace to Lake Lenape County Park in Mays Landing. Explore 4,867-acre Maple Lake Wildlife Management Area, south on County Route 557.

MORE INFORMATION

Open 7:30 A.M. until a half-hour after sunset. Group camping is available by calling the park. The Warren E. Fox Nature Center is open 8 A.M. to 4 P.M. daily; call 609-625-1897. The Veterans Cemetery holds a Memorial Day service every year.

33 EDWIN B. FORSYTHE NATIONAL WILDLIFE REFUGE

Explore a birder's paradise, with mystical marshes, a cozy woods trail, and stunning views of Atlantic City.

Features

Location Galloway, NJ

Rating Easy

Distance 5.3-mile loop

Elevation Gain 300 feet

Estimated Time 2.5 hours

Maps USGS Oceanville; fws.gov/refuge/Edwin_b_forsythe

GPS Coordinates 39° 27.902' N, 74° 27.026' W

Contact Mailing addresses: Edwin B. Forsythe National Wildlife Refuge, P.O. Box 72, Oceanville, NJ 08231; 609-652-1665; fws.gov/refuge/edwin_b_forsythe. Friends of Forsythe National Wildlife Refuge, P.O. Box 355, Oceanville, NJ 08231; 609-652-1665; friendsofforsythe.org

DIRECTIONS
From Garden State Parkway, take Exit 48 for US 9 (toward Port Republic/Smithville). Continue onto US 9 South (New York Road). After 5.7 miles, the sign for the wildlife refuge entrance is on the right; turn right at the sign onto East Lilly Lake Road to reach the parking lot (800 East Lilly Lake Road). The large paved lot has space for more than 60 cars.

TRAIL DESCRIPTION
This immense refuge stretches nearly 50 miles (and 7,000 acres) from around Oceanville to Holgate, Manahawkin, Forked River, and Mantoloking. It was created to protect migratory birds, and 82 percent is wetlands. Predictably, tens of thousands of migrating ducks, geese, wading birds, and shorebirds linger here in spring and fall, feasting on the rich resources. Many species spend the winter here, and peregrine falcons and ospreys use the nesting platforms. Trees (pitch pines, oaks, and white cedars) dominate 5,000 acres, providing homes for deer, box turtles, and foxes. Be prepared from mid-May through mid-October when ticks and biting insects abound. Winter brings a calm, meditative feel. Fall and spring bring riots of color from leaves and flowers.

This hike is in the Brigantine Unit, with five well-marked routes from which to choose. You'll travel popular Songbird Trail through a variety of upland habitats, coming back on Wildlife Drive, where you can either explore other trails or end the hike.

Stop at the visitor contact station beyond the self-pay kiosk (fee for the Wildlife Drive auto tour only; hikers get in free) for an informative journey through impressive exhibits on the value of barrier islands, salt marshes, and more. An educational film in the station describes the birds of the refuge. Orient yourself to the area via a wooden floor map and a viewing guide to points north, south, east, and west. Flush toilets are available at the station, which also has a fountain to fill water bottles.

Head to the left of the outdoor toilets to the posted trail map and signs to the Songbird Trail loop. A cinder path leads through a picnic area to some wooden steps. Turn left at the bottom of the steps onto the gravel road. The way to blue-blazed Songbird Trail is well marked. Turn right at the gate (blue arrow) onto Wildlife Drive, a one-way dirt road that circles the entire refuge. (*Caution*: Watch out for cars—you are walking against traffic.) Cross a bridge over a pond, bordered by waving reeds. Pause on the bridge to watch the swans (get out your binoculars), and in winter, try to identify the blue and red berries. Private homes sprawl to your left. At about 0.7 mile, at a metal gate and small parking

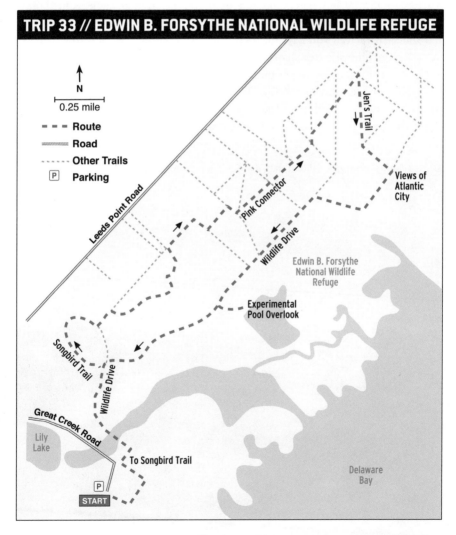

TRIP 33 // EDWIN B. FORSYTHE NATIONAL WILDLIFE REFUGE

N
0.25 mile

- - - Route
===== Road
------ Other Trails
P   Parking

Leeds Point Road

Pink Connector

Jen's Trail

Wildlife Drive

Views of Atlantic City

Edwin B. Forsythe National Wildlife Refuge

Experimental Pool Overlook

Songbird Trail

Wildlife Drive

Great Creek Road

Lily Lake

To Songbird Trail

Delaware Bay

P
START

area, turn left and go around the metal gate, following the blue arrow and the Songbird Trail sign. (You could go straight at the gate onto Jen's Trail, a 0.75-mile loop with attractive views of the refuge.) The blue-blazed trail enters the woods.

The white sand treadway is pretty in the green pine forest. Turn right at the blue arrow onto a narrow, curving path with rolling ups and downs, surrounded by the fresh scent of pine. Watch for roots and slippery moss. At the next blue arrow, turn right; a wire fence is on your left. Follow the fence and turn left where it ends at a bench and blue arrow. (Wildlife Drive is straight ahead if you want to return.) A graceful path leads up a gentle slope to another blue arrow; turn right here. As the woods close in, look for triple- and even quadruple-trunked trees. The path soon opens up into a small clearing with soft grasses beneath your feet.

At the Y intersection, go left at the blue blaze, back into the woods. Songbird Trail becomes a narrow dirt trail that undulates past 10-foot-high, red-berried American holly trees. At a field, the trail splits; simply follow the blue arrow to the right. In this open area with low bushes, pause and look up—you may spot an eagle. A field on your right, lined by stately pines, contains milkweed pods and berries that are colorful in winter. Blue arrows lead you left and then right, back into the woods. The trail slopes down past more fantastic tree shapes and holly. At the same wire fence as before, blue arrows lead to the right, and then right again, before pointing left. Emerald-green moss shines against white sand just before a T intersection with an unnamed trail; blue arrows indicating Songbird Trail lead you to the right. Cross a wide, unnamed road that cuts through the woods. (At 2.0 miles, watch for pink blazes that lead back to

Atlantic City shines across the fields of the Edwin B. Forsythe National Wildlife Refuge.

Wildlife Drive, if you want to shorten the hike.) Proceed to the next blue arrow and turn left, which puts you on a narrow, rolling dirt trail, with a bench on the right. Continue following the blue arrows through an area with lovely foliage in autumn. (*Note*: Because of ticks and insects, this trail is not recommended from mid-May through mid-October unless you take precautions.)

At the intersection with an unnamed trail, continue right on blue-blazed Songbird Trail. Periodic patches of white sand highlight the brown and green woods. A metal bench perches on the left atop a slight rise at a T intersection with an unnamed trail. Keep left to continue on Songbird Trail; white-blazed Jen's Trail feeds in here. Another blue arrow directs you to curve to the right onto a wide, sandy path (check for deer and red fox tracks). A bench beneath two fir trees makes for a peaceful rest overlooking a pond.

Suddenly the trail intersects Wildlife Drive, the 7-mile road that circles the refuge (3.2 miles). Turn right, but pause for views of Atlantic City, shining straight ahead across the marsh and bay. The city glimmers with its own personality, changing from hour to hour. The road is unshaded. Watch for cars. An open field stretches to the left, and a "scrub-shrub" area is to the right (a habitat in between a meadow and a forest, which eastern meadowlarks, cottontail rabbits, butterflies, and some other animals prefer). Turn left at the sign for Experimental Pool Overlook (3.9 miles) and linger on the viewing platform with its spotting scope. You may see snow geese and Atlantic brants (geese). Enjoy another view of Atlantic City to your right.

Continue on Wildlife Drive, heading to the parking lot. The private homes on the right signal that the lot is close. Cross a bridge over a pond, looking for resident swans. You can recycle your brochure in the mailbox on the trail. Turn left at the metal gate, turn right at the headquarters sign, then go up the steps and through the picnic area to the parking area.

DID YOU KNOW?

The Jersey Devil is rumored to have been born in the small town of Leeds Point. Tales of this ferocious creature have terrified New Jersey children of all ages for years (see "Have You Seen the Jersey Devil?" on page 180). Leeds Point is about 3 miles away and worth the trip. While there, drive to the end of Oyster Creek Road for dinner at the family-friendly Oyster Creek Inn Restaurant and Boat Bar and a magnificent sunset overlooking Great Bay.

OTHER ACTIVITIES

The Wildlife Drive auto tour at Edwin B. Forsythe National Wildlife Refuge on 800 East Lilly Lake Road is worth the $4 entrance fee, especially near sunset. (Pay and get a dashboard tag at a self-service kiosk near the visitor contact station. Refuge employees do check for tags.) Park and walk Leeds Eco-Trail over the tidal salt marsh. Climb Gull Pond Tower. See osprey nesting platforms and dozens of swans. Follow eBird (bird-tracker app) sightings at friendsofforsythe.org. Visit historic Smithville a few minutes away on US 9, with many shops and restaurants.

MORE INFORMATION

Fishing and hunting are allowed at designated locations. Seven trails allow leashed dogs. Three trails are universally accessible. Biking is on designated bike trails only.

HAVE YOU SEEN THE JERSEY DEVIL?

Deep in the tall, unmoving pines, on a sugar-sand path, mysterious footprints appear. Larger than those of a horse, the footprints are cloven and made by a creature with two legs. As you proceed cautiously on the path, deeper into the Pine Barrens, thick pine straw muffles your footfalls. The preternatural quiet of the Pine Barrens transforms to an eerie hum; the silence achieves a presence, an actual tangible quality. As you creep past fire-blackened trunks and mysterious deep holes of cold, blue water, you hear it: an inhuman scream of rage and hatred, an unearthly cry. You freeze as a breeze lifts your hair— not a cool, refreshing breeze, but a hot, acrid wave, made by a devil with large, leathery wings. Then, too late, you see it: the red-eyed creature with a dragon-like tail, sharp, glittering teeth, and talons of steel begins its attack. The Jersey Devil has struck again.

More than 2,000 sightings of the Jersey Devil have been reported since 1735, when Jane Leeds of the Pine Barrens in South Jersey gave birth to an unwanted thirteenth child. At the end of her rope, Leeds reportedly screamed, "Let this one be a devil!" And it was. According to lore, the beautiful baby sprouted wings, a thick coating of body hair, and ferocious hooves, claws, and teeth. The creature then demolished its mother and the midwives and maimed and killed onlookers before flying from the house to live forever in the desolate Pine Barrens.

This 10-foot-tall, kangaroo-like creature with the face of a horse, the head of a dog, and wings like a bat, plus claws and a pointed tail, is allegedly seen to this day by travelers on Garden State Parkway and the Atlantic City Expressway and by hikers in the Pine Barrens. But Jersey Devil phobia reached its peak in January 1909. Hundreds of sightings were reported throughout the Delaware Valley area, even in the cities of Camden and Philadelphia. Livestock were slaughtered, mysterious footprints traipsed across snow-covered rooftops, schools in lower New Jersey and Philadelphia closed or suffered poor

The Jersey Devil, as depicted in the *Philadelphia Post* in 1909 by a police sketch artist. The creature was described by a couple who sat in bed and watched it cavort on the roof of one of their outbuildings for 15 to 20 minutes.

attendance, and mills shut down when workers refused to leave their homes. Variously described as "a large, flying kangaroo," "an ostrich-like creature," and "a deer with wings," the reported monster terrorized trolley car passengers, firefighters, and dogs. Bloodhounds refused to track it. A thousand eyewitness accounts were compiled that year.

In 1820, Joseph Bonaparte, Napoleon's older brother, claimed he saw the Jersey Devil near his home in Bordentown, New Jersey. In the early 1800s, the American Revolution hero Stephen Decatur claimed he saw the creature fly across the sky within firing range and shot it with a cannonball, but the beast kept going. Other reports have come from forest rangers, anglers, foragers, taxi drivers, campers, and paddlers.

Some say the Jersey Devil's supernatural origins boil down to politics, plain and simple, beginning in 1677, with Daniel Leeds's arrival from England. Leeds settled in Burlington, New Jersey, and published an almanac that relied on astrology. His Quaker neighbors deemed this evil and thus began a feud in which Leeds was labeled "Satan's Harbinger." Leeds's son Titian took over the almanac and came up against competing almanac publisher Benjamin Franklin. A publicity battle ensued, and Franklin won. Daniel Leeds became a target of anti-British fervor (his family sided with Great Britain), and by the time of the American Revolution, the "Leeds Devil" symbolized sedition. The fervor eventually faded, as it often does, until the early twentieth century, when T. F. Hopkins, a Philadelphia publicist, opened a 10-cent museum at Ninth and Arch streets. There, Hopkins displayed the "Leeds Devil," captured "after a terrific struggle." The poor caged and chained creature was simply a kangaroo upon which Hopkins had slapped wings. Being promoted as a living dragon that "Swims! Flys! Gallops!" catapulted the creature into lasting lore.

Strange things happen in the Pine Barrens. Counts build castles on isolated islands, and famous aviators crash (see the Carranza Memorial and Apple Pie Hill sections of Batona Trail; southjerseytrails.org/2013/03/25/batona-trail-carranza-memorial-to-apple-pie-hill -tabernacle-nj). Dyslexic forest rangers fight the evil of man (see *Idiot!*, a novel by Christopher Klim, Hopewell Publications, 2007). In a sparsely populated land of crumbling walls and rusted machinery, remnants of once-thriving factories and towns, the quietness of the Pine Barrens can unnerve the average person accustomed to clamor. Is it any wonder that imagination begins to fill the gaps of quietude with tales of the supernatural?

For more on the Jersey Devil, see *The Jersey Devil*, by James McCloy and Ray Miller Jr. (Middle Atlantic Press, 1976), and the online magazine *Weird N.J.* (weirdnj.com/ stories/jersey-devil).

34 BIRCH GROVE PARK

An intricate web of trails explores almost two dozen small ponds teeming with birds and wildlife.

Features 🚶 💧 🏕 ✂ 🚴

Location Northfield, NJ

Rating Easy

Distance 3-mile loop

Elevation Gain 50 feet

Estimated Time 1.5 hours

Maps Pleasantville USGS; southjerseytrails.org/2019/12/01/birchgrovepark

GPS Coordinates 39° 22.536' N, 074° 33.830' W

Contact Birch Grove Park, 1675 Burton Avenue, Northfield, NJ 08225; 609-641-3778; cityofnorthfield.org/recreation/birchgrove.asp

DIRECTIONS
From Garden State Parkway, take Exit 36 for Northfield/Margate City and merge onto Tilton Road. Drive 1.3 miles and turn right at the light onto Burton Road. Just past the baseball fields, turn right onto Joyce Pullan Way. Follow this road around the baseball fields and past the Northfield Museum. Closest parking to the trailhead is on the right, either just before or just after the green "Closed dusk to dawn" sign. The parking lot has room for more than 75 cars.

TRAIL DESCRIPTION
Birch Grove Park encompasses 271 acres in the midst of Northfield, a mainland town opposite Atlantic City. The site includes many of the usual accoutrements of a suburban park—baseball fields, picnic tables, and a playground—plus a small-town historical museum. But your visit focuses on the back section of the property, which features a few miles of nature trails built mostly within a loop road. Despite the ball fields and playground, the park here is far from the usual, and a view from the air shows why: close to two dozen small ponds are clumped together, each one in a rectangular or a wedge shape. Each pond was originally a clay-mining pit, used as part of the Somers Brick Yard, which produced about 80,000 bricks a day and operated from 1900 until sometime during the Great Depression. When the brickyard stopped production, the pits filled with water and nature began to take over. The city eventually seized the property for unpaid taxes, and a park was opened in the 1950s that included a campground (sadly, permanently closed in 2019) and a web of hiking trails around the ponds. This

is an easy place to explore, no matter which route you follow; wander to your heart's content and, if you get tired, just follow the road back.

Start your adventure at the southeastern edge of the hiking area, behind a baseball field and past the small history museum. Your parking spot is near a long pond. Walk a short distance along the pond to reach its southern end, then turn east. Pass the first trail junction and turn left at the second junction onto the red-blazed trail, which heads onto an isthmus between two ponds, always a delight to walk down (if not a delight to spell). Be careful of the tree roots along the way, which are important for holding

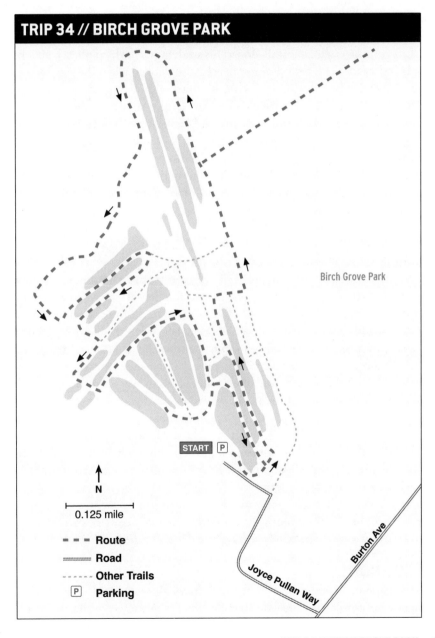

everything together but can ruin your day if you trip over one of them. Watch for waterfowl that hang out here, such as double-crested cormorants or green herons in spring. Also notice the covered footbridge on the next trail to the west. Resist the urge to rush over to it now; you'll get there! The red-blazed trail you're on crosses a footbridge and hits a T intersection. Turn right and see a strangely elevated tree whose roots suspend it well above the ground, as if it is standing up on four or five legs.

The trail then reaches the loop road that serves as the border for most of the trail system. Turn left and follow the road. The break from the lakes gives you a chance to admire the forest succession that has taken place, as this area has been regrowing for seven or eight decades. About 0.2 mile from your last turn (0.6 mile into the hike), a slightly elevated, overgrown road heads into the woods on your right. If you have prepared for ticks, turn right and walk down this straightaway, which offers a view of some wetlands and an idea of what this forest may have all looked like if the clay had not been dug out. (*Note*: It's best to skip this when it's filled with high grass in summer.) Keep watch for pine warblers, easily mistaken for New Jersey's state bird, the goldfinch; goldfinches have mostly black wings, and pine warblers' wings often look gray. When you come to downed trees or you've had enough of this stretch of forest, retrace your steps to the loop road and turn right. The road goes around the northernmost section of trail and two long ponds before swinging south, then southwest, and curving sharply to the southeast. Just after this sharp curve, turn left to leave the road and cross a footbridge to reenter the heart of the trail system (1.8 miles).

Once again, walk down the isthmus between two long ponds. With good fortune, you may spot an egret or a heron. Pass the first trail to the right and take the second right turn to swing around the east side of the pond to follow the other side in the direction you just came. The trail drops slightly and crosses a footbridge before rejoining the road. Turn left to walk along the road and follow the curve to the right as the road skirts the edge of another pond before turning south to pass between two more ponds. The road heads down a long straightaway here (past the old campground), but you'll abandon it to turn left and head into the small bit of land among six different ponds (2.2 miles). Really take your time on this quarter-mile stretch, which is another common haunt of wading birds and offers water views in every direction. Take the first right to follow the east side of the pond, which will lead you down a blue-blazed trail over a trio of long footbridges to the main parking area.

Just before entering the parking area, turn right and head for the boardwalk along the southern edge of the lake. Pass a memorial to four high school football players who tragically died in a car accident. Small fishing piers offer a quiet spot for reflection if they are not being used by anglers.

Backtrack to the beginning of the boardwalk, continuing straight between two more ponds. After passing the first pond on your right, turn right and finally cross the covered bridge spotted earlier. At the base of the pond, turn right and walk to the parking lot (3.0 miles).

DID YOU KNOW?

European nations, Canada, and the United States all once highly prized beaver fur, particularly for stylish hats. Indeed, Abe Lincoln's famous stovepipe hat was made from

This tree is not standing on its tiptoes; rather, the clay has eroded from under the roots.

beaver fur. The desires of fashion nearly resulted in beavers being hunted into extinction. The New Jersey legislature protected the beaver in 1903, but it took the importation of around 1,500 beavers in the 1930s to stabilize the population. Beavers are now common throughout the state and can be found along many of the hikes in this book, including this one.

OTHER ACTIVITIES

Birch Grove Park also allows fishing (the lakes are stocked twice each year) and mountain biking. Sadly, as of 2019, the park is no longer open for camping. A 10- to 15-minute drive brings you to Margate, the home of Lucy, the World's Largest Elephant, newly fixed up and once again open for tours (lucytheelephant.org). Ten minutes south, you'll find the Somers Mansion Historic Site, the oldest house in Atlantic County (hours vary; nj.gov/dep/parksandforests/historic/somersmansion.html) and the Atlantic County Historical Society Library and Museum—open Thursday to Saturday—which has a fascinating historical collection (atlanticcountyhistoricalsocietynj.org).

MORE INFORMATION

Open year-round; hours are seasonal. Pets are not allowed in the park.

The Southern Shore is part of New Jersey's Outer Coastal Plain. You won't stub your toes hiking here, because much of the region is flat and covered with sandy soil, especially in the area of the Pinelands that bleeds briefly into the northern part of the Shore, and on the Atlantic Ocean beaches themselves.

Cape May County has the distinction of being the southernmost county in New Jersey and is almost completely surrounded by water. The county's western coastline meets Delaware Bay, and its eastern and southern coastlines embrace the Atlantic Ocean. With 30 miles of beaches, Cape May County attracts many vacationers. Tourism is the county's single largest industry, although lima beans once covered 5,000 acres. The town of West Cape May still calls itself the lima bean capital of the world and hosts an annual lima bean festival. Growing vineyard grapes is more common in the area now than in years past.

Cape May County is a very popular destination for birders—one of the world's most celebrated migratory junctions. Every autumn, the county's unique wind patterns and geography bring millions of migrating hawks, seabirds, shorebirds, and songbirds, not to mention butterflies and dragonflies. Cape May and Cumberland counties are a natural stopover for more than 120 different species of birds.

On the Delaware Bay side, which includes the entire coastline of Cumberland County and the western coastline of Cape May County, the region changes to salt marshes, mud flats, and wetlands. On 6,000 acres of coastal wetlands, the nonprofit Wetlands Institute, based in the town of Stone Harbor, provides a wonderful overall education on life in the salt marshes and the marshes' importance (see "Salt of the Earth: Salt Marsh Ecosystems" on page 199 and Trip 39).

The Delaware Bay side—also known as the Bayshore, with 42 miles of beachfront coastline—is quite a different animal from the Atlantic Ocean side. Usually bypassed by beachgoers headed to the ocean, the communities here are smaller; some are even disappearing due to rising sea levels. Cumberland County, where the shore is entirely

Facing page: Migrating monarch butterflies can be seen by the thousands in October, such as this one off Thompson's Beach in southern New Jersey.

on the Delaware Bay side, is served only by state and county routes. In contrast, the Atlantic City Expressway takes you directly to Cape May County, via Exit 0.

But what the Bayshore lacks in people, it more than makes up for in wildlife. In May and June, millions of Atlantic horseshoe crabs come to Delaware Bay to spawn (see Trip 37). Tens of thousands of red knots, a type of migratory bird, depend on the horseshoe crabs' eggs for refueling on their flight from South America to the Arctic. Other migratory shorebirds that rely on these eggs are the ruddy turnstone, semipalmated sandpiper, sanderling, dunlin, and short-billed dowitcher. To preserve these vitally important horseshoe crab populations, please participate in the horseshoe crab rescue program called reTURN the Favor (returnthefavornj.org).

The Bayshore is also prime oystering ground. The wetlands in the community of Bivalve in Cumberland County were once known as the oyster capital of the world.

Also impressive is the Southern Shore's preponderance of wildlife management areas—according to the New Jersey Department of Fish and Wildlife, 23 in Cape May and Cumberland counties combined. It follows that fourteen conservation organizations have offices in the Bayshore.

The ecological importance of the Southern Shore and its sandy, marshy beauty is undisputed.

35 BELLEPLAIN STATE FOREST

Lose yourself in this long woods walk, with tunnels of mountain laurel, soothing lakes, and interesting wetlands.

Features 🚶 🐕 💧 🔍 🎿 ⛺ 🏊 ⛱

Location Woodbine, NJ

Rating Moderate to Strenuous

Distance 10.3-mile loop

Elevation Gain 300 feet

Estimated Time 5 hours

Maps USGS Tuckahoe; nj.gov/dep/parksandforests/maps/belleplainstateforest.html

GPS Coordinates 39° 14.908′ N, 74° 50.549′ W

Contact Mailing address: Belleplain State Forest, P.O. Box 450, Woodbine, NJ 08270; 609-861-2404; nj.gov/dep/parksandforests/parks/belleplainstateforest.html

DIRECTIONS

If going south, take Garden State Parkway to Exit 17 to US 9 and then to County Route 550. If going north, take NJ 55 South, to NJ 47, to NJ 347, and then to County Route 550. Follow signs to the forest (One Henkinsifkin Road). The parking lot holds about 30 cars.

TRAIL DESCRIPTION

Belleplain is 21,254 acres of pine-oak and Atlantic white cedar forest, interspersed with lowland hardwoods, plantations of evergreens, swamps, three ponds (Hands Mill, Pickle Factory, and East Creek), and one lake (Nummy). The Civilian Corps of Engineers created Lake Nummy from a cranberry bog in 1933. At this National Audubon Society Important Bird Area, you can see bald eagles, barred owls, Cooper's hawks, and many songbirds, including a proliferation of yellow-throated warblers. Choose from more than 40 miles of trails. On this hike, you'll get a good leg-stretch and an overview of the forest by taking North Shore, Goosekill, and East Creek trails and coming back to North Shore. In April, enjoy white and purple wood violets, twittering birds, and the blooming golden club in East Creek Pond. In May and June, a profusion of mountain laurels bursts into clouds of white and pink, and the aquatic, carnivorous yellow bladderwort floats on ponds, as do bullhead pond lilies. In midsummer, pick highbush blueberries. The forest is part of the Pinelands but not the Pine Barrens (see "Get Away from the Crowds in the Pine Barrens and the Pinelands" on page 143), which allows for richer soil conditions and more growth. Belleplain State Forest is also part of the New

Jersey Coastal Heritage Trail (see "The Ultimate Multiuse Trail: New Jersey Coastal Heritage Trail" on page 164).

Start directly from Belleplain State Forest headquarters on Henkinsifkin Road. Be sure to grab a map (the free New Jersey Audubon Belleplain State Forest Birding Map is the most detailed) from the ranger station. Facing the headquarters building, walk to the right onto orange-blazed North Shore Trail, a lovely, narrow dirt path through the woods. Read about lichens on the nature signs that line the way. Continue on North Shore Trail and turn right (0.3 mile) at a circle to get on green-blazed Goosekill Trail (unmarked here, but follow the square yellow marker that soon appears as the trail widens to a surface made of tiny stones). Walking on these root-free flat trails is a delight. Turn right at the now-visible green blaze toward the two-lane, paved County Route 550. Turn left on the road for a short walk across a small culvert. Turn left at the "Gypsy Moth Killed Oak Salvaged 1988" sign and a guardrail, at the metal sign for the yellow-and-white-blazed Champion Trail (0.8 mile).

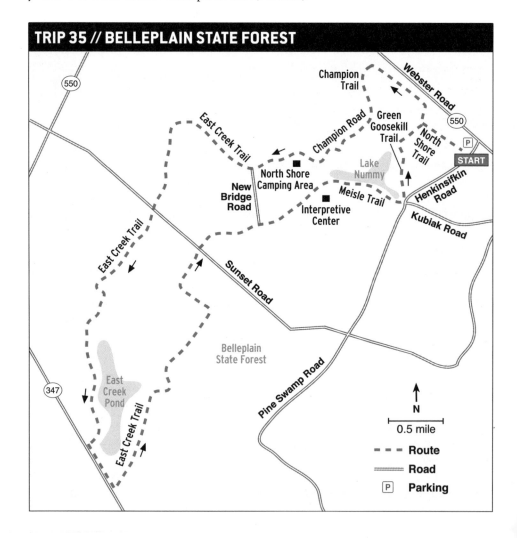

TRIP 35 // BELLEPLAIN STATE FOREST

Champion Trail, a dirt path, turns off almost immediately to the left, but don't take it. Instead, walk straight onto the paved, shady road (called Champion Road, not blazed), which is closed to cars. You'll feel like you're on the Avenue des Champs-Élysées. On the left is the North Shore Camping Area, with a few picnic tables, restrooms, and a drinking-water pump, open in season, Memorial Day to Labor Day (1.6 miles). On the right is Ballfield Pavilion and a large athletic and recreation field. Turn left here at the stop sign and head toward a 60-car parking lot, playground, picnic tables, swimming beach, and restrooms, fronted by glistening Lake Nummy. Take a moment to look around at this impressive complex. Side trip completed, walk back to the stop sign, turn left, and in a few yards, just before the bridge, turn right onto white-blazed East Creek Trail (2.0 miles). (*Note*: You can drive to Lake Nummy and park there if you want to start here and make the hike 2.0 miles shorter.)

Hike into the woods on the shaded, white-blazed dirt path. Turn right at the fork; be careful of roots as you admire the mountain laurels. Soon a short boardwalk leads over a primordial-feeling swamp. In winter, all is quiet as you walk into the sun past moss and large, red-berried American holly trees. Cross one-lane paved New Bridge Road (2.7 miles) onto white-blazed East Creek Trail on the other side. Pine straw hushes your footfalls. At the four-way intersection in the forest of mountain laurels and tall pines, keep straight on East Creek Trail. A footbridge spans a stream. Walk across a dirt road, keeping straight on the white-blazed trail (orange-blazed Cedar Trail is to your right). Two overlapping trees caress the path. At another dirt road, keep straight to stay on the white-blazed trail. A fire ditch is to the left. Cross one-lane paved Sunset Road (3.7 miles) and pick up East Creek Trail on the other side, still nestled deep in the woods. Some patches of the treadway can be muddy and flooded here in spring, but a nine-trunked tree on the left is your reward.

The shaded trail continues to meander through the woods and understory, eventually traversing a one-lane paved road into the woods on the other side. Mountain laurels begin to crowd the path. Cross a dirt road. Soon two T intersections pop up in quick succession—turn right on each. Very quickly after, white-blazed East Creek Trail turns left. (In leafless seasons, East Creek Pond peeks through the trees.) Tread a boardwalk over a small swamp and proceed straight. The quiet here is pervasive, other than the faint murmur of cars. The route begins to follow East Creek Pond on the left (4.9 miles) and becomes a bit rooty and muddy. Enter a small tunnel of mountain laurels as the path eventually winds to the pond and follows the water's edge. You can walk to the shore at periodic inroads. A fuchsia-colored metal bench, the only one on the trail, allows full enjoyment of the scene.

Back on the white-blazed trail, enter the gravel parking lot at the East Creek Pond boat ramp on NJ 347 (5.5 miles) at the south end of East Creek Pond. Walk down the ramp and look for April-blooming golden club along the water's edge, as well as bald eagles, ducks, and turtles. To begin the loop back, turn left on busy NJ 347 and walk across a bridge (road shoulders are ample), stopping to admire the expanse of the creek below. Go past East Creek Group Cabins on the left. Look closely as you pass a telephone pole on the left and you'll see a white arrow guiding the way. About one minute

A December moon rises above Lake Nummy in Belleplain State Forest.

(750 feet) past the group cabins, the trail sign points to the left, back into the woods, on East Creek Trail again (5.9 miles).

Soon the traffic sounds fade on the flat path, framed by huge mountain laurels (make that mental note about visiting in spring). Keep straight. The trail can be very muddy and often flooded in spring, but walk-around paths are provided. Footbridges and boardwalks aid passage through serene swamps. At the T intersection, go left, following the white arrows. The path is flat, lined with moss, and hugged by trees. Go left to follow the white arrow at the overgrown field on the right. Walk by a pretty field before popping back into the woods at the white arrow and fire ditch.

Cross paved Sunset Road (7.9 miles) onto the path on the other side, and then walk across a cute footbridge. At the Y intersection, go left at the white arrow. At the next Y intersection soon after, go left to follow the white arrow, admiring the carpet of green moss. A recycling center for campers appears on your right just before the trail ends in a T intersection at a paved road. Turn left and then quickly right onto paved Deans Branch Road/Meisle Road. Lake Nummy is on your left, and the interpretive center is on your right (8.9 miles). If the center is open, go in and explore. Otherwise walk down the road, keeping the center on your right. Sit on the benches, stroll on the dock, and admire the lake, beautiful at any time. Look for yellow pond lilies and floating bladderwort in season.

Go straight on paved Meisle Road, past the nature markers. Toward the end of the lake, turn left at the orange blaze on a tree; although not marked as such, this is Meisle Trail.

A pleasant, gentle path pads through the Virginia pines, with the lake on the left. (A foot-bridge helps with the muddy parts.) At the T intersection, go left onto a dirt road called Green Goosekill Trail (green metal square, 9.4 miles). Then continue straight on the green-blazed trail, ignoring yellow-blazed Nature Trail on the left. Admire the highbush blueberries, sheep laurel (which has a special "spring-loaded" pollination system—when an insect lands, the anthers pop out and shower it with pollen), and the common green-brier (with gorgeous blue or red berries in fall). (*Caution*: Sheep laurel is toxic if eaten.) In summer, inhale the perfume of sweet pepperbush blooms. Walk over a culvert pipe in a few hundred yards and then turn right onto orange-blazed North Shore Trail (10 miles). Look for frogs as you pass a muddy swamp, with a stream flowing to your right. At the Y intersection, go right and return to the headquarters parking lot.

DID YOU KNOW?

A beaver dam sits not far down Tom Field Road (or Narrows Road), which is a dirt trail leading left off East Creek Trail (before East Creek Pond), about 0.5 mile after Sunset Road. The town of Woodbine, where Belleplain is located, started as a Jewish agricul-tural community for Russian families displaced by the pogroms of the 1880s.

OTHER ACTIVITIES

Thirty minutes away in Millville is Wheaton Arts and Cultural Center (1000 Village Drive), known for glass creations, and Millville's arty Glasstown Arts District. To the south, in Dennis, is 8,000-acre Dennis Creek Wildlife Management Area; farther west in the town of South Dennis is Beaver Swamp Wildlife Management Area on Beaver Dam Road (off NJ 47), with bald eagles. About 15 miles north, in Heislerville, are East Point Lighthouse (call 856-785-0349 for hours) and Heislerville Wildlife Management Area.

MORE INFORMATION

Open dawn to dusk. Seasonal entrance fees may apply for parts of the park from Me-morial Day to Labor Day—check the park's website to see if fees are currently in effect before you go.

36   FORT MOTT STATE PARK

A walk through an 1890s battery, one of the earliest bird refuges in the country, and a Civil War POW cemetery make this a unique hike in the state!

Features

Location Pennsville, NJ

Rating Easy

Distance 3.1-mile loop

Elevation Gain 250 feet

Estimated Time 2 hours

Maps USGS Delaware City; Fort Mott History Trail: nj.gov/dep/parksandforests/parks/docs/interpretive%20trailguide%20_Fort%20Mott_MEDRES.pdf; nj.gov/dep/parksandforests/parks/fortmottstatepark.html

GPS Coordinates 39° 36.180′ N, 075° 33.015′ W

Contact Fort Mott State Park, 454 Fort Mott Road, Pennsville, NJ 08070; 856-935-3218; nj.gov/dep/parksandforests/parks/fortmottstatepark.html

DIRECTIONS

From I-295, take Exit 1C for County Route 551 South toward Salem. Drive 3.4 miles and then turn right onto Mahoney Road. After another 0.8 mile, turn right onto South Broadway. In 0.4 mile, turn left onto Fort Mott Road. Drive 3.1 miles and then turn right onto the driveway for Fort Mott. The parking lot is on your left, with room for approximately 75 cars.

TRAIL DESCRIPTION

From the building of Swedish Fort Elfsborg in 1643 to the World War II bunker at Cape May Point (see Trip 37), the Delaware River has always been heavily defended along the New Jersey side. Fort Mott was involved in this long line of defense, part of an ambitious late-1800s plan to defend the river via three forts—Fort Mott, Fort Delaware, and Fort DuPont—in the buildup to the Spanish-American War. This hike takes you on a tour of the New Jersey link in that three-fort chain, Fort Mott.

After parking in the lot, head west and pass through the car gate, which has the current hours for the park. Interpretive signs just inside the gate help you get oriented. If you have children, they have likely gone right past the signs and are already climbing the set of stairs on the opposite side of the trail. Here are the remains of Battery Gregg; climb up for a view from the observation station at the top.

When you return to the ground, turn left and then immediately right down the paved roadway, away from the fortifications. The tower on your right was used as a fire control tower to tell the batteries where to fire. The buildings on the left now house the ranger station, bathrooms, and a small museum. Stop in for a map and to learn more about Fort Mott before continuing your exploration. (Pick up the Fort Mott History Trail interpretive guide; it will give you a lot more information about the sights than can fit in this description.) Back outside, turn left and walk to the end of the road. The field ahead of you was the military parade field. To the right, the large building served as the post headquarters.

Turn around and head back the way you came, going by the museum and ranger station again. After you pass the remains of the moat, now filled with cattails and other marsh-loving plants, keep a sharp eye out to the right. A set of stone steps with a wooden handrail lead up the forested hill; climb them to summit the hill. This is the beginning of the

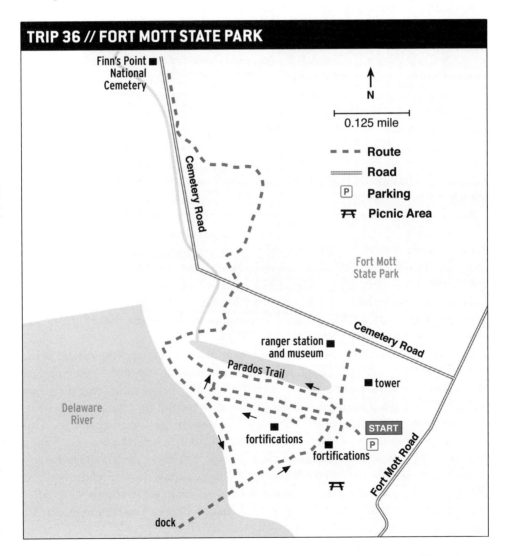

TRIP 36 // FORT MOTT STATE PARK

Finn's Point ■
National
Cemetery

N

0.125 mile

- - - Route
══════ Road
P Parking
🎪 Picnic Area

Cemetery Road

Fort Mott
State Park

Cemetery Road

ranger station ■
and museum

Parados Trail

■ tower

Delaware
River

■
fortifications

START
P

■
fortifications

Fort Mott Road

🎪

dock

unblazed Parados Trail. The trail then follows along the ridge of this hill, known as the Parados, which was manmade and used, along with the moat, as part of the rear defenses of the fort. It's now a heavily wooded island in the sky, a great spot to watch for the many birds that frequent the area year-round or visit during migration.

The trail from the Parados loops over the top of a tunnel and puts you on the fortifications. Resist the urge to explore them now; instead use the grassy ramp to descend toward the river and onto a paved path. Turn right and walk to the very end of the fortifications. Here, you will see an arrow pointing to the nature trail. Follow the arrow down the gravel service road, which is the beginning of the nature trail. The service road quickly shrinks to a stone pathway.

Crossing the park road, enter the former Killcohook National Wildlife Refuge, set aside by President Franklin D. Roosevelt during the Great Depression as a breeding area for migratory birds. Its status was revoked in 1998, as dredge spoils placed by the Army Corps of Engineers had destroyed much of the original wetlands. This quiet nature trail still is a choice spot for bird-watching, and the shade is a welcome respite from the other exposed trails around Fort Mott. When the pathway ends, turn right for a short walk up the road to Finn's Point National Cemetery (1.2 miles). Here are buried thousands of Confederate prisoners of war (POWs) in unmarked graves, as well as some of their Union guards, all of whom died at nearby Fort Delaware. Military veterans of later periods are also buried here and, curiously, a few German POWs from World War II who were imprisoned in the United States. Just behind the cemetery, you'll find Delaware. Seriously. The dredge spoils raised the bottom of the Delaware River here so much that it now is above the water mark, creating more than 500 acres that are, legally, Delaware, thanks to a charter granted by King Charles II in 1681 (and a lot of wrangling in courts ever since).

Backtrack to the cemetery entrance and down the nature trail to the paved path in front of the fortifications. Stay on that path as it heads along the Delaware River. Alternatingly admire the river views and the front of the fort, which is remarkably well concealed as grassy hills. When you reach the Fort Mott Ferry Pier, walk out toward the end in nice weather and enjoy the river breezes. Here, in season, a ferry travels to Fort Delaware on Pea Patch Island. The stone fortifications on the island in front of you are where the Confederate soldiers buried in the graveyard were imprisoned. Continue along the paved path until you pass between the fortifications.

Turn left and enter Battery Harker by a door at the back corner, being careful of the pigeons that hang out here. Climb the wooden steps to the top of the gun emplacements. The trail winds around a disappearing gun battery before summiting the grassy top of the hill. A disappearing gun is designed to drop behind the defensive walls when it is fired, protecting it from enemy fire while it is reloaded. Follow along the crest that will take you from Battery Harker to Battery Arnold, located behind a shared defensive structure. The elevation here allows for clear views of the river to the left and of Battery Arnold to the right. When you reach the end of Battery Arnold, curve slightly right and then go straight to enter two small gun batteries, as well as an observation pillbox. After you dead-end at the second of the two small batteries, Battery Krayenbuhl, backtrack to the set of wooden steps and descend to ground level. Turn left and go through the tunnel for views of the Peace Magazine and the Western Fire Control Tower. Backtrack through the tunnel and head straight down the paved path that runs between the gun emplacements and the Parados. Where you can, peek into windows to see some of the inner workings of the batteries. To your left, watch for the tunnels in the Parados that were used to bring ammunition into the batteries. At the end of the fortifications, take the short walk back to the parking area. Picnic tables and a playground offer a pleasant spot for a break before your next adventure.

DID YOU KNOW?

Fort Mott was named for Gershom Mott, who was born in Lamberton, New Jersey, near Trenton, and served as an officer in the United States Army. He rose from a second lieutenant in the Mexican-American War to a major general of volunteers by the end of the Civil War and had a reputation as being both competent and brave. The fort, originally named the Battery at Finn's Point, was renamed in his honor in 1897.

OTHER ACTIVITIES

Take the ferry from here or from nearby Fort DuPont in Delaware to Fort Delaware State Park, better known as Pea Patch Island, right in the middle of the Delaware River. This island houses a Civil War–era fort and POW camp (many of the prisoners arrived from the Battle of Gettysburg) and has museum displays, a nature trail, cannon demonstrations, and more. The Forts Ferry Crossing schedule varies slightly each year but usually

These ruins sit along the northern side of the fortifications.

runs on weekends from late April until late September, and from Wednesday to Sunday from mid-June to Labor Day. For information and tickets, see delawarememorialbridge .com/ferries-landing-page. Finn's Point Rear Range Light, one of New Jersey's eleven remaining lighthouses, is just a few minutes away and is very occasionally open to climb. The lighthouse is in Supawna Meadows National Wildlife Refuge, which has trails that can be explored.

MORE INFORMATION

The park has no entrance fee. Hours vary by season. Leashed dogs are allowed in the park, but the hike described is not suitable for dogs.

SALT OF THE EARTH: SALT MARSH ECOSYSTEMS

Salt marshes are one of the most productive ecosystems on earth. They protect the mainland from flooding and erosion, filter sediment and pollutants, afford a safe nursery for many species of coastal fish and shellfish, provide food and nesting for migratory birds, and house mammals, insects, and diamondback terrapins. As far as ecosystems go (and there are 24 types of ecosystems), salt marshes are to coastal ecosystems what Iowa cornfields are to terrestrial ecosystems. But instead of feeding pigs, cows, and humans, salt marshes feed muskrat, mink, raccoons, snowy egrets, ospreys, great blue herons, swans, sparrows, and crustaceans. Common cordgrass even supports the air-breathing coffee bean snail as it slowly climbs along the grassy stalk at high tide. Unfortunately for the snail, the birds crunch and eat it, as the shell helps grind up food in their stomachs.

How can an environment so salty support a single living thing, let alone so many? It seems that halophytes (salt marsh plants) love salt, or to be more precise, they process it well. Plants such as cordgrass manage salt stress with salt-excreting glands and mechanisms to reduce water loss and promote high water-use efficiency. Salt marsh plants also have the ability to deliver oxygen to belowground roots, much like trees in the Amazon do during times of high water.

The tides also promote life. As a transitional habitat between ocean and land, salt marshes receive plenty of tidal water—twice a day, in fact. Water decays the plant life, which creates soft marsh substrate ("pluff mud") and, eventually, dense layers of peat. Fiddler crabs, marsh snails, insects, fish, and mussels further shred the organic material. Bacteria, fungi, and small algae break down what remains. The tide goes out, carrying nutrients back to the sea, where they feed fish and other coastal organisms.

Over time, the buildup of organic material from repeated decay acts like a giant sponge, absorbing and holding water that would otherwise erode the shoreline and flood the coast and all its inhabitants. Salt marshes absorbed water from Hurricane Sandy, which slammed into New Jersey's southern coast in 2012, and surely saved some homes from flooding. The dense organic material also filters pollutants.

The salt marsh is the backbone of the beach, the barrier between sand and solid land. This is especially important in New Jersey, which has 245,000 acres of salt marsh, mostly along Delaware Bay and the Atlantic coasts of Cape May and Atlantic counties.

Outright destruction, such as from farming (mainly salt hay), has been greatly diminished by federal and state legislation. But other dangers exist, such as pollution from overpopulation along the coast and improper mosquito and flood control that either dries up or floods the marshes.

As the sea levels continue to rise, the nurturing, nutritive, protective, and self-sustaining salt marshes will keep pace—as long as we let them.

37 CAPE MAY POINT STATE PARK AND SOUTH CAPE MAY MEADOWS

Enjoy sand dunes, marshes, woods, beaches, birds, and butterflies at the end of New Jersey, surrounded by the sea.

Features

Location Cape May Point, NJ

Rating Easy

Distance 3.4-mile loop

Elevation Gain 100 feet

Estimated Time 1.5 hours

Maps USGS Cape May; Cape May Point State Park: nj.gov/dep/parksandforests /maps/capemaypointstatepark.html; South Cape May Meadows: nature.org/en-us /get-involved/how-to-help/places-we-protect/south-cape-may-meadows

GPS Coodinates 38° 56.060′ N, 74° 56.954′ W

Contact Cape May Point State Park mailing address: P.O. Box 107, Cape May Point, NJ 08212; 609-884-2159; state.nj.us/dep/parksandforests/parks/capemay.html. South Cape May Meadows: The Nature Conservancy, 200 Pottersville Road Chester, NJ 07930; 908-879-7262; nature.org/en-us/get-involved/how-to-help/places-we -protect/south-cape-may-meadows

DIRECTIONS

Take Exit 0 (yes, zero) off Garden State Parkway toward Cape May on NJ 109. Turn right onto Bank Street and then left onto Broad Street. Turn right onto County Route 633, which becomes County Route 606. Turn left onto 215 Lighthouse Avenue (County Route 629). A large parking lot is on the left (space for about 200 cars). You'll see the Cape May Lighthouse.

TRAIL DESCRIPTION

Cape May Point State Park is managed by the New Jersey Division of Parks and Forestry. The Nature Conservancy manages the adjacent South Cape May Meadows, a nature preserve. Both properties are on major migratory routes for seabirds, shorebirds, and songbirds. The Cape May Peninsula acts as a funnel for birds migrating along the Atlantic Flyway. From mid-May to June, the shorebirds and songbirds return. Summer hosts nesting American oystercatchers, least terns, piping plovers, and black skimmers. Magnificent hordes of airy dragonflies and vividly colored monarch butterflies float through in late summer and early fall. In fall, hundreds of hawks power past this premier migration route, headed south. Horseshoe crabs lay eggs here in May and June

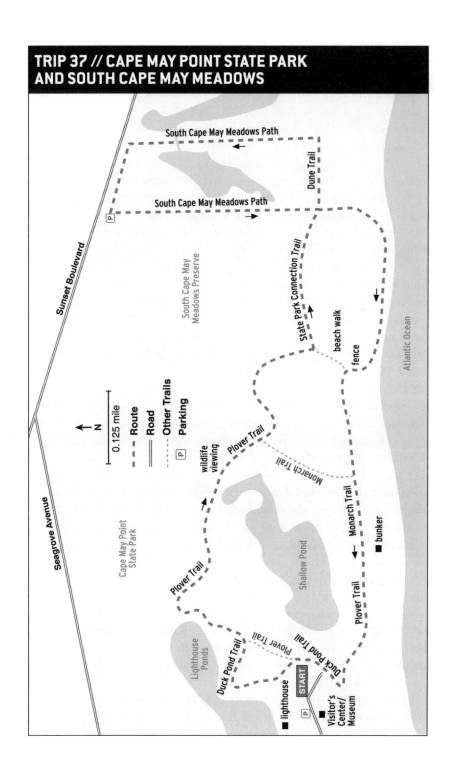

TRIP 37 // CAPE MAY POINT STATE PARK AND SOUTH CAPE MAY MEADOWS

South Cape May Meadows Path

South Cape May Meadows Path

Dune Trail

Sunset Boulevard

Atlantic Ocean

South Cape May Meadows Preserve

State Park Connection Trail

beach walk

fence

0.125 mile

N

Route
Road
Other Trails
P Parking

wildlife viewing

Plover Trail

Monarch Trail

Seagrove Avenue

Cape May Point State Park

Shallow Pond

Monarch Trail

bunker

Plover Trail

Plover Trail

Lighthouse Ponds

Duck Pond Trail

Plover Trail

Duck Pond Trail

START

lighthouse

P

Visitor's Center/ Museum

during their annual migration. (See information about reTURN the Favor, a horseshoe crab rescue program, on page 188 in the Southern Shore section opening.)

All year long, visitors can enjoy the dunes, ocean, freshwater wetlands, woods, meadows, and ponds.

Take blue-blazed Plover Trail and red-blazed Duck Pond Trail through the highlights of the park, using a connector trail to South Cape May Meadows. Enjoy a beach walk past a World War II bunker before heading back to the parking lot with a bird observation deck and lighthouse.

Start from the Cape May Lighthouse parking lot. (*Note*: In summer, the lot fills quickly, so get there early.) The 157-foot lighthouse, with 199 steps, is open seasonally ($12 for adults; $8 for children ages 3 to 12; free for children younger than 3). Parts of the trail are exposed to sun, so you may want to bring a hat for added sun protection. In summer, bring bug spray and remember to apply the spray to your feet to guard against chigger bites. (Chiggers are tiny red mites whose bites cause maddening skin irritation.)

Stop at the visitor center for maps and other information. Flush toilets are available here. Walk to the end of the parking lot, toward the evergreens, and go straight onto the combined red-, yellow-, and blue-blazed trails (Duck Pond, Monarch, and Plover trails, respectively). Cross the raised boardwalk through cedars and a pretty foliage archway, stopping to read the nature signs about the great blue heron, great horned owl, muskrat, and more. Get your bearings at the comfortable bench, noting the decorative reeds and plants, such as shadbush and pitch pines. Then turn left onto red-blazed Duck Pond Trail, universally accessible, toward a pond with ducks, swans, and perhaps an osprey.

A bird blind on your right may or may not be open, depending on the season. The pitch pines are impressive and shady. Note the sassafras trees, red-leaved in fall, and eastern red cedars. Lighthouse Pond quickly comes into view; take advantage of the observation deck for a close-up look at the swans. The trail splits into three branches (0.3 mile); turn left on the combined blue- and yellow-blazed trails (Plover and Monarch) away from the parking lot. Still on a boardwalk, observe the different kinds of trees: black gum, with deep-red leaves in fall; persimmon (uncommon in New Jersey); and sweet gum, with its star-shaped leaves. Cross a bridge with a pretty view of the pond to the left. Benches afford a comfortable view of the water and a big field.

Past the pond, the boardwalk turns to a dirt path. Stay on the combined Plover and Monarch trails. Garter snakes may twist through the dirt in front of you. Enter an open area featuring a pond, wetlands, and ducks, and cross it on a boardwalk onto a dirt path again. On the right, the shallow pond shimmers in the sun; a cozy thicket is on the left as you walk this fun, narrow route. When you reach the upcoming woods of white oak and black gum, take a seat on the convenient bench for an excellent view of the pond and lighthouse. At the intersection, climb the wildlife viewing platform to watch swans eat, preen, and glide (0.8 mile).

Return to the intersection and turn left onto blue-blazed Plover Trail. After about 200 yards, go over the bridge. Take the boardwalk through an open marsh, turning around to orient yourself to the ever-present lighthouse. Head into the woods, looking for persimmon trees, and at the intersection with an unnamed dirt road (1.1 miles), turn right. Continue on Plover Trail, over another bridge with another excellent view of

The crashing waves of the Atlantic Ocean are hard to resist. Cool your hike-weary feet in the surf.

the lighthouse. Go left through a gap in the fence at the large sign for 0.25-mile State Park Connection Trail, also blazed blue (1.2 miles); you are now entering South Cape May Meadows, a nature preserve and migratory bird refuge, via State Park Connection Trail. (*Note*: This trail is not on the state park map.) Head to the pond for more ducks (mallards, American black ducks and wigeons, gadwalls, and shovelers), and walk the sugar-sand trail through an open field.

At the next fence, go straight to explore South Cape May Meadows. (A right turn leads to the beach.) You are now on South Cape May Meadows Path. Keep the fence on your right. At the next intersection, go left (the path sports a brown blaze here). In late summer and early fall, enjoy the monarch butterflies floating about, part of their annual migration toward central Mexico, more than 2,000 miles away. You'll see a pond on the right with houses in the distance.

Stroll a bit farther to some benches and an observation deck (1.7 miles). Look in the sky for turkey vultures and other raptors, such as eagles, ospreys, falcons, and hawks. Scan the meadow for songbirds—warblers, wrens, and sparrows. Look at the water's edge for great egrets and terns feeding in the shallows. Swans and ducks float farther out. Listen to the roar of the ocean nearby and smell the salty breeze.

Refreshed, begin walking on a bridge between two ponds. This ordinary-looking footbridge covers an important water control structure that can change water levels in the wetlands during storms or drought. Employees use two special hooks to add or remove boards that raise or lower water levels on either side of the bridge. Lowering the levels during Hurricane Sandy handily absorbed 10 inches of rain. Manipulation during migration or nesting facilitates the survival of waterfowl. Take a moment to check out this marvel of water control and watch a turtle or two.

At the gate and paved road (Sunset Boulevard, 1.9 miles), turn left onto a gravel path that parallels the road, and you'll encounter The Nature Conservancy's large parking lot. Don't enter the lot, but turn left to reach the conservancy's kiosks and building with a mossy "living roof." Check the posted schedule for programs. Turn left, staying on South Cape May Meadows Path (blazed white here, 2.0 miles), heading into the sun toward the birdhouses and over another water management bridge on a long, straight, exposed treadway. Stop on the bridge and watch snapping turtles navigate the water control boards beneath.

At the next intersection (Dune Trail, 2.4 miles), keep straight to head to the Atlantic Ocean, which pops up beyond the hill, shimmering and salty. Stroll down the fenced path and turn right onto the sand, toward the lighthouse, keeping an eye out for your return path on the right. In summer, piping plovers, with their black-banded necks and plaintive calls, skitter on the sands, searching for mollusks. During nesting season in spring, be careful of their eggs, laid in shallow depressions in the sand, because the federal government now classifies piping plovers as an endangered species. Enjoy the ocean, pausing to dip your toes in the water.

At the split rail fence, look for a sign for Cape May Point State Park. (2.7 miles). Leave the beach and follow it. At the next intersection, go left (2.8 miles) on blue-blazed Plover Trail, which will eventually return you to Cape May Point State Park. Pass a pond to the right, where you can enjoy more bird-watching. If you look left at about 3.1 miles, out to the Atlantic Ocean, you will see a World War II bunker, built in 1942 when the park was a military base. At low tide, the gun turrets at the front are visible. The sea will eventually claim the bunker, which was once 900 feet inland. If you'd like to take a path through the dunes to check out the bunker before it disappears, now is your chance.

Otherwise, head toward the lighthouse. Tall bushes on either side of the trail provide shade, and puddle ducks paddle in a pond to your right. Follow Plover Trail into the lighthouse parking lot, stopping to climb the wooden hawk-watching platform, where 30,000 raptors pass annually, and read the informative signs about the plants, bats and other mammals, and birds of the coastal dunes.

DID YOU KNOW?

Storms in the twentieth century eventually washed away most of the Victorian-style resort town of South Cape May (remnants lie on the ocean floor). Entrepreneurs and conservation groups began to rebuild at the end of the century. Cape May Point has beautiful quartz pebbles (commonly called "Cape May diamonds") created by thousands of years of waves—search for them in the sands.

OTHER ACTIVITIES

Hike 2.5-mile Diamond Beach Trail at West Cape May's Higbee Beach Wildlife Management Area (west end of New England Road). Chill at Cape May Point's Sunset Beach, and watch for dolphins around a submerged concrete ship (502 Sunset Boulevard). To the north lie short trails at Lizard Tail Swamp Preserve (406 Courthouse–South Dennis Road in Cape May Courthouse) and Eldora Nature Preserve, which includes a boardwalk (2350 NJ 47, also called Delsea Drive, in Delmont). Shoppers, historians, and foodies will enjoy the Victorian charm of restored Cape May.

MORE INFORMATION

Cape May Point State Park and South Cape Meadows are both open dawn to dusk. The beach is open for nature viewing only from March 15 through August 31. The visitor center is advertised as fully accessible.

38 MAURICE RIVER BLUFFS PRESERVE

Rugged, watery beauty awaits on this loop hike through forested wetlands and along the bluffs of the Maurice River.

Features 👤 🐕 💧

Location Millville, NJ

Rating Moderate

Distance 5.5-mile loop

Elevation Gain 400 feet

Estimated Time 3 hours

Maps USGS Dividing Creek; njhiking.com/nj-hiking-maps/maurice-river-bluffs /Maurice-Bluffs-Trail-Map.pdf; nature.org/content/dam/tnc/nature/en/documents /MauriceRiverBluffs-trail-RELEASE.pdf

GPS Coordinates 39° 21.207′ N, 75° 02.009′ W

Contact The Nature Conservancy, 200 Pottersville Road, Chester, NJ 07930; 908-879-7262; nature.org/en-us/get-involved/how-to-help/places-we-protect /delaware-bayshores-maurice-river-bluffs-preserve

DIRECTIONS

Get onto NJ 42 from I-76 East. After 1.5 miles, merge onto NJ 55 via Exit 13 toward Glassboro/Vineland. After 33.0 miles, merge onto NJ 47 (North Second Street) via Exit 27 toward Millville. In about 2 miles, turn right onto East Vine Street. Drive 0.2 mile and then turn slightly left onto North Brandriff Avenue. In 0.5 mile, stay straight to go onto County Route 555 (South Race Street). County Route 555 becomes Silver Run Road (County Route 627) in a bit more than 1 mile. A little more than 1.5 miles after that, turn left at the large green-and-white sign for Maurice River Bluffs Preserve and reach the parking lot, which is on the right at 1200 Silver Run Road. The lot holds about 50 cars. No bathroom facilities are available.

TRAIL DESCRIPTION

This 525-acre preserve nestles along the 34.5-mile Maurice River, an important watershed that includes some of the state's largest contiguous wild rice marshes. This habitat has no shortage of birds: nesting ospreys, bald eagles, songbirds, and waterfowl. Also look for freshwater odonates (carnivorous insects, such as dragonflies and damselflies). As you hike through oak-pine forests, fields, and freshwater marshes and along the river, watch for red foxes, river otters, and muskrat.

This perimeter hike circles the entire preserve on Blue, Orange, Red, White, and Yellow trails (all of which are blazed accordingly), starting and ending at the explanatory kiosk in the parking lot. Read the kiosk map and consider taking a photo of it for reference. In general, the route is well marked, with many wooden steps, but some parts loop creatively; you may be confused, but follow the markings and you won't get lost.

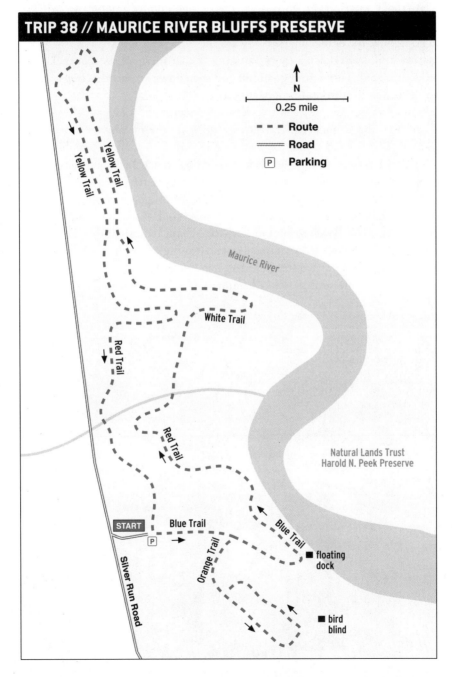

TRIP 38 // MAURICE RIVER BLUFFS PRESERVE

N

0.25 mile

- - - Route
===== Road
P Parking

Maurice River

Yellow Trail

Yellow Trail

White Trail

Red Trail

Red Trail

Natural Lands Trust
Harold N. Peek Preserve

START

Blue Trail

Blue Trail

P

floating
dock

Silver Run Road

Orange Trail

bird
blind

From the map kiosk in the parking lot, turn right onto Blue Trail. Enjoy the woods on a narrow, rooty path with a steep dropoff to the left. At the T intersection, turn quickly left onto a wider path, still Blue Trail. The pines make a tunnel above a flat, sandy path. At the next intersection, turn right at the arrow onto Orange Trail (0.2 mile). A charming picnic table sits beneath a tree. Just beyond the table, go right at the fork.

A narrow, grassy path offers no shade until it enters a grove of fragrant cedars and pines. At the T intersection, go right at the orange marker among twisted trees and descend a small ravine. Soon, a rope-railing bridge appears, crossing a deep ravine. Pass it and go right at the orange markers toward the bird-blind loop.

A narrow trail leads down a rooty bank into a charming hollow that makes you feel splendidly isolated. Turn left to go uphill and then down six wooden steps. Take a side trip to the bench to admire the marshy area.

Back on Orange Trail, descend two sets of wooden steps. Linger at the covered bird blind on the right, complete with seats, overlooking the marshy river (0.6 mile). Go uphill on eight steps and rest at the picnic table with a view of the marsh. At the map and direction arrows, bear right at the fork (still on Orange Trail; left leads to the rope-railed bridge). The path narrows through twisted trees. Turn left at the T intersection, away from the parking sign. The grassy path leads through quiet pines. At the next Y intersection (0.9 mile), turn right toward the bird blind. Keep following Orange Trail until it intersects Blue Trail; turn right onto Blue Trail, away from the parking sign and Orange Trail (1.1 miles). (*Note*: From January through July, Blue Trail is sometimes closed to protect nesting bald eagles. You can use Alternate Blue Trail by heading straight across the intersection onto the faint connector path through the pines—blue

Many steps and bridges help ease the ups and downs on this hike.

trail markings are visible once you enter the pines, and the map posted in the park shows the path.)

This section of Blue Trail is delightfully wide and sandy. Note the birdhouse or bat house sitting on a pole to the right, and reach the ruins of an old concrete building on your right. At the next Y intersection, the river shines in front of you. Go left here, following the blue marker. (*Note*: Stay off the private property to the right.) Sit at a picnic table atop the hill to enjoy the river and dock (1.3 miles). Then take the concrete steps down the steep bank and walk on the large floating dock you just saw, with benches to contemplate river life; look for eagle's nests.

The trail continues along the water's edge and a pretty beach. (*Caution*: This part of the hike is very rooty.) Follow a series of steps for fine views of the river. Stay on Blue Trail as you climb up and down the riverbanks on a series of steep steps.

Blue Trail narrows through the woods, with gentle ups and downs and a calming look at the river from the bluff sections. At the T intersection at a kiosk, go left, staying on Blue Trail for some steep ups and downs. Go up seven steps, turn left, and then descend. At the next intersection, turn right at the trail signs and map to follow Red Trail (1.8 miles), with the river on your right. Note the large sand-mining pit on the left. At the bank, turn left and take the gently sloped path down. Turn right to continue on Red Trail.

Cross a small wooden footbridge, welcome in this swampy area. Go left at the Y intersection up a bank. At the left-pointing arrow on the Red Trail sign, turn right, away from Red Trail; you will soon see a White Trail marker at a posted map; turn right onto White Trail (2.3 miles). Where the white-blazed trail meets the marsh, look for small "haystacks" signaling a muskrat's home. Via a rooty, uphill jaunt, reach a land point with excellent views of the river.

At the next white blaze, turn left downhill to continue the river walk and to explore the sandy crescent beach. Follow the white blazes uphill to a picnic table high on the bluffs overlooking the river. Continue on White Trail, with the river on both sides, onto a narrow peninsula. Carefully navigate the steep chute between banks to explore remains of an old dock.

Turn left at the marker to continue on White Trail and turn right almost immediately onto narrow Yellow Trail (2.7 miles), which curves through the woods, with two large concrete cisterns on the right (you'll loop back to them). With high banks to the left and the river to the right, this section feels wild and isolated. The path curves sharply to the right, down steps. (*Caution*: In late fall, leaves make the steps slippery.) Pass the remains of four concrete columns on the right and a big concrete slab on the left, and then climb some steps uphill for an impressive river view.

At the Y intersection, take Yellow Trail to the right, up and down steep steps. Follow Yellow Trail, enjoying another attractive river scene at the bottom of more steps, until you reach a sandy four-way intersection; go straight here. As you walk flat Yellow Trail through the forest, you'll hear the cars on Silver Run Road.

At the next four-way intersection, Yellow Trail curves to the left up a steep bank. In late fall, the ground is covered with blooming club moss—these plants are actually tiny evergreens. Walk a charming, narrow, elevated path above two small valleys and then go down a steep bank to flat terrain. Turn quickly right at the concrete cisterns, head to the next four-way intersection, and go right, toward a posted map. Here, you've completed the loop (4.4 miles).

To return to the parking area, take a right at the Y intersection immediately past the map to get onto Red Trail (marsh on your left). Stay on Red Trail and go right at the Y intersection, through the woods. Turn left on Red Trail at the next junction, with signs and three wooden posts (don't go straight on the red-blazed trail here, even though you could). Pass the sand-mining pit and deep ravine from before. Turn right at the Y intersection to go downhill toward the bridge. Cross the marshy area on a footbridge; turn right at the Red Trail sign. Steep banks close in on either side. Go up a hill, keeping straight, toward a posted map. At the next intersection, turn right on Blue Trail toward the sign for the parking area (5.0 miles), enjoying the narrow up-and-down path.

DID YOU KNOW?

The Maurice River is a critical link between the Delaware Estuary and the Pinelands National Reserve (see "Get Away from the Crowds in the Pine Barrens and the Pinelands" on page 143). A functioning drive-in theater entertains at the Delsea Drive-In, the last such theater in the state (2203 South Delsea Drive, Vineland).

OTHER ACTIVITIES

Explore two peaceful sites in Millville that have raptors and Atlantic white cedar bogs: Harold N. Peek Preserve, across the Maurice River (2100 South Second Street), and Buckshutem Wildlife Management Area, on NJ 49. Don't miss the 5-mile wetlands walk and museum at Bayshore Center at Bivalve. Drive to the virtually abandoned town of Sea Breeze, once a thriving resort (take County Route 601 and turn left when the road splits).

MORE INFORMATION

Open 6 A.M. to 7 P.M. (Gate is locked at closing time.) For information about a separate mountain biking trail, see nature.org/content/dam/tnc/nature/en/graphics/maps/bluffs -bike-trails.pdf.

39 GLADES WILDLIFE REFUGE: TAT STARR TRAIL AND BALD EAGLE TRAIL

This hike offers a chance to explore the diverse natural world of the riparian region, where salt water and fresh water meet.

Features 👥🐕💧

Location Newport, NJ

Rating Easy

Distance 3.9 miles round-trip

Elevation Gain 100 feet

Estimated Time 2 hours

Maps USGS Cedarville, USGS Dividing Creek; natlands.org/glades-wildlife-refuge; ExploreNLT app

GPS Coordinates Tat Starr Trail trailhead: 39° 15.896′ N, 75° 09.968′ W; Bald Eagle Trail trailhead: 39° 15.677′ N, 75° 07.550′ W

Contact Natural Lands, 1031 Palmers Mill Road, Media, PA 19063; 610-353-5587; natlands.org/glades-wildlife-refuge

DIRECTIONS

Tat Starr Trail: On NJ 55 South, take Exit 27 toward Millville. Merge onto NJ 47 South (North Second Street). After 2.5 miles, turn right onto County Route 555 (East Main Street). In 0.3 mile, turn left onto Cedar Street to follow County Route 555. Drive 5.6 miles and then turn left onto Newport–Center Grove Road. Drive 4.4 miles and, at the T intersection, turn right on Baptist Road. In a quarter-mile, turn left onto Fortescue Road. The trailhead is 2.4 miles farther. Roadside parking only has room for three to six cars.

Bald Eagle Trail: To get to the second trailhead from Tat Starr Trail, head north on Fortescue Road. In 2.1 miles, turn right onto Hall Street and then right onto Methodist Road. Drive 0.7 mile and turn right onto Main Street. Follow Main Street for 1.9 miles and turn right onto Turkey Point Road. After 1.6 miles, turn right at the stop sign to stay on Turkey Point Road. The trailhead is on the right, just after the curve, at 0.2 mile. Roadside parking only has room for three to four cars.

TRAIL DESCRIPTION

Along the southern coast of New Jersey, away from the crowds on the ocean shore, lies a beautiful area known as the Bayshore. Even among those who venture to the far corners of the state, it is a location rarely explored. This riparian region, a marshy land where fresh water and salt water join together in the salt marshes, hosts a smorgasbord of life: insects, birds, and maritime creatures. The vast natural resources—from salt hay to oysters—first drew Native Americans and then colonists to the region. It later became a place that helped reestablish the bald eagle in New Jersey and continues to serve as a buffet for the birds along the great migration route that comes up the East Coast.

Glades Wildlife Preserve (property of nonprofit Natural Lands) is one of several preserves along the Bayshore and features four hiking trails and several water trails. In this trip, you will travel the most popular routes: Tat Starr (2.4 miles) and Bald Eagle (1.5 miles) trails.

Glades Wildlife Preserve is a fantastic site to explore, but only if you are well prepared. Limited hunting is allowed here by permit except on Sundays, so be sure to wear blaze orange during hunting season or visit on a Sunday. From late spring to early fall, any day without a strong, consistent breeze will make you the prey of the most vicious of the Bayshore's wildlife—mosquitoes and biting flies—which can quickly ruin your outing. Ticks are here in abundance. Tat Starr Trail also goes out over tidal areas, so time your hike to avoid high tide, or you'll find your trek much shorter than you planned. Check the tides online for Dividing Creek, New Jersey, to get the tide schedule for the day you'd like to visit. Sturdy waterproof boots are a necessity, as these trails can be very wet.

Tat Starr Trail begins at a small pull-off by the side of the road, where a trailhead sign greets you. Walk around the car gate to begin your journey, following the green trail markers labeled "Trail" with arrows. Start on an old road, which rapidly narrows to a pathway. Admire the holly trees and keep an ear out for birds as you walk through this

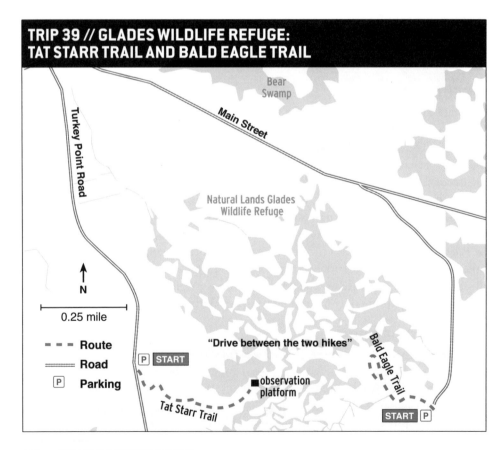

TRIP 39 // GLADES WILDLIFE REFUGE:
TAT STARR TRAIL AND BALD EAGLE TRAIL

shady, wooded area. Be aware of where you step, as puncheons are in several spots that can be wet and muddy. The trail dead-ends in a T at an old road labeled Russell Lane on maps, but no longer open to traffic. Here, turn left onto a much wider walking trail (0.5 mile). A sign to your left explains forest succession. The trail continues almost due east, and the trees quickly thin out to be replaced by tall phragmites, more commonly known as reeds, which dominate many marshy areas. These towering plants can reach 15 feet high and block out light, stopping other plants from growing in the vicinity.

You are now in the salt marshes, with a whole new range of birds and wildlife to look out for, including herons, snapping turtles, and muskrat (muskrat trapping has deep roots in the area, and a few local towns still host annual muskrat dinners). Ospreys nest here, and bald eagles can be seen on patrol at times. Step up onto the boardwalk for a better vantage point. Until the turnaround, the trail crosses a series of boardwalks and bridges that bring you up above most of the phragmites and help keep your feet dry. It's unlikely you'll be looking down much, as a mesmerizing landscape of water, mud, grass, and reeds stretches out to the horizon in nearly every direction. The scenery is broken in just a few places by small dead trees and tree stumps, which are promising spots to scan carefully for birds while providing a hint of otherworldliness to the marsh.

A little less than a mile brings you to a drop off the boardwalk, where the trail continues along a clearly flattened area of grass. No markers exist here, but the route is easy to follow and impossible to get lost on. If you failed to check the tidal charts, this is likely where your hike will end, as this part of the trail, always squishy, is often underwater. With some preparation (or luck), you can continue onward, deep in the salt marshes toward the observation tower, perhaps the most rewarding section of trail on the refuge. Climb the tower (1.2 miles) and enjoy the view across the salt marsh before retracing your steps back to the parking area.

A 10-minute drive from the parking area brings you to the other side of the salt marshes and the trailhead for Bald Eagle Trail. This is another popular route for birding, particularly if you are looking for bald eagles or other raptors of the bird variety (the trail will be little help with raptors of the dinosaur variety). Go past the gate and down the wide road that makes up this trail, a welcome change from the narrow paths at Tat Starr. Bald Eagle Trail quickly transitions to marshlands as you head into the now-familiar gauntlet of phragmites (0.2 mile). In fall, admire the red leaves on the maples that tower over the trail to the left. The right offers the more foreboding scenery of the salt marsh with dead trees sticking up.

The trail splits (0.5 mile) to make a small loop, the candy part of this lollipop route. Stay to the left to follow along a stockade of trees that separates this slightly elevated area from the marsh beyond. The trail circles a small pond in a "bowl" to your right, a great spot to see ducks and other swimming birds. The back end of the pond, the farthest reach of Bald Eagle Trail, offers a few more chances for views out deep into the marshes. Then complete the loop, bearing left to walk back toward the parking lot.

DID YOU KNOW?

In winter, frogs burrow into leaves and hibernate: their breathing and heartbeat stop, ice crystals form in their bodies, and they produce "antifreeze" to keep their cells from

A boardwalk leads out into the scenic salt marshes.

freezing. Frogs love the seasonal vernal pools at the refuge. These wetland areas are covered by water during winter and spring, but are dry in summer and fall. On this property, The Nature Conservancy has built "ditch plugs" in old agricultural ditches. Ditch plugs work similarly to plugs in bathtubs; they are used to slow the pools' drainage by trapping water in these ditches.

OTHER ACTIVITIES

Drive down to Turkey Point in the refuge to climb the bird-watching tower and to cross the footbridge for another look at the heart of the property. The two other refuge hiking trails, Warfle Farm Trail and Maple Street Trail, are along the road to Turkey Point. Visit 5-mile Shaws Mill Pond, where you can enjoy a tree frog symphony in June and look for eels in the pristine 28-acre pond (Railroad Road/Ackley Road over railroad tracks to intersection with Shaws Mill Road; park entrance beyond). Visit Egg Island Wildlife Management Area, near Fortescue (County Route 553, left on Maple Street).

MORE INFORMATION

Open sunrise to sunset. Trail maps are available at kiosks. The main information kiosk is at Turkey Point Road and Maple Street. Wear blaze orange during hunting season. From late spring through summer, avoid the trails on this trip or come very well protected against mosquitoes and biting flies.

40 MAURICE RIVER BICYCLE AND WALKING TRAIL

A paved path along the Maurice River beckons hikers with wetlands, the ruins of a hydroelectric plant, and maybe even some bald eagles.

Features

Location Millville, NJ

Rating Easy

Distance 3.2 miles round-trip

Elevation Gain 100 feet

Estimated Time 2 hours

Maps USGS Millville; cumauriceriver.org/wp-content/uploads/2021/03/MRT-Map-Only.pdf

GPS Coordinates 39° 23.597′ N, 075° 02.373′ W

Contact City of Millville Parks Department, 12 South High Street, Millville, NJ 08332; 856-825-7000; millvillenj.gov/129/Parks. Citizens United to Protect the Maurice River and Its Tributaries, Inc., P.O. Box 474, Millville, NJ 08332; 856-300-5331; cumauriceriver.org

DIRECTIONS

Driving: From NJ 55, take Exit 27 for Millville. Keep right and merge onto NJ 47/North Second Street. Follow this for 2.3 miles and then turn right onto Ware Avenue. Turn right after the first baseball field and then immediately turn left into the parking lot. Parking is available for about twenty cars. More parking is available on the opposite side of the river in a pair of small lots.

Public Transportation: Bus route 408 runs from Philadelphia to Millville. Exit the bus at NJ 47 and East Pine Street. Walk two blocks south to East Main Street and then two blocks west to the headquarters of Citizens United to Protect the Maurice River and Its Tributaries to get a trail map. Check njtransit.com for details.

TRAIL DESCRIPTION

Maurice River Bicycle and Walking Trail (MRBWT) is paved, flat, and short but offers a lot of variety in that brief distance. Begin by parking in the public lot in front of the baseball field. Take the sidewalk west, turning right at the corner of left field; 150 feet from the corner of the fence, turn left to cross Ware Avenue at the crosswalk. In front of you is the Maurice (pronounced "Morris") River, which you will follow upstream. Start the upstream walk now, heading north to reach Main Street. Here, turn right to recross Ware Avenue. The second building on your right is the headquarters of the

Citizens United to Protect the Maurice River and Its Tributaries (17 East Main Street). Stop in for a trail map during normal business hours Monday to Friday. The map is also available at the organization's website (cumauriceriver.org).

Backtracking across Ware Avenue, turn right to cross East Main Street and walk under the archway to enter Captain Joseph Buck Waterfront Park, named in honor of the founder of Millville, a veteran of the American Revolution. Continue to follow the river path until you reach a statue of the gentleman himself on your right. Just past this, a boardwalk leads to a beautiful arched bridge over the Maurice River (0.4 mile). Cross the bridge, stopping along the top of the arch to check for any birds in the area—a good habit for your entire walk along this trail.

At the end of the bridge, take the ramp down to the paved path and then continue upstream past the playground (any children or children-at-heart with you can stop on the way back). You are now, officially, on MRBWT. Keep alert for the bikes. The trail passes under a graffitied road bridge, after which you'll quite suddenly find yourself with the river on one side and wetlands on the other. This is the heart of the hike. Be sure to stop frequently to scan each side of the trail for a wide variety of birds, especially red-winged blackbirds and various wading birds. The "big one" that brings folks here can often be found along the riverbanks: the bald eagle. While bald eagles are no longer on the endangered species list, seeing one in the wild is still a thrilling experience.

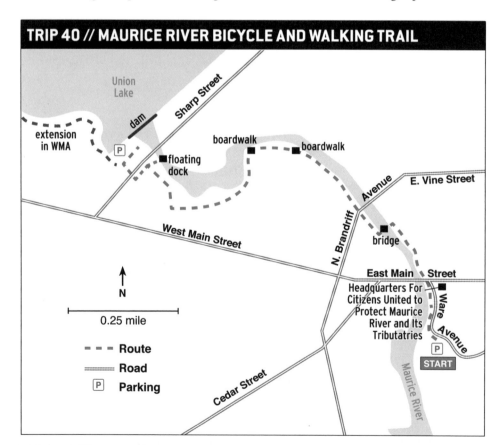

While keeping an eye out for an eagle, take a moment to notice the remains of several industrial buildings on the opposite bank, including the ruins of a hydroelectric plant. As you cross a footbridge, look for herons and egrets to your left. At 1.1 miles, MRBWT splits; stay right to stay on this hike. You'll lose your view of the river and be hemmed in by wetlands on each side while you traverse a series of short footbridges (keeping right once again at a second split).

At 1.4 miles, MRBWT emerges at Sharp Park, which houses a few baseball fields. Resist the urge to turn around; instead stay to the right side of the parking lot and pick up the paved path again that skirts the edge of it. Large, fenced-in stone ruins sit in the middle of the parking lot. As you near Sharp Street, turn right and follow the paved path down to the floating kayak launch docks, where you can walk out and admire the Maurice River from over the water. Backtracking to the front of the parking lot, listen for the rush of the water going over the dam at Union Lake, your next stop. Walk southeast along Sharp Street, crossing the entrance to Sharp Park and continuing on the sidewalk until you are opposite the fenced-in parking lot. Cross the street carefully here (no crosswalk) through the gate to enter Union Lake Wildlife Management Area (WMA). Head toward the noise for a chance to properly admire a human-made waterfall, the exit point for water from this massive 5,000-acre lake, popular with anglers and paddlers alike.

This 1.6-mile mark is the official turnaround point for the hike, but if you want to stretch your legs a bit more, look for a gap in the fence at the western corner of the parking lot. Go through and turn right to follow the outside of the fence. A few steps up an incline brings you to the miles of unmarked trails of Union Lake WMA. (Don't forget your blaze-orange clothing during hunting season). The trails downhill along the

The river and wetlands areas along this trail are a popular spot to look for bald eagles.

lakefront are the best part of this wild maze of pathways. If ending at the turnaround, backtrack across Sharp Street and reenter MRBWT past the baseball field. Traverse the little bridges and pass the wetlands, go under the road bridge, recross the arch bridge, and make your way back to the parking area.

DID YOU KNOW?

Glassblowing has been an important industry in New Jersey since before there was a United States of America. The first successful glassblowing enterprise was set up in Millville around 1739 by Casper Wistar, who made glass bottles, window glass, and even glass globes for some of Ben Franklin's experiments. Today, Wheaton Arts and Cultural Center (1000 Village Drive) keeps this tradition alive, allowing folks to watch glassblowing, see historical and artistic blown glass, and even learn how to blow glass themselves.

OTHER ACTIVITIES

The beautiful art deco Landis Theater in nearby Vineland (830 East Landis Avenue) offers concerts and other entertainment. Vineland also features the Palace of Depression (265 South Mill Road). This castle was built out of junk during the Great Depression (hence, Palace of Depression) by George Daynor, who operated it for years as a tourist attraction. It fell into disrepair and was knocked down in the 1960s, shortly after Daynor's death. But in the mid-1990s, a man named Kevin Kirchner decided to rebuild the Palace, a labor of love that took him decades to bring to fruition. Kirchner died suddenly in 2021, but his son Kristian has taken up the mantle and plans to reopen the Palace for tours (the-palace-of-depression.business.site).

MORE INFORMATION

Citizens United to Protect the Maurice River and Its Tributaries offers guided bird-watching walks along MRBWT. A map and a trail guide are available at the organization's office or at cumauriceriver.org/conservation-wildlife/trails/maurice-river-bicycle-walking-trail.

The Delaware River region represents a balanced mix of rural and urban, with cities, forests, wooded stretches, and a plenitude of waterways—the queen of which is the Delaware River.

The Delaware forms the entire boundary between New Jersey and Pennsylvania, and parts of the river are designated a Wild and Scenic River by Congress. The Delaware River is the longest free-flowing river in the eastern United States, running 330 miles from New York through Pennsylvania, New Jersey, and Delaware on its way to the Atlantic Ocean. The Delaware River flows past forests, farmlands, villages, and cities, and it links some of the most densely populated sections of the United States.

Most counties in the Delaware River region are also linked by a well-developed transportation system, NJ Transit, enabling travel and commuting to work in nearby Philadelphia. You'll find overlapping loyalties to sports teams here, as well as to recreational and historical subjects. For instance, the site where General George Washington and his troops crossed the Delaware River on December 25, 1776, lies in both New Jersey and Pennsylvania (see Trip 45). The canal that opened up this area to trade in the 1800s runs along both sides of the Delaware River. On the New Jersey (eastern) side, it stretches 70-plus miles, from Milford to New Brunswick, and is called the Delaware and Raritan Canal (see "From Mules to Multiuse: Today's Delaware and Raritan Canal State Park" on page 40). On the Pennsylvania (western) side, it runs 60 miles, from Easton to Bristol, and is called the Delaware and Lehigh Canal.

This region is also the home of Princeton University, Rowan University, and New Jersey's state capital of Trenton.

Physiographically speaking, the Delaware River region falls into the Inner and Outer Coastal plains. A narrow strip on the western side of the region lies in the Inner Coastal Plain. The Inner Coastal Plain is relatively flat, with many meandering rivers. Pleasantly wooded, the northern part has forests of mixed oak, upland pine, beech-oak, and red maple–sweet gum. The southern part segues to Virginia pine, white cedar swamps, hardwood swamps, and marshes. The Inner Coastal Plain occupies about 14 percent of the area of New Jersey and contains about 14 percent of the state's population.

The narrow strip in the Inner Coastal Plain is separated from the Outer Coastal Plain by a low ridge with bumpy hills, called "cuestas." The Outer Coastal Plain occupies the remaining portion of the Delaware River region and is also relatively flat. The forest communities consist of southern mixed oak, upland pine and oak, red maple–sweet gum, and Virginia pine. Nearer the coasts and in the Pinelands, the mix shifts to coastal white cedar swamps, pitch-pine lowland forests, hardwood swamps, Pine Barrens shrub swamps, and marshes.

The Pinelands creep into the eastern sections of Gloucester, Camden, and Burlington counties. In fact, Black Run Preserve (Trip 47) in Burlington County calls itself "the Gateway to the Pinelands."

Each county in the Delaware River region has a wealth of waterways beyond the Delaware River. Camden County has the urban Cooper River (Trip 48). The more remote Salem County boasts Alloway Creek; the Cohansey, Salem, and Maurice rivers; and Parvin Lake (see Trip 46). Bustling Burlington County includes the Mullica River (see Trip 42), Rancocas Creek, and Assiscunk Creek. Mercer County, the site of Princeton University, benefits from Assunpink Creek and Crosswicks Creek. Raccoon Creek lies in Gloucester County. Gloucester and Salem counties share Oldman's Creek. The waterways spill over into a cooling network of creeks and streams, nestled deep in the woods.

Dozens and dozens of national parks, state parks, state forests, and recreation areas lie in the five counties that make up the Delaware River region. Spring brings showy displays of wildflowers and blooming shrubs and trees. Raspberries, blackberries, and blueberries ripen in summer. Fall shines with colored leaves against the October sky, and migratory songbirds, swans, and ducks abound. In winter, trails beg to be skied and bare branches expose striking vistas. Forests hide beavers, deer, groundhogs, foxes, raccoons, and more.

The Delaware River region has something for everyone, from secluded rambles to urban adventures.

41 WENONAH WOODS

More than 6 miles of trails ring this small town, where you'll cross dozens of footbridges while looking out for beavers, a Japanese teahouse, and old railroad ruins.

Features 👨‍🦯 🐕 ♿ 💧 🎣

Location Wenonah, NJ

Rating Easy

Distance 5.7-mile loop

Elevation Gain 350 feet

Estimated Time 3–4 hours

Maps USGS Woodbury; wenonahenvironmentalcommission.org/trail_system.htm

GPS Coordinates 39° 47.150′ N, 75° 08.715′ W

Contact Wenonah Environmental Commission, 1 South West Avenue, P.O. Box 66, Wenonah, NJ 08090; 856-468-5228; wenonahenvironmentalcommission.org

DIRECTIONS

Take NJ 55 to Exit 56B for Woodbury/Westville, merging onto Delsea Drive/NJ 47 North. Immediately get over to the left lane and turn left at the light onto Bankbridge Road. Follow Bankbridge Road for 1.5 miles until it ends at a light. Turn right onto Glassboro Road and take the first left onto East Mantua Avenue. In 0.2 mile, turn left onto South Princeton Avenue. In 0.4 mile, turn left onto East Pine Street. Streetside parking for only six to eight cars is available between the turn and the trailhead, but nearby roads provide plenty of streetside parking.

TRAIL DESCRIPTION

At first glance, Wenonah seems like a pretty typical small South Jersey town in the Philadelphia metro area. It's a little more than 1 square mile with about 2,300 people and a lot of beautiful old homes. But thanks to some farsighted locals half a century ago and the dedicated work of the Wenonah Environmental Commission, magic lurks in these woods. A little more than 20 percent of the town has been set aside forever as public land, and more than 6 miles of trails wind through that "ring of green," crossing dozens of footbridges. The trails are not marked with colored blazes, but posts at each major intersection label changes in trail names and exits.

Park your car and walk to the end of East Pine Street and the trailhead for George Eldridge Trail. You won't take that trail quite yet; instead, leave the pavement, walking straight on the road along the post fence. Pass a house and then go through a gap in the fence to enter the trail system on the right onto Comey's Lake Trail, which explores the old Oakwood Estate. Turn left as the trail heads north along the lake (it should be to your right), going up and down in stretches. The trail turns left, goes uphill a few steps, and immediately turns right again. It crosses a bridge over Camel's Back Run. At the intersection, bear left to check out the rebuilt Japanese Tea House, originally constructed by Robert Comey as a centerpiece of his estate. Turning back toward the trail, you can see the remains of a small amphitheater. Return to the intersection and take the trail south to follow the other shore of the lake, stopping at the fishing dock to admire the water, which once held a floating carousel.

Retrace your steps north for about 40 feet; then turn right to head east on George Eldridge Trail. Traverse an expansive boardwalk that was built in response to some very

TRIP 41 // WENONAH WOODS

busy beavers that flooded this area. Pass the two intersections of Monongahela Loop (it is often too muddy to hike) and Indian Trail (leads to a short road walk to Tall Pines Preserve, if you'd like to lengthen your hike), and turn left at 0.8 mile on Monongahela Brook Trail toward Marion Avenue. This trail heads west, crossing Marion Avenue. You'll then carefully cross a long, newly rebuilt footbridge over a swamp. Keep an eye out here for birds that enjoy these surroundings, such as ducks and red-winged blackbirds.

At 1.3 miles, George Eldridge Trail passes an old bridge abutment and the intersection for short Garden Trail (which features a Victorian frog pond uncovered during trail construction) before turning sharply south onto Mantua Creek Trail to parallel the railroad tracks. The trail curves under an impressive railroad bridge (a popular place for fishing) and then heads back north along the other side of the tracks. Keep a sharp eye out for a left turn to stay on Mantua Creek Trail shortly before it reaches South West Avenue (a connector trail continues straight to that road).

Mantua Creek Trail suddenly changes from shady to sunny. From the size and number of the downed trees, you can imagine how cool and shadowed this stretch of trail used to be. That all changed in September 2021 when a rare EF3 tornado ripped through Gloucester County, destroying the forest here (the Enhanced Fujita [EF] Scale measures the strength of tornadoes from 0 to 5). Back in the shade, 2.1 miles brings you to Clay Hill, where you climb an old railroad embankment.

Mantua Creek Trail ends at West Mantua Avenue. Turn right and proceed east along the road for 200 feet. Cross Mantua Avenue and walk down the paved road that runs past the baseball field. After passing the pump house and kayak launch, turn right onto Breakback Run Trail. This takes you on a bumpy walk for a half-mile along a creek—watch your footing when the trail drops down!

At 3.3 miles, Breakback Run Trail dead-ends at Maple Street. Cross the street and turn left, soon traversing the bridge over Wenonah Lake. Just after the bridge, turn right onto Wenonah Lake Trail. The trail loops around the lake (open for swimming in summer; check wenonahlakeassociation.com for details), with the back end sometimes very soggy depending on the weather and the activity level of the beavers. As Breakback Run Trail approaches the parking lot, head onto Frank Eggert Trail, which loops for a half-mile past another pretty creek and back around to this intersection.

Returning to the trail intersection, head south and arrive at a parking lot at 4.4 miles. Walk through town back to your car. Go down Jefferson Street and turn left onto Mantua Avenue. Admire the many Victorian houses in the center of town. Many sport a sign from the local historical society showing the year they were built. After crossing the railroad tracks, follow the paved walkway diagonally through Wenonah Park, taking care to watch out for a lion (his name is Ramsey). Proceed south along South Clinton Avenue until it reaches Pine Street. Turn left and arrive at your car.

DID YOU KNOW?

When Robert Comey built the original Japanese Tea House, the lake was slightly larger, so rowboats and canoes could dock at the base of the structure. Comey would throw parties featuring an orchestra playing from the teahouse, which was decorated with

Damage along Mantua Creek Trail from a 2021 EF3 tornado.

hundreds of Japanese lanterns. At other times, entertainment might include private performances by singer Enrico Caruso or comedian Groucho Marx, friends of Comey.

OTHER ACTIVITIES

The Wenonah Environmental Commission and the Gloucester County Nature Club offer many activities throughout the year, including an annual moonlight hike, a Fourth of July hike, a Mad Hatter's Tree Party, and an annual bird count. Tall Pine State Preserve, one of the newest state parks in New Jersey, is a few minutes away and explores the rebounding natural world on a former golf course that was once owned by Philadelphia Eagles football legend Ron Jaworski.

MORE INFORMATION

Open dawn to dusk. Maps can be obtained for a few dollars at the Wenonah Borough Hall during business hours. Fishing is allowed in Mantua Creek along Mantua Creek Trail at the southern portions of the trail system.

MULLICA RIVER TRAIL:
ATSION TO QUAKER BRIDGE

Enjoy a lengthy, leg-stretching hike along the Mullica River in the flat, preternaturally beautiful, and quiet Pine Barrens of Wharton State Forest.

Features

Location Shamong, NJ

Rating Moderate to Strenuous

Distance 9.9-mile loop

Elevation Gain 320 feet

Estimated Time 4.5 hours

Maps USGS Indian Mills; nj.gov/dep/parksandforests/maps/wharton-area.pdf

GPS Coordinates 39° 44.522' N, 74° 43.539' W

Contact Wharton State Forest, Atsion Office, 744 US 206, Shamong, NJ 08088; 609-268-0444; state.nj.us/dep/parksandforests/parks/wharton.html

DIRECTIONS

Take I-295 South to US 130 via Exit 57B-A toward Bordentown/Burlington. In 0.13 mile, merge onto US 130 North via Exit 57A on the left toward Bordentown. In 1.0 mile, turn right onto Farnsworth Avenue (County Route 545). Follow this for 0.25 mile and then turn right onto US 206 South. Go 17.5 miles, then take the second exit of the roundabout to stay on US 206 South. In 11.0 miles, turn left at a big brown sign that reads "Wharton State Forest, Atsion Office." (A Global Positioning System [GPS] device will say Vincentown.) A dirt parking area has room for at least 50 cars.

TRAIL DESCRIPTION

Mullica River Trail is in the heart of the Pinelands in 115,000-acre Wharton State Forest, one of four state forests in the Pinelands National Reserve (see "Get Away from the Crowds in the Pine Barrens and the Pinelands" on page 143). The trail encompasses key aspects of the Pinelands: a river, cedar swamps, pine trees, sand roads, and flat paths. You'll probably have the path mostly to yourself, with much to see and hear. In spring, tree frogs sing, and mountain laurel, pyxie, and turkey beard bloom. In early summer, note the rare bog asphodel, a lily with small bright yellow flowers that's found only in the Pine Barrens. Spot red-bellied turtles in the water. Watch for turkeys and pygmy pines—mature pygmy pines are only 4 to 10 feet high. (*Note*: This area is extremely buggy from May to October.)

You'll take yellow-blazed Mullica River Trail, purple-blazed Beaver Pond–Quaker Bridge Trail, and green-blazed Wilderness Camps Connector Trail in a lollipop and then retrace your steps. Some of the turns are tricky because of fire ditches, hunters' roads, and false trails made by ATVs, so be alert. If you don't see a blaze for a while, backtrack. You are walking into the sun, so use sun protection.

Yellow-blazed Mullica River Trail begins at the trail sign in front of the ranger station, which was the Atsion General Store until World War II, when gasoline scarcity forced it to close. Pick up a map at the trail sign. Turn left on the trail and walk by restored Atsion Mansion and the ruins of the concrete Wharton barn and a chicken coop on the left. At a yellow-blazed metal post on your right, you can go left to visit the composting outhouse. If nature does not call, proceed on the dirt road, past the gun club on the right and the cemetery and historical, still functioning, white church on the left. The graves date back to the late 1800s.

Follow the yellow blazes on short metal posts and turn left into the woods at a double yellow blaze. The path is soft with pine straw. In 0.7 mile, cross yellow-blazed railroad tracks and a wide dirt path, then head toward the "9 miles to Batsto" sign. Continue on the moss-lined path through a pine forest. Mountain laurels hug the edges. At the Y

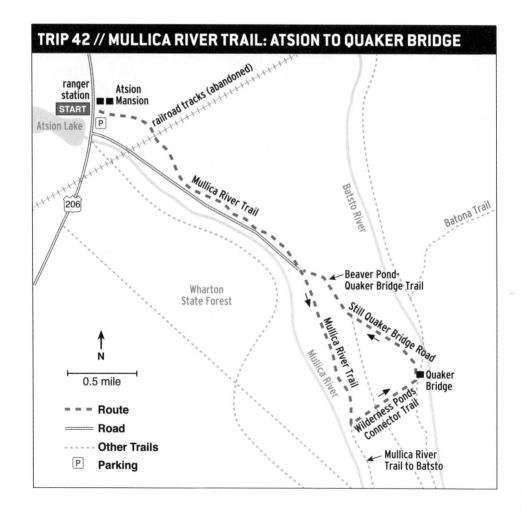

TRIP 42 // MULLICA RIVER TRAIL: ATSION TO QUAKER BRIDGE

intersection, go right to follow the yellow blazes. At the four-way intersection, go right again, still following yellow blazes. (*Caution*: Do not go straight, which will take you into the woods.) At the next four-way intersection, cross the road to follow the yellow-blazed path; soon after, cross another dirt road and go into the woods. At the "8.5 miles to Batsto" sign, turn right. Enjoy the calm pines.

(*Note*: A confusing welter of hunting and ATV roads is coming, so read and then hike carefully.) At a T intersection with double yellow blazes, curve right for a few steps on the dirt road and then go straight, keeping the water and sand pit to your right. A Y intersection appears immediately; take the right fork toward the yellow-blazed tree, away from the sand pit. Go right at the next fork; the yellow blaze crops up soon. (If you find yourself at the dirt road for cars, back up and find the yellow blaze.)

The sandy path bumps pleasantly up and down. Cross a dirt road and enter the woods at the yellow blaze. Walk through striking fire-damaged pines. A private property sign appears on the left. Soon you reach the "8 miles to Batsto" sign. A very narrow path meanders through the woods, with a spookily picturesque marsh-pond-bog to the left (2.2 miles). The path comes to a T intersection at a dirt road; go left at double-yellow blazes onto the road, and then cross a small bridge. Right after the bridge is a double yellow blaze on a tree. A few yards past that, a yellow blaze on a metal post leads you into the woods to the right.

A stream on the right follows this narrow path. Pass the "7.5 miles to Batsto" sign. In December, bare, white trees are stark against the blue sky. Reach a huge, sandy circle with many spokes. Stay straight, keeping the water on your right. A wide path brings yellow blazes and tall shrubs on the right. At another big intersection with many paths, go straight, toward the yellow blaze. (Do not take side paths into the forest.) The Mullica River curves prettily through the trees to your right, a picture postcard for the Pine Barrens. You might see a red fox.

At the Y intersection (double yellow blazes), turn left, away from the river. In a few hundred yards, turn right at the T intersection toward a yellow blaze that leads you down a sandy road. At the next Y intersection, go right and again admire the lovely river. Two big wooden signs pop up: "Beaver Pond–Quaker Bridge Trail" and "Mullica River Trail" (3.0 miles). Turn left here (away from the river) to get on purple-blazed Beaver Pond–Quaker Bridge Trail, heading toward Batona Trail and Lower Forge Camp.

Beaver Pond–Quaker Bridge Trail is a pleasant and very meditative little path through the woods. Keep straight on the purple blazes at all times. Traverse several fire ditches (trenches dug to stop or slow wildfires or brushfires, which can devastate, and have devastated, the Pine Barrens. Cross a one-lane dirt road and go into the woods. Keep an eye out for the double green blazes of Wilderness Camps Connector Trail on the right; they appear within sight of a big open area with sand roads (4.6 miles). (If you reach the open area, backtrack.) Turn right at the green blazes onto a narrow woods path. Lichens and moss continue to decorate the green-blazed trail. Cross a fire ditch and enter a burned area with low shrubs. Cross four more fire ditches. Two big wooden trail signs appear at a three-way intersection; turn right to follow yellow-blazed Mullica River Trail (5.4 miles). One of the other paths connects to Batona Trail (see Trip 49). The third route leads to Batsto Village, a 5-mile one-way journey.

Here, Mullica River Trail is an attractive, moss-lined woods route, as narrow as a balance beam, and deliciously crowded by pines. Note the reindeer moss. Signs for Atsion appear every 0.5 mile. After the sixth fire ditch, the trail intersects with a big sandy road, with the river gleaming ahead. Turn right toward the two big signs for Mullica River Trail and Beaver Pond–Quaker Bridge Trail, which you passed earlier, and go back the way you came. It's a bit tough to follow the signs, but just keep watch for the yellow blazes. At the circle with the trail spokes, take the far-left spoke, blazed yellow. At the sand pit and water, go straight. Watch for a yellow blaze on the left as the road curves right; take that left path into the woods and keep following yellow blazes to the parking lot.

DID YOU KNOW?

On the other side of US 206 lies 100-acre Atsion Lake, a recreation facility with swimming, camping, cabins, and more. Nature trails are wheelchair accessible. Per-car fees of $5 to $20 apply; nj.gov/dep/parksandforests/parks/atsionrecreationarea.html. Nearby Atsion Mansion, built in 1826 as a summer home for the ironmaster Samuel Richards, is open for tours; call 609-268-0444 for information.

OTHER ACTIVITIES

Hike Piper's Corner Preserve, a transitional forest between hardwoods and the Pine Barrens; part of the Rancocas Conservancy. Visit resident critters at Woodford Cedar Run Wildlife Refuge, an environmental education center and rehab facility for injured wildlife. (The refuge is at 4 Sawmill Road in Medford. Call 856-983-3329 for more

Ghostly bare branches frame a lake in the Pine Barrens in late afternoon.

information.) Many eateries line US 206 North, and a winery is on US 206 South. Enjoy farmers markets in season and wholesale nurseries.

MORE INFORMATION

Open dawn to dusk. This hike is along one of many trails in Wharton State Forest. Five are designated specifically for mountain bike use: nj.gov/dep/parksandforests/trailguides /docs/Wharton-Trails.pdf.

43 PRINCETON BATTLEFIELD STATE PARK AND INSTITUTE WOODS

A shady hike through a birding oasis is paired with a walk across a historic American Revolution battlefield.

Features 👥 🐕

Location Princeton, NJ

Rating Easy

Distance 4.2-mile loop

Elevation Gain 75 feet

Estimated Time 2.5 hours

Maps USGS Princeton; nj.gov/dep/parksandforests/maps/princetonbattlefield-area.pdf; njtrails.org/wp-content/uploads/2013/04/InstituteWoods4.pdf

GPS Coordinates 40° 19.765′ N, W 74° 40.580′ W

Contact Princeton Battlefield State Park, 500 Mercer Road, Princeton, NJ 08540; 609-921-0074; nj.gov/dep/parksandforests/parks/princetonbattlefieldstatepark.html. Institute Woods, c/o Outdoor Action Program, 350 Alexander Street, Princeton University, Princeton, NJ 08544; 609-258-6230; outdooraction.princeton.edu /places/institute-woods

DIRECTIONS
From I-295, take Exit 68A and merge onto Princeton Pike. After 3.4 miles, turn right onto the driveway for Princeton Battlefield State Park. The parking lot has room for about eighteen cars. (*Note*: No public parking is allowed at the Institute for Advanced Study, owner of Institute Woods.)

TRAIL DESCRIPTION
More than 240 years ago, the ground here became enshrined in history when it saw the last action of the "Ten Crucial Days" of the American Revolution that began with George Washington and his troops crossing the Delaware River on December 25 (see Trip 45). The Battle of Princeton was the third in a trio of battles that made the colonists believe they could win the war against the British. Today, Institute Woods is known not only for its history but also for the remarkable variety of birds that can be found here, especially during migration season. This hike takes you to a historic home (now the park office) that stood during the Battle of Princeton, a historical Quaker meetinghouse and cemetery where a signer of the Declaration of Independence is buried, and down Pipeline Trail, Far Trail, and River's Edge Trail to a swinging bridge. It then brings you back to the battlefield via Near Trail, Marsh Trail, Founders' Walk, and Trolley Track Trail

before making a loop around the site. Trail blazes are sporadic to nonexistent, so a trail app for your phone is a helpful tool to keep track of where you are.

After parking near Thomas Clarke Farm, head up toward the old farmhouse, which served as a hospital during the Battle of Princeton and is preserved as Clarke House today. If it's open, stop in for an overview of the battle. After your stop, backtrack west of the farmhouse and look for a low stone post in the ground, which points you down a grassy trail west-southwest toward the meetinghouse. Cross two trails before reaching the parking lot of the Stony Brook Meeting House, built in 1723. The cemetery across the path contains the unmarked grave of Richard Stockton, a signer of the Declaration of Independence.

The small path in front of the meetinghouse takes you back to the trail system. Turn right onto Pipeline Trail and at 0.4 mile enter Institute Woods, where most of this hike takes place. These 589 acres of woods, permanently preserved in 1997, feature a wide array of plants, including some impressive trees. While hiking, keep an eye out for beech, tulip, hickory, and birch, as well as oak and maple.

Quite a grid of trails exists back here, but stay right at the first intersection, go left when the trail splits, and then walk past three other trail intersections, staying on

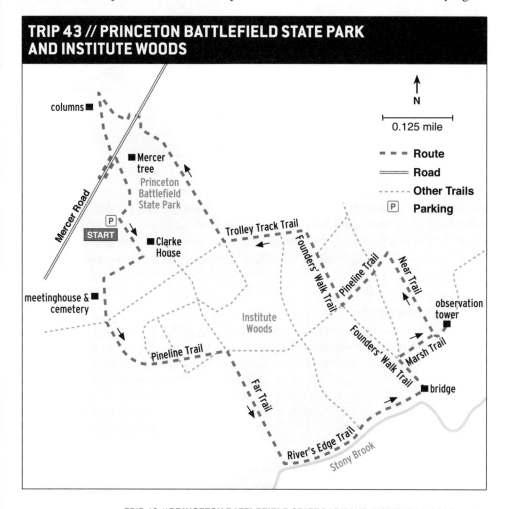

TRIP 43 // PRINCETON BATTLEFIELD STATE PARK AND INSTITUTE WOODS

N

0.125 mile

- - - Route
=== Road
----- Other Trails
P Parking

columns ■

■ Mercer tree
Princeton Battlefield State Park

Mercer Road

P
START

■ Clarke House

Trolley Track Trail

Founders' Walk Trail

Pineline Trail

Near Trail

observation tower

meetinghouse & ■ cemetery

Institute Woods

Pineline Trail

Founders' Walk Trail

Marsh Trail

Far Trail

■ bridge

River's Edge Trail

Stony Brook

A swinging bridge crosses Stony Brook by the intersection of River's Edge Trail and Founders' Walk Trail.

Pipeline Trail the entire time. Pass a large field on your right. Just after the field, but not along the edge of it, turn right onto Far Trail, 0.9 mile into the hike.

This trail can be overgrown in summer (beware of ticks!), with some wet spots at other times of the year, so hike carefully. Keep an eye out on the left for tulip, hickory, and maple trees. Far Trail eventually brings you all the way back to Stony Brook. Here, take the imaginatively named River's Edge Trail east. The river gurgles away on your right while you pass Middle Trail and some sweet gum trees with their distinctive, spiky "gumballs" that carry the tree's seeds. Sweet gums, the bane of people with non-driving lawnmowers, are an important habitat for many kinds of butterflies and moths, as well as—surprisingly—a popular food source for many species of birds.

Arrive at the junction of Founders' Walk. Turn right and cross Stony Brook on the wonderful little swinging suspension bridge. A small path on the other side leads 0.1 mile for a view of the Delaware and Raritan Canal, but you might opt to sit on the steps here at the bridge and take a break or eat a snack. Younger hikers (and young-at-heart hikers) might want to cross and recross the bridge a few times before continuing.

Heading back to the intersection before the bridge, hike northwest a short distance on Founders' Walk before turning right at the blue arrow blaze onto Marsh Trail. Step over a wooden footbridge that's doing a very poor job of being a bridge anymore and arrive at wider Near Trail. Turn right and quickly find yourself at a bird observation deck overlooking a swamp in the Charles Rogers Wildlife Refuge Area. This is a great spot to look for wetlands-loving birds, including red-winged blackbirds.

Descend from the observation deck and continue on Near Trail, past the point where it intersects with blue-blazed Marsh Trail. In the warm months, you might find this tread-way blanketed in invasive Japanese stiltgrass, which likes disturbed areas and crowds out native species. At 2.4 miles, arrive at the junction of Pipeline Trail. Turn left and walk on this much clearer trail, passing three trail junctions before turning right on wide Founders' Walk. Proceed to the end of this trail, where you'll find a rock monument and a bench to sit on with a view of the Institute for Advanced Study buildings at Princeton University.

After your break, head west on Trolley Track Trail, which marks the right of way of a trolley line that operated between the cities of Trenton and Princeton. At 3.0 miles, turn right to go north. Leave both the cool of the woods and the Institute Woods property, reentering the open fields of Princeton Battlefield State Park.

Hike past still-active farming fields (resist picking from the rows of corn) and arrive at paved Mercer Road. After crossing the road (use the crosswalk), look for columns in the distance to your northwest. Leave the trail and walk across the lawn toward them. Behind the columns is a mass grave of American and British officers who died here in the Battle of Princeton. The pillars, left as a monument to those who fought, were originally from a mansion in Philadelphia and were brought here in 1900 to become part of another mansion, which has since been demolished—aside from the facade.

Cut back across the lawn to the paved trail along the road. Follow the trail to the cross-walk over Mercer Road and then head northeast toward the fenced-in tree. This is a descendent of the Mercer Oak, which was where General Hugh Mercer was shot during the battle. Mercer County, where Princeton is located, is named in his honor. Finally, cut across the field to the parking area near the Clarke farmhouse where this hike started.

DID YOU KNOW?

While battles in Massachusetts (Lexington, Concord, Bunker Hill), New York (Saratoga), Pennsylvania (Germantown), and Virginia (Yorktown) are better known, New Jersey saw more fighting during the American Revolution than any other colony, including here at Princeton, two battles at Trenton, the Battle of Monmouth, and scores of smaller skirmishes. For this reason, some historians refer to the state as "the Crossroads of the Revolution."

OTHER ACTIVITIES

Visit Princeton University's Nassau Hall, which dates to 1756, and walk the historic campus. Princeton Record Exchange, one of the largest and best-stocked music stores in the state, is a mecca for music lovers. Explore Princeton Cemetery, which includes many notable burials, including Grover Cleveland (the 22nd and 24th U.S. president); Aaron Burr (Thomas Jefferson's vice president, who famously shot Alexander Hamilton); John Witherspoon, a signer of the Declaration of Independence; and the renowned American theologian Jonathan Edwards. Stop by Morven Museum & Garden, the former home of Richard Stockton—another signer of the Declaration of Independence—and the site of New Jersey's governor's mansion from 1944 to 1981.

MORE INFORMATION

No admission fee. Both parks are open dawn to dusk. Clarke House has limited hours.

44 LAURIE CHAUNCEY TRAIL

This hidden haven—deceivingly placed on the perimeter of a corporate park in Princeton—showcases a creek, three-pony truss bridge, rock outcroppings, and an oasis of green.

Features

Location Princeton, NJ

Rating Easy

Distance 2.7-mile loop

Elevation Gain 200 feet

Estimated Time 1.5 hours

Maps USGS Princeton; njtrails.org/wp-content/uploads/2013/06/LaurieChaunceyETS2.pdf

GPS Coordinates 40° 21.085′ N, 74° 42.565′ W

Contact ETS Corporate Headquarters, 660 Rosedale Road, Princeton, NJ 08541; 609-921-9000. Trail information: njtrails.org/trail/laurie-chauncey-trail-at-ets

DIRECTIONS

On I-95 North, take US 206 North via Exit 7B toward Lawrenceville/Princeton. Go 4.0 miles and turn left onto Province Line Road. Travel to the concrete barrier at the end of the road (about 2 miles) and park along the shoulder, which has room for about five or six cars.

TRAIL DESCRIPTION

This hike is unusual because it's part of the lunchtime strolling grounds of the Educational Testing Service (ETS), and, as such, is not known by many hikers. ETS is the organization that develops and scores academic tests: SAT, GRE, PSAT, and more. (Say a friendly hello to those who walk sporting ETS name badges.) The trail winds through an abundance of red maples, ashes, and tulip poplars, and partially follows Stony Brook and some impressive granite outcroppings. This trip includes an ecotone (watch for the signs), a transition area between two different ecological communities. Animals like ecotones because of easy access to multiple habitats and food sources. Look for deer; foxes and raccoons come out at dusk.

Spring brings fairy-tale greenery and shade-loving wildflowers. Pick raspberries in summer. Golden leaves float in Stony Brook in fall. Winter brings a beauty of its own, but the rocks and leaves can be a bit slippery. A bonus in any season is the rare three-pony truss bridge at the end of the hike. (A pony truss bridge allows traffic through the truss, but the top of the bridge is not joined together with cross braces, so tall vehicles can pass easily. Most pony truss bridges have only one span, but a three-pony has three spans, rendering it longer than a one-span.)

Park along the road near the concrete barrier, which permanently closes the other side of the road to traffic (you'll hike it later).

Walk south, away from the barrier, about 275 feet, to a sign for Laurie Chauncey Trail on the right. Enter the woods and go straight at the next trail marker. The dirt path slopes down gently to a bridge on your left. Don't take the bridge; go straight instead, and then follow the unblazed trail as it curves to the right.

A stream is on your left as the path continues down a gentle slope; be careful on the rocks. Cross a bridge with Stony Brook on your right. Ignore steps to the left—they lead up to the ETS building. The creek is beautiful, and you can linger here next to the impressive rocks that appear on your left. Soon after this, watch for a little path on the right where you can walk out onto the rocks in the water, large enough to perch on

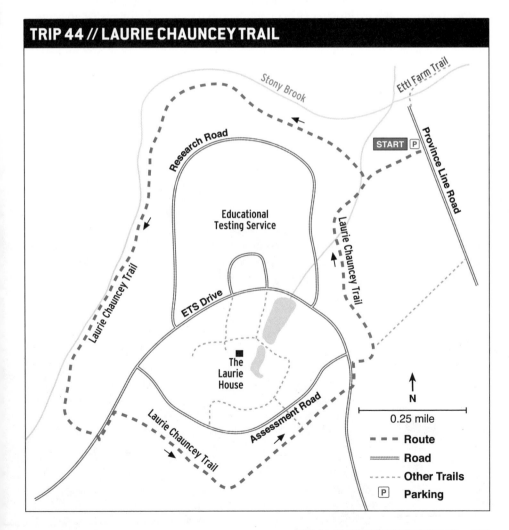

TRIP 44 // LAURIE CHAUNCEY TRAIL

without getting wet, and bask in the sun as it plays on branches of overhanging trees. At the junction (0.2 mile), go right, following the flat, grassy path along the creek. A road is on your left. Soon two more sets of steps to the ETS building appear on the left; ignore them. Maneuver a stream crossing on stepping-stones, and then traverse three bridges on this pretty, winding, narrow dirt path.

Cross another bridge at a tree with carvings—do not take the path to the left. Here, Laurie Chauncey Trail is gorgeous, grassy, and green as it intersects with a series of jogging trails. At a four-way intersection, with a power line above, go straight at the trail marker to stay on the route. Jogging trail 9 is to your right. Walk through a tunnel of bushes, and at the next trail marker, go left onto paved ETS Drive (jogging trail 20 is to your right). Cross the road (1.4 miles). In 100 yards, a trail marker leads you right into the woods on a grassy path that turns into a wide dirt one. At the trail junction, go straight, and then follow the wide dirt path as it bends to the left onto a grassy boulevard. At the four-way intersection, go straight—jogging trail 2 is to your right. At the three-way intersection (jogging trail 3 to your right), go straight and onto an open path that leads to the ETS parking lot (1.7 miles). Read the sign explaining what an ecotone is, and then see a real ecotone. Note the mowed swatch of grass (actually a pipeline right of way) that neatly divides the woods from a meadow filled with tall mountain mint: a prime example of a transitional area between two communities of plants and animals—and improbably located at the edge of a parking lot.

Walk across the ETS campus to get onto the trail again (don't worry; it's allowed). Go straight toward the flagpole. When you reach the road (ETS Drive), cross it (2.0 miles). Turn left to walk along the shoulder of the road and soon come to a marker for Laurie

The trail winds along Stony Brook, through verdant forest.

Chauncey Trail where Assessment Road and ETS Drive meet (2.1 miles). Turn right onto the trail, which is now a wide, mowed grassy path with a sign for Laurie Chauncey Trail. A gorgeous field is to the right. At the next trail marker, turn left into the shady woods and cross a miniature bridge. At the Y intersection, go straight onto a pebble-and-dirt path with a ditch on the left. Cross two more bridges and walk slightly down-hill into an area lush with skunk cabbage. At the next Y intersection, turn right, still slightly downhill, and cross two more bridges, before going uphill and down on a nar-row dirt path. A building appears to the left through the trees. Cross one final bridge, and at the T intersection, turn right at the trail sign. Go uphill and then turn right at the next trail sign (2.5 miles) to return to Province Line Road.

Bonus: Put your pack in the car. Walk past the concrete barrier and go about 0.8 mile down the closed paved road. Feel free to walk on the yellow line, as this road is perma-nently closed to traffic. You'll soon come to the three-pony truss bridge over Stony Brook. The road continues on the other side of the bridge. If you have time, before the bridge, watch for a path to the right marked "Stony Brook Trail"—a pleasant way to extend your hike. (*Note*: On the map, it's labeled Ettl Farm Trail.)

DID YOU KNOW?

You can buy a local guide to sixteen of the best trails through preserved open spaces in Princeton: *Walk the Trails In and Around Princeton*, by Sophie Glovier (Princeton Uni-versity Press, revised edition, 2017). The revised edition includes the newest trails.

OTHER ACTIVITIES

Carson Road Woods, on Carson Road, has 4.4 miles of trails through a beech forest, with streams and meadows. Explore Institute Woods at the Institute for Advanced Study, next to Princeton Battlefield State Park (see Trip 43). Hike 48 poems (yes, poems) at the Scott and Hella McVay Poetry Trail on Rosedale Road at the Johnson Education Center (opengreenmap.org/greenmap/new-princeton-green-connections/scott-and-hella-mcvay -poetry-trail-27888).

MORE INFORMATION

Open dawn to dusk. Bridge buffs, take note: twelve historical and unusual bridges exist in Mercer County. Extend your day with a trip to one or more: historicbridges.org /b_a_list.php?ct=&c=&ptype=county&pname=Mercer+County,+New+Jersey.

45 WASHINGTON CROSSING STATE PARK

Enjoy excellent river views where George Washington and his troops crossed the Delaware, and then stroll on historic Continental Lane Trail on this hike to the park's northern section.

Features 👥 🐕 💧 📷 ⛷ ❄ ⛺ 🚹

Location Titusville, NJ

Rating Easy

Distance 3.9 miles round-trip

Elevation Gain 350 feet

Estimated Time 2 hours

Maps USGS Pennington; state.nj.us/dep/parksandforests/parks/maps/WashingtonCrossingAreaMapFinalDraft.pdf

GPS Coordinates 40° 17.810' N, 74° 52.090' W

Contact Washington Crossing State Park, 355 Washington Crossing–Pennington Road, Titusville, NJ 08560; 609-737-0623; nj.gov/dep/parksandforests/parks/washingtoncrossingstatepark.html

DIRECTIONS

Take I-95 to Exit 1 toward Lambertville/NJ 29 North. Go left at the fork, merging with River Road (NJ 29). In about 3 miles, turn left at the light (near restaurant and gas station) onto Washington Crossing–Pennington Road and then immediately turn right (before the bridge into Pennsylvania) into the spacious parking lot (at least 50 cars).

TRAIL DESCRIPTION

Journey back through time in 3,575-acre Washington Crossing State Park, where the friendly ghosts of American Revolution soldiers speak to you at every turn. You may catch a glimpse of bewigged George Washington himself during the many historical reenactments. Fifteen miles of trails wind through the park. See the spot where General Washington and his soldiers crossed the icy Delaware on the night of December 25, 1776. Walk Continental Lane Trail, the route over which Washington's troops began their march to Trenton and won a morale-boosting battle. (The Trenton Battle Monument is on North Warren Street in Trenton.)

The park is eminently walkable in every season. In fall, the river and canal reflect the shimmer of colorful deciduous trees. Cross-country skiing beckons in winter, as well as the December 25 reenactment of Washington and his men crossing the Delaware. Enjoy events and performances at the Open Air Theatre in summer. Wildflowers paint the park in spring. The visitor center, museum, and historical Johnson Ferry House are a few minutes away by car (355 Washington Crossing–Pennington Road).

This hike starts briefly on Green Dot Trail (blazed green) and then follows Red Dot Trail (blazed red) up and down, over bridges, and through the forests and fields to reach the natural area and nature center in the remote northern section of the park. The return trip follows Blue Dot Trail (blazed blue) to Red Dot Trail.

Leave the parking lot, where Pennsylvania peeks at you across the Delaware River, and walk toward the bridge and historical Nelson House (enter, if it's open). Follow the red

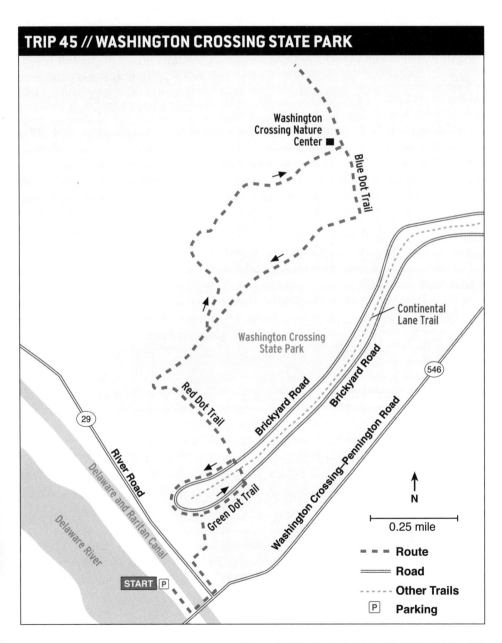

TRIP 45 // WASHINGTON CROSSING STATE PARK

Washington Crossing Nature Center ■

Blue Dot Trail

Continental Lane Trail

Washington Crossing State Park

Red Dot Trail

546

29

Brickyard Road

Brickyard Road

Washington Crossing–Pennington Road

River Road

Delaware and Raritan Canal

Green Dot Trail

N

0.25 mile

Delaware River

START P

- - - Route
=== Road
----- Other Trails
P Parking

brick path to the left, cross the pedestrian bridge over the Delaware and Raritan Canal, and turn left onto the paved walkway, which soon becomes dirt Green Dot Trail. Cross a paved road to stay on this trail. Turn right (0.4 mile) onto wood-chip Continental Lane Trail, flanked by welcoming woods, which marks a route that Washington's army marched (you are on this historic trail for only 0.1 mile). Turn left onto Red Dot Trail and stay on it, watching carefully for red blazes and trail markers at junctions and crossings. Cross a paved road (open field to the right) and enter the woods through a gap in a fence, walking along a meadow. Almost immediately on the left, turn onto Red Dot Trail; that trail quickly intersects Green Dot Trail; continue straight on Red Dot Trail through the deep, lovely woods. (Turn right on Green Dot Trail if you want to go to the picnic/playground area and the visitor center.)

Head downhill through the quiet green woods. At the bottom of the hill lies an impressive, sometimes-dry creek bed. Turn left on Red Dot Trail (0.8 mile) and then right to cross the wooden footbridge. Veer right (straight) after the bridge, still on Red Dot Trail (Yellow Dot Trail is to the left), and climb a small hill. Then turn left to stay on Red Dot Trail. At the crossroads with Blue Dot Trail, keep straight on a well-worn, narrow, furrowed path, flanked by sentinel trees.

Cross Blue Dot Trail again and descend a rooty downhill slope. To the left is an open field in the distance. Follow Red Dot Trail across another bridge, and cross Blue Dot Trail twice more. Keep going straight, past the bench on your right, and turn left onto the paved road (1.9 miles) to visit the nature center's exhibits. Staff members raise bees out back, and an outdoor solar dryer is on the site. (This solar dryer is an all-season passive solar energy structure made of wood, metal, and plastic that uses sunlight to dry nuts, seedpods, and flowers to use in the park's nature programs.) A covered pavilion to the left seats about 30.

Retrace your route on Red Dot Trail to the junction with Blue Dot Trail (2.3 miles); veer left onto Blue Dot Trail. After a few hundred feet, veer right to stay on the trail. On a gentle downward slope canopied by trees, go toward signs for the nature center's theater. Exit the woods and turn right on a paved road (2.5 miles). The Open Air Theatre, which offers music and plays in nice weather, is about 200 yards to your left, toward the parking lot and bathrooms. Stay straight on Blue Dot Trail, walking across grass now, and then turn left on the blue-blazed trail and continue beneath the lacy canopy of trees.

At the trail intersection, turn left onto Red Dot Trail (2.9 miles). Retrace your steps from here, following Red Dot Trail until it reaches Green Dot Trail near the pedestrian bridge. Step to your right to view where George Washington and his soldiers crossed the Delaware in 1776 (sign and monument). Then go over the pedestrian bridge and back to the parking area.

DID YOU KNOW?

The park has an observatory and a museum. An artist's paradise is 20 minutes away in Hamilton at the beautifully landscaped, nonprofit 43-acre Grounds for Sculpture (80 Sculptors Way; 609-586-0616).

Washington Crossing Bridge marks the area where, on the night of December 25, 1776, George Washington crossed the Delaware River, the first move in a surprise attack organized by Washington against the Hessian forces in Trenton, New Jersey.

OTHER ACTIVITIES
Drive 15 minutes for a 1-mile hike to Goat Hill Overlook (administered by Washington Crossing State Park), with excellent views of the Delaware River and bridges. To visit the museum across the river from where you parked, drive or walk over the narrow bridge to Washington Crossing Historic Park in Pennsylvania (1112 River Road, Washington Crossing, PA 18977; 215-493-4076). See several historical buildings and replicas of boats used by the Continental Army. If visiting in December, check out the popular reenactment of the crossing of the Delaware (washingtoncrossingpark.org).

MORE INFORMATION
Open 8 A.M. to 7 P.M. Primitive group campsites are available to rent. Fishing is allowed in designated areas. Bicycles and horses are not permitted on hiking trails. The park is partially accessible for people with disabilities; call the visitor center for details: 609-737-0623.

46 PARVIN STATE PARK

Don't miss the wildflowers and blooming trees and shrubs in spring; the egrets fishing in the lake in spring, summer, and fall; and the charm of an isolated swamp trail in any season.

Features

Location Elmer, NJ

Rating Moderate to Strenuous

Distance 9.3 miles round-trip

Elevation Gain 375 feet

Estimated Time 5 hours

Maps USGS Elmer; state.nj.us/dep/parksandforests/parks/maps/ ParvinFinalDraft2_reduced_Area_broc.pdf

GPS Coordinates 39° 30.658′ N, 75° 07.912′ W

Contact Parvin State Park, 701 Almond Road, Pittsgrove, NJ 08318; 856-358-8616; nj.gov/dep/parksandforests/parks/parvinstatepark.html

DIRECTIONS
From NJ 55 North or South, take Exit 35 toward Glassboro/Vineland and follow signs to the park (about 30 miles from the exit). The parking lot holds at least 50 cars.

TRAIL DESCRIPTION
Parvin State Park is one of the parks built by the Civilian Conservation Corps (CCC), an outgrowth of the New Deal program created by President Franklin D. Roosevelt during the Great Depression. The CCC constructed the main beach complex, a parking lot, campsites, and cabins. In summer, the 2,092-acre park is rich with campers and bird songs. Here at the edge of the Pine Barrens, several miles of trails through cedar swamps, holly groves, pine forests, and laurel thickets delight in all seasons (except perhaps summer, peak bug season). Spring is a heady mix of blooms and perfumes from more than 200 kinds of flowering plants, plus wild azaleas, dogwoods, mountain laurels, and magnolias. Visitors can lounge on the beach and swim in Parvin Lake in season ($2 walk-in entry fee to beach from Memorial Day weekend through Labor Day).

On this hike, start on green-blazed Parvin Lake Trail and wander deep into secluded areas on Parvin Lake Trail, orange-blazed Knoll Trail, red-blazed Long Trail, brown-blazed Black Oak Trail, blue-blazed Forest Loop Trail, and back on Parvin Lake Trail, getting an interesting overview of both the swamp hardwood forests and pine forests. Even in the parking lot, you'll hear birds shriek and, in September, see hawks soar.

Cross the road to the park office in front of the beach and Parvin Lake. Stop in and pick up a map and a guide to birds. Gender-neutral flush toilets are outside the office.

Facing the lake, turn left onto a trail constructed from red bricks; the bricks end and the trail becomes sandy, flat, green-blazed Parvin Lake Trail (trails are mainly identified by color only). Walk along a green metal fence that parallels the road. Then cross a field and go over a footbridge with an inviting pagoda to the left. Cross White Bridge (built by the CCC), and the path changes to dirt as it winds around the lake into the woods.

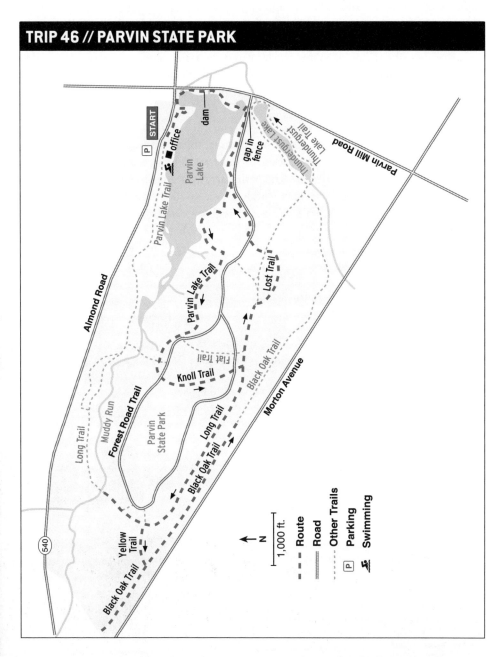

TRIP 46 // PARVIN STATE PARK

Walk past a dam where you may spot some birds fishing. Head toward a floating dock, stopping to rest on perfectly placed benches overlooking the lake. Nature signage makes the trail educational as you continue your hike, walking toward two floating docks separated by a parking lot (0.7 mile at lot).

After enjoying the docks, cross a bridge over the lake. At the trail junction with a yellow-blazed connector trail and blue-blazed Forest Loop Trail, stay right on Parvin Lake Trail (0.9 mile). Check out the cabins for rent on the left. The lake narrows to a tributary as the woods encroach and turn swampy. At a four-way intersection, at the sign for the Island Point picnic area, go straight to continue on green-blazed Parvin Lake Trail.

The lily pad–covered lake comes into full view again on the right. Note the nature signs that describe the plants along the hike and the stately column of trees (1.0 mile). Keep on the green-blazed trail, ignoring feeder trails to the left. The trail intersects a paved road with camping and picnic areas on the right, all part of the Jaggers Point camping site (1.4 miles). Fill your water bottle at the pump to your left. Turn right on the paved road, turn right at the green sign, and then quickly turn left at the playground. At the next trail junction, stay on the green-blazed trail (do not go left at the campground area). Lake views disappear. At the next trail junction, turn left to stay on the green-blazed trail (no trail sign). The path narrows as shrubs encroach and sounds recede. Go more deeply into the quiet woods over a wooden footbridge, and reach the 2-mile green trail marker. Cross a wooden bridge over swampy water. At the paved intersection, go straight—you are now entering orange-blazed Knoll Trail (2.4 miles).

Secluded woods embrace you as the trail narrows, hugged by low shrubs. Watch out for low-hanging branches at the wooden bridge. Cross a paved path, keeping straight on

An egret awaits dinner at Parvin Lake dam.

the orange-blazed trail. The woods open up as you traverse two footbridges. At the paved road (the blue-blazed trail, 2.8 miles), go straight, still on Knoll Trail. At the next junction, turn right onto red-blazed Long Trail (2.9 miles). Sit on a moss-covered log and have lunch. As you continue on beautiful, elevated Long Trail, the atmosphere becomes quieter along the sandy edge of the Pine Barrens; tall, thin pines grow from a crazy jumble of blowdown. Enjoy the peaceful seclusion and red-headed woodpeckers.

At the four-way junction, Long Trail ends at a red-blazed connector trail (3.8 miles); turn left on this connector trail (a bit confusingly shown as yellow on the map), which is a wide, soft path through the forest. At the next junction, turn left (road and houses to the right) onto brown-blazed Black Oak Trail (4.0 miles). Swampy areas are covered with carefully placed branches to walk on. The brown-blazed trail ends in a swamp, with Morton Avenue on the right (4.8 miles). You are alone, a rare occurrence in today's world. Stay a while and enjoy the solitude.

When you're ready, turn around so that Morton Avenue is now on your left. Walk to the end of the brown-blazed trail going the other way (pass the junction at 5.6 miles). Expect some intricate spiderwebs, as almost no one walks here. Black Oak Trail dead-ends at houses and private property (5.9 miles). Backtrack to the junction with the red-blazed connector trail and turn left onto the connector trail (6.2 miles). At the next junction, turn right to continue on red-blazed Long Trail (6.6 miles).

Soon you walk over plank footbridges, and the path becomes sandy. At the junction, turn right onto the red-blazed trail (orange-blazed trail is to the left). Cross a dirt road—keep straight on the red-blazed trail. Pass a pink-blazed connector trail to your left (7.5 miles). The path becomes wide and flat. Light-orange-blazed Lost Trail appears to your right, but keep straight on red-blazed Long Trail. At the next junction, turn right on Long Trail as it narrows. Observe an odd-shaped blowdown.

At a four-way intersection, take light-orange-blazed Lost Trail on the left because Long Trail was closed here as of September 2016 due to storm damage. Still following the light orange blazes, go right at the split, toward the paved road. A sign for the Jaggers Point campground is to your left. Turn right onto the paved road, which is blue-blazed Forest Loop Trail (8.2 miles). Pass a forest regeneration area sign on the right. Soon on the left is familiar, civilized, green-blazed Parvin Lake Trail. Turn left onto it (8.8 miles). Go down a short hill and turn right at the path; the hike is now a retrace on Parvin Lake Trail.

Along the way, enjoy the highbush blueberries and the plopping of frogs in the lake. Pause at the large root ball (mass of exposed roots and dirt) of an uprooted tree; fish jump in the branches that sprawl across the lake. Watch the sunset and look for egrets fishing at the dam before you cross the road and return to the parking area.

DID YOU KNOW?

During World War II, Parvin State Park was a camp for German prisoners of war and a summer camp for children of displaced Japanese Americans. Remains of Native American encampments dot the area. Hike around the other lake in the park, Thundergust Lake, on yellow-blazed Thundergust Lake Trail.

OTHER ACTIVITIES

Explore the eighteenth- century sawmill and gristmill and the former homes of mill workers at Fries Mill Ruins in the Manumuskin River Preserve near Millville. Also in Millville, explore 5,000-acre Union Lake Wildlife Management Area (County Route 552).

MORE INFORMATION

Open sunrise to sunset. Seasonal entrance fees may apply from Memorial Day to Labor Day—check the park's website to see if fees are currently in effect before you go. A snack bar is open in season. Swimming is permitted from Memorial Day through Labor Day when a lifeguard is on duty. Pets must be leashed. The park is partially accessible for persons with disabilities; for details, call 856-358-8616.

47 BLACK RUN PRESERVE

Walk through a patch of pine barrens that sits close to a busy highway corridor but feels a million miles away.

Features 👥🐕💧🏞️🎿🚴

Location Evesham, NJ

Rating Easy

Distance 5-mile loop

Elevation Gain 100 feet

Estimated Time 2–3 hours

Maps USGS Clementon; blackrun.org/printable-map; interactive map: blackrun .org/map

GPS Coordinates 39° 50.757′ N, 74° 53.991′ W

Contact Friends of the Black Run Preserve, 123 East Main Street, P.O. Box 1124, Marlton, NJ 08053; 609-451-0580; blackrun.org

DIRECTIONS

Take I-295 South to Exit 36A toward Berlin onto NJ 73 North/South. Go 7.0 miles and turn left onto Braddock Mill Road. Continue for 0.66 mile before turning right onto Tomlinson Mill Road. At 0.07 mile, take the second left onto Braddock Mill Road and follow the road for 0.62 mile. Keep left at the fork to continue on Braddock Mill Road. Go 0.02 mile and turn left onto Kettle Run Road at the stop sign; 179 Kettle Run Road is on the left, past the larger parking lot (space for twenty cars) for Black Run Trail on the right. The dirt lot accommodates about twelve cars.

TRAIL DESCRIPTION

Through the intense efforts of local citizens and Friends of the Black Run Preserve, this former cranberry farm in Marlton has been slowly changed into a regional recreation destination. The trails are popular with hikers, mountain bikers, and bird-watchers, and an orienteering course is available, too. Friends of the Black Run Preserve puts on a series of popular programs, from sunset photography sessions to yoga to drum circles. The preserve itself sits on the edge of Pinelands National Preserve and, despite its proximity to the Philadelphia metropolitan area's heavy suburban sprawl, gives a good feel for what the deep pine barrens many miles away are like.

From the parking lot, walk east toward Kettle Run Road. Just after the last parking space, take the trail to the right, proceed 200 feet, and cross Kettle Run Road. Walk through the main parking lot and through the back gate onto blue-blazed Peaceful

Partners Trail. Follow this old farm road past the kiosk and around the curve over a large bridge. You'll often find the handiwork of beavers under this bridge, as they keep building a dam that keeps getting removed only to be built again. To your right is a beaver pond, an old cranberry bog that has gone from a nearly waterless swamp to a proper pond in the years since the preserve opened, a beautiful example of the impact that beavers can have on the topography of a landscape.

At the first trail junction just past the bridge, turn left onto the dirt road (look for the Bike Route sign) and then quickly turn right onto Bog Trail (red blaze with a white dot). This trail takes you through a closely hemmed-in forest of pitch pines, giving you the feeling that you are deep in the pine barrens rather than five minutes from the congested NJ 73 corridor. Follow Bog Trail all the way to its end, where it rejoins Peaceful Partners Trail (0.6 mile). Turn left and follow the blue blazes for 0.1 mile; then head left on white-blazed Kettle Trail. At the junction with the yellow-blazed trail, keep right to stay on Kettle Trail for another 0.2 mile until it dead-ends at Peaceful Partners Trail.

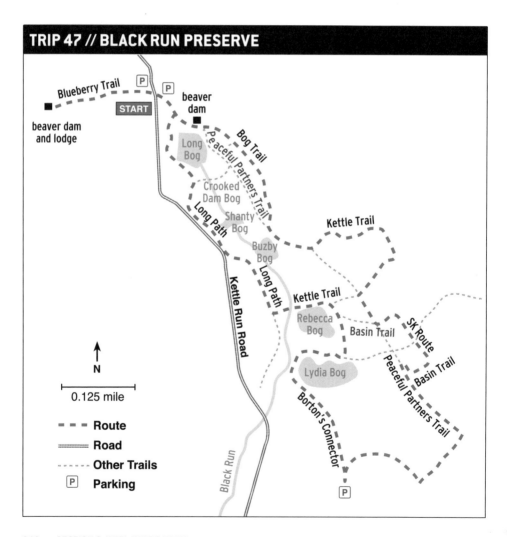

TRIP 47 // BLACK RUN PRESERVE

Once more back at the blue-blazed trail, turn left, walk another 500 feet, and turn left onto red-blazed Basin Trail, a short loop that takes you through open, grassy areas. Turn left onto Peaceful Partners Trail one final time (1.5 miles). Stick with the blue blazes as they cross and recross REI White Trail (designed for mountain biking) half a dozen times. Peaceful Partners Trail reaches the eastern border of the preserve, makes a sharp right turn, and continues southwest before eventually passing a touching memorial to a local youth and arriving at yellow-blazed Bortons Connector Trail near the southern parking lot for the preserve (2.3 miles). Turn right here to take the connector trail back into the heart of the preserve.

After 0.2 mile, the trail reaches a large circle of logs and veers left before continuing along the edge of an old cranberry bog, a perfect spot to look for hunting birds. Just before Bortons Connector Trail ends, watch for a very secret parking area with room for only one car (and that spot is filled 24 hours a day, 365 days each year). Just after, turn right to follow the red blazes (2.8 miles) for more views of bogs. The wooden structures sticking out of the water are sluice gates, which were used to regulate the amount of water in the bogs. At some of them, you can still hear the water rushing through the gate and going underneath your feet.

At the next intersection, turn left onto a connector trail (blazed red with a white stripe) and then turn left when the trail splits (3.1 miles). A bench here is a great spot for a snack and for watching wildlife, which can range from deer to birds to beavers. Back on the trail, take the next left to get on white-blazed Kettle Trail once more, heading west for about 350 yards before turning right onto red-blazed Long Path (3.3 miles).

Follow Long Path past a black-blazed trail and a nature trail before turning right where Long Path and the black-blazed trail overlap. Pass a bench honoring President John F. Kennedy (4.0 miles) on black-blazed Black Run Trail and turn left to continue following only the red blazes. This stretch of Long Path can be tricky, with lots of roots sticking up as you navigate along the top of an old bog dike with wetlands on either side.

Long Path travels along the back side of the first bog you passed. Keep an eye out to your right for beaver activity and, with luck, a beaver swimming. The trail curves to the right, heading east back to the main trail kiosk. (*Note*: Long Path has been rerouted away from the water, a result of a beaver lodge and a lot of flooding along the original right of way.) Exit the trail at the kiosk; turn left and recross the main parking lot and Kettle Run Road back to your car (4.4 miles). Don't drive away yet though! Instead, head past another trail kiosk at the back of the parking lot. It's a straight shot down this trail, Blueberry Trail, for a third of a mile. Pass through woods before coming out on top of another old cranberry bog dike (4.7 miles). Where the route dead-ends, admire the beaver lodge in front of you. To the right, behold one of nature's finest works of architecture: a large, curving beaver dam that holds back a sizable pool of water. If you visit near dawn or dusk, you may even get a chance to meet the architects. When you have had your fill of this spot, backtrack once more to your car in the parking lot (5.0 miles).

DID YOU KNOW?

The roots of Evesham Township go back to the 1600s. You can get a taste of that history at The John Inskeep House in Marlton. Its oldest sections date to 1771, possibly built

A pair of beaver lodges along Lower Schaefer Bog

on the foundations of a house that was built here in 1725 and burned. (10 Madison Court, eveshamhistoricalsociety.org).

OTHER ACTIVITIES

Fifteen minutes away in Medford is the Dr. James Still Historic Office Site and Education Center (210 Medford–Mt. Holly Road, drjamesstillcenter.org), the first New Jersey state historic park to honor an African American. James Still began life as the child of poor former slaves and became a successful medical practitioner (he made herbal medicines) and the largest landowner in Medford. The site preserves his office and his story, as well as the stories of other local African Americans, including that of William Still, James's younger brother, who ran the Underground Railroad in Philadelphia for many years. The property also features a short nature trail and a garden with some of the plants that James Still used.

MORE INFORMATION

Open dawn to dusk. Check the website of Friends of the Black Run Preserve (blackrun .org) or the organization's Facebook page (facebook.com/blackrunpreserveteam) for news and upcoming events, which can include guided hikes, nature walks, or photography outings.

48 COOPER RIVER PARK LOOP

Stretch your legs on an urban and suburban adventure over bridges, past playgrounds and woods, and through neighborhoods.

Features 🚶🐕💧🗺️🎿✳️🏕️🚌🎣

Location Cherry Hill, NJ

Rating Easy

Distance 7.8-mile loop

Elevation Gain 200 feet

Estimated Time 3.5 hours

Maps USGS Camden; camdencounty.com/wp-content/uploads/2017/07/COOPER-RIVER-3-23-16.pdf

GPS Coordinates 39° 55.660′ N, 75° 03.964′ W

Contact Camden County Board of Freeholders, Office of Constituent Services, Courthouse, Suite 306, 520 Market Street, Camden, NJ 08102; 866-226-3362; camdencounty.com/service/parks/cooper-river-park

DIRECTIONS

Driving: From I-295, take Exit 34B for Marlton Pike/NJ 70 West. After 3.9 miles, take the second exit on the right for Cuthbert Boulevard South. Take the first right onto North Park Boulevard. After 0.5 mile, turn left into the parking area for Cooper River Park. The large lot probably has 200 spaces.

Public Transportation: Take PATCO trains to the Collingswood, Westmont, or Haddonfield stop; see area map at train station for walking directions. Take NJ Transit bus routes 406, 413, 450, or 451 to the Cooper River Park bus stop; consult bus stop map for walking directions.

TRAIL DESCRIPTION

Cooper River Park epitomizes New Jersey: urban and suburban living side by side. Where else can you see a juvenile hawk drying its wings on someone's freshly mowed front lawn? Other contrasts appear as you walk the loop around Cooper River and wind through the pretty streets of Haddon Township, passing a yacht club, an outdoor carnival, miniature golf, food trucks, playgrounds, private homes, war memorials, large auto dealerships, and more. The 346-acre park in Camden County is truly an urban adventure that spans several municipalities (Cherry Hill, Collingswood, Pennsauken, and Haddon Township) and boasts eight parking lots. It's also part of the Camden

GreenWay, a network of thirteen trails that, when complete, will link communities throughout the Camden County area to Philadelphia.

The park is bounded by North Park and South Park drives, US 130, and Grove Street. The loop trail is mainly asphalt and parallels North Park and South Park drives,

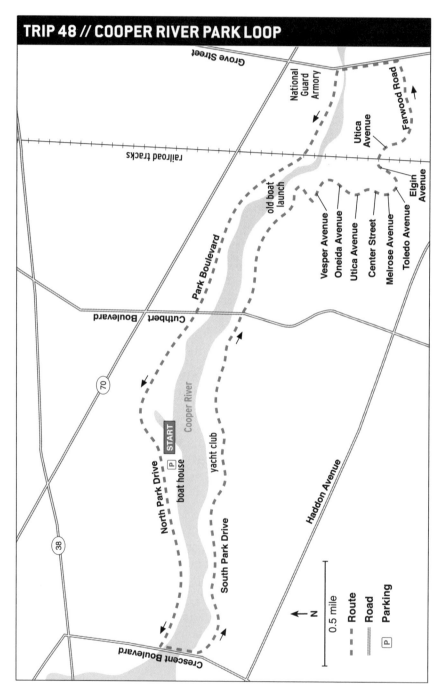

TRIP 48 // COOPER RIVER PARK LOOP

except for the residential jaunt, which extends the mileage, through Haddonfield. The park itself is a swath of green between the trail and the river.

Start at the Cherry Hill parking lot, which has a restaurant with a beer garden. (Ignore any directional arrows painted on the pavement that may linger from the COVID-19 era.) Proceed west on the asphalt trail (the river is on your left). You can stop at any point and walk down to the generous river or take advantage of the park's many amenities, including playgrounds, boat rentals, running tracks, volleyball courts, pavilions, and picnic tables. Ground-up tires make the surface of the playgrounds soft and eco-friendly.

As you pass the benches that conveniently dot the trail, be mindful of bicyclists. Cooper River shimmers to the left past a series of stone steps leading down to a soccer field. Trees line the route for a while, as you pass portable toilets, food trucks, and boat and kayak rentals, but soon you'll need your hat for protection from the sun. The impressive, orange-colored Camden County Boathouse, home to several New Jersey rowing clubs and available for party rentals, is on your left (0.4 mile). Walk around the building for a lovely river view and a stroll on the docks.

Back on the trail, commercial buildings line North Park Drive on your right, a wonderful urban contrast to the dewy green of the park. Picnic tables rest under 100-year-old trees. Look straight down North Park Drive at the Oz-like Philadelphia skyline shining in the distance. Follow the path over the Cooper River Bridge (1.1 miles), where US 30 and US 130 meet. Be sure to stop in the middle of the bridge for a moment to drink in the sight of the river. The sign for Camden city limits is on the other side of the bridge. Veer left once you cross the bridge, staying on the asphalt trail, which winds past a pavilion and viewing tower toward the river. At the parking lot, turn left. You are now walking east on South Park Drive.

South Park Drive, technically in Collingswood, is an attractive residential street. Soon, on your left, is a mowed path around tall greenery. Follow the path to a hidden wooden bridge and pond: a cool, shady reprieve (1.1 miles). The semicircular path curves back to the trail. Admire a dolphin statue and other works in an outdoor sculpture display (2.3 miles). In the parking lot for the Cooper River Yacht Club rests a huge old anchor, and more sculptures are visible nearby. Hopkins House—whose still-standing west wing was built in 1737—is next (250 South Park Drive). The other half of the building was built by the Civilian Conservation Corps (CCC) during the Great Depression, using the footprint of the original east wing, which had been constructed in 1720. This building served as the office for the park for many decades. Walk around back and admire the wide, green expanse and the giant trees leading to the river. Take advantage of the picnic tables and shade. A bit farther along you'll see a breathtakingly big weeping willow and a mimosa tree at the water's edge. At the traffic light, cross Cuthbert Boulevard at the crosswalk (3.0 miles) to continue on South Park Drive. More residential areas are to the right. The trail is quieter and more peaceful here, the river narrower and wooded. You may see a hawk or an eagle. Proceed to the circular stone platform on your left and walk down the short dirt path to a meadow the length of several football fields. The river, which seems to disappear, is through the trees ahead. Explore a bit if you'd like. Otherwise, return to the asphalt trail.

The trail curves generously left at a large yellow arrow. Here, make a side trip by taking the dirt path on your left (3.8 miles), which veers left to another huge meadow. Both expansive meadows are surprising finds in this urban setting. Walk the meadow, keeping slightly to your left and watching for a barely visible path through the woods. Take the path and be rewarded by solitude and peace at an old stone boat launch on the sleepy river. Retrace your steps to the yellow arrow and turn left. In a few hundred yards reach Vesper Avenue, where the residential part of the loop, on sidewalks, begins. The neighborhoods are delightfully varied in style.

Turn left onto Vesper Avenue and then curve right as Vesper changes to Oneida Avenue, where you continue on the sidewalk. At a T intersection, turn left onto Utica Avenue and then take the first right onto Center Street. After two blocks, turn left onto Melrose Avenue (4.4 miles). At a T intersection, turn left onto Toledo Street, which curves and becomes Elgin Avenue (the river is to your left, but you can't see it yet). At another T intersection, turn left onto Locust Avenue. Then turn right onto Utica Avenue (4.8 miles) and carefully walk over the still-active railroad tracks. Cross Coles Mill/Windsor Road (the street has two names and the street signs change from red to white). Utica Avenue curves to the right and becomes Farwood Road—stay on this road. Do not take Farwood Circle.

Cross Longwood Street and Cedar Street. At the T intersection, turn left onto Grove Street (5.4 miles). Walk across the bridge over the river. Steps, built by the CCC (who also constructed the lake), offer a shady spot for a snack or rest. Those with sharp eyes may spot some relics of the CCC's work around the park (in addition to the aforementioned Hopkins House wing). Past the steps, turn left onto the asphalt trail again (5.7 miles) and walk behind the National Guard Armory along the river. Continue under a picturesque railroad bridge (6.1 miles). A parking lot and a dog park (Pooch Park) appear soon. Commercial businesses line the road on the right, and the wide river flows on your left. When you cross Cuthbert Boulevard (7.1 miles), you are 0.7 mile from your car. A boat launch and a pleasant viewing area pop up on the left. Pass a 9/11 memorial, a Holocaust memorial, a Polish war memorial, and several other monuments. Traverse an arched bridge to Veteran's Island to appreciate a few more monuments and scenic views before strolling over a small bridge to reach the parking lot.

DID YOU KNOW?

Across the street from the monuments lies an underground building, the former office of Malcolm Wells, considered to be a pioneer in underground and eco-friendly architecture. Petty's Island Preserve floats in the Delaware River between Camden (New Jersey) and Philadelphia. New Jersey Natural Lands Trust is cleaning up this former CITGO Petroleum Corporation facility, now home to rare plants and to eagles, hawks, falcons, and other wildlife. Public access is planned eventually, but for now, access is offered via ticketed guided hikes organized by the Center for Aquatic Sciences at Adventure Aquarium. For more information, future dates, or tickets, go to aquaticsciences.org/pettys-island.

A young hiker enjoys swinging by the water and admiring the sailboats on a warm summer's day.

OTHER ACTIVITIES

Visit Dinosaur Discovery Park in nearby Haddonfield, where the world's first nearly complete dinosaur skeleton was excavated. (The park is at the dead end of Maple Avenue, just off Grove Street.) Hike adjacent Pennypacker Park. In Camden, stroll the waterfront to see the Battleship New Jersey Museum and Memorial, Adventure Aquarium, Camden Children's Garden, Stingray Beach Club (touch and hand-feed a stingray), and the marina promenade. Many places to eat are along NJ 73. Thirty minutes northwest lies 250-acre Palmyra Cove Nature Park (1335 NJ 73, Palmyra).

MORE INFORMATION

Open dawn to dusk. Rent canoes and kayaks from the Cooper River Yacht Club; call 856-869-9145. The park does not list trails as universally accessible, but some parts of the asphalt path could be maneuvered.

BATONA TRAIL: SAND AND WATER TRAIL AND 1808 TRAIL

Hike through the heart of a massive cedar swamp and then deep in the pitch-pine-filled woods of the Pine Barrens.

Features

Location Hammonton, NJ

Rating Moderate

Distance 7.3-mile loop

Elevation Gain 350 feet

Estimated Time 3 hours

Maps USGS Atsion; nj.gov/dep/parksandforests/maps/wharton-area.pdf

GPS Coordinates 39° 38.645′ N, 074° 38.800′ W

Contact Wharton State Forest, Batsto Office, 31 Batsto Road, Hammonton, NJ 08037; 609-561-0024; state.nj.us/dep/parksandforests/parks/wharton.html#trails

DIRECTIONS

From the Atlantic City Expressway, take Exit 28 toward Hammonton. Keep to the left and turn left onto 12th Street (NJ 54). Drive for 2.1 miles and then turn right onto Central Avenue. In 1.7 miles, turn right onto White Horse Pike/US 30 and then immediately turn left onto Pleasant Mills Road. Continue on Pleasant Mills Road for 7.2 miles and then turn left onto Batsto Road. Take the first left onto the driveway for Batsto Village. The large parking lot has room for more than 140 vehicles.

TRAIL DESCRIPTION

This hike combines four trails to create a loop of a little more than 7 miles through the heart of the Pine Barrens: Sand and Water Trail (orange blazes), 1808 Trail (green blazes), Buttonwood Camp Connector Trail (blue blazes), and Batona Trail (pink blazes). Along the way, you'll experience the deep quiet of a cedar swamp and acre after acre of pitch pines.

Cross the parking lot and enter the Batsto Village visitor center to pick up a map. The center includes a well-developed museum about the Pine Barrens and Batsto, an iron-works town from before the American Revolution. You can also visit a small gift shop, request to see an informational film, and buy tickets for tours of Batsto Mansion (save those for after your hike).

Leaving from the back of the gift shop, walk straight toward the large information kiosk along the paved path. Head left and look for a gap in the rail fence. Exit through the gap and traverse the field diagonally, angling south-southeast away from Batsto

Village. (Don't worry; you can explore the village after the hike!) Keep an eye out for the post with an orange blaze at the tree line that marks Sand and Water Trail. Follow the trail, keeping an eye out on the right side for prickly pear cactus, a cactus native to New Jersey. Arrive at paved Batsto Road (no parking!) and cross the road to reach the official trailhead for Sand and Water Trail. The orange-blazed trail heads through a burned area (this spot is often the site of prescribed burns) before entering treeline and stepping up on some puncheons. This first part of the route in the woods is far from beautiful—not much except scrub pines and greenbrier (sticker bushes).

In a very short time, greenbrier gives way to cedar swamps. The Atlantic white cedar is an evergreen that can grow up to 75 feet tall and loves low wetlands and swamps. What makes it different from many trees, particularly in the Pine Barrens, is that it grows very straight. This lightweight wood was highly prized in colonial times, particularly for shipbuilding because it's rot resistant and can last a long time. Hike through a spectacular series of stands of cedar and take time to admire them. Make sure you step up to cross the small footbridges, and stay alert so you don't miss your turn onto green-blazed 1808 Trail (1.2 miles).

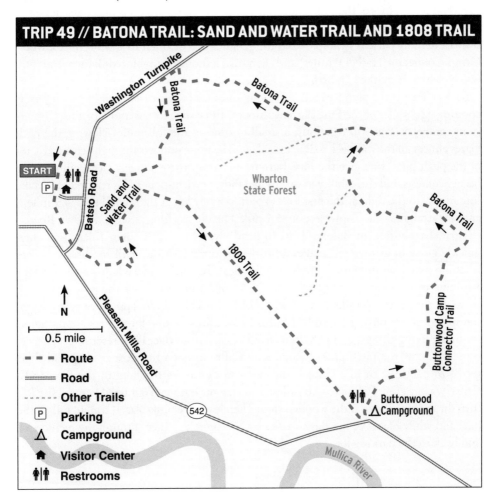

Notice that the green-blazed trail is on top of a long, narrow rise of land, the remains of an old stage road built in 1808 that gives the trail its name. This slight rise now provides a dry-footed, ecologically friendly way to penetrate deep into the cedar swamp in a way very few other trails in New Jersey do. Enjoy your special look at this unusual terrain. Cedar swamps have a bit of magic about them, as sounds seem to be absorbed into the trees and what little light makes it to the floor must be filtered through the tops of the giants. Snow or light rain provides extra magic. The myriad of little bridges along the way add to the ambiance. Where benches provide the opportunity, take a few minutes to sit and soak it all in.

Finally leaving the swamps behind, enter Buttonwood Campground at 2.8 miles. You can turn right here and cross the road for lunch or a snack by the Mullica River at the Crowley's Landing picnic tables. When you are ready to continue, come back to where 1808 Trail ends and head left through the campground. Past Site 5, enter blue-blazed Buttonwood Camp Connector Trail, which follows sand Burnt Schoolhouse Road. Don't worry much about traffic, as large, semipermanent puddles and deep ruts have made the road virtually impassable by vehicles at this time. You are now among the usual pitch pines of the Pinelands, but watch for scattered stands of cedars along the side of the road here as well. Notice how branches grow much lower on the trunks outside the densely packed swamp. Avoid the puddles and bear left to stay on Buttonwood Camp Connector Trail (4.0 miles) and then turn left onto pink-blazed Batona Trail (4.1 miles), which is marked "North."

Batona Trail is the premier (and only) long-distance backpacking trail in South Jersey, covering 52.7 miles of the Pine Barrens through three state forests and a Nature Conservancy property. You will travel just a small portion of the full trail, following the pink blazes almost all the way back to Batsto Village. The route wanders through acres and acres of the pitch pines that give the Pine Barrens its name. These scraggly trees will win few beauty contests, but their ability to survive in sandy, nutrient-poor soil is remarkable. Make sure to stay to the right at the first fork (4.5 miles); stay left at the second fork (4.9 miles); and stay straight at the T intersection (5.1 miles) before reaching paved Tylertown Road.

Turn sharply left on Batona Trail to head away from Tylertown Road; and then quickly go right as the trail makes a 90-degree turn. Cross a small footbridge before reaching paved Washington Turnpike (6.3 miles). Turn left and walk down the road for a minute or so before turning left into the woods and away from the pavement once more. In the next 0.75 mile, traverse a pair of firebreaks—ditches put in to help control the spread of fire during controlled burns or wildfires. While forest fires are not good for many living things, a pine barrens needs them to survive. Fires reset forest succession and allow the pitch pines (which require fire to open their cones to spread their seeds) to continue to reproduce—and here, to dominate the flora of the Pinelands. Cross Washington Turnpike (7.0 miles) and stay on Batona Trail until you see the left turn for Batsto Village at the wooden sign. Then leave the pink-blazed trail to follow the blue and white blazes of the Batsto Lake trails a short distance through the picnic area and back to the parking lot.

DID YOU KNOW?

While the Batsto visible today largely shows the agricultural pursuits that it followed under the ownership of the Wharton family, the roots of the village are in ironmaking in the 1760s. At various times, the furnace here made cannonballs for the Continental Army and firebacks for fireplaces at George Washington's home in Mount Vernon. Under the Richards family, Batsto saw its greatest success in iron and later, when iron production moved west into Pennsylvania, in glassmaking.

OTHER ACTIVITIES

Batsto Village is a gem. Explore the village, check out the small museum, and tour Batsto Mansion. Many other trails leave from Batsto as well, including the three colored loops (red, white, or blue) of Batsto Lake Trail: Batsto Lake Red Trail (this 1-mile route with a crushed-stone base is rated ADA accessible), Tom's Pond Trail, and Mullica River Trail—which stretches to Atsion. (Part of Mullica River Trail is covered in Trip 42.) The Mullica River or nearby Wading River make for wonderful paddles by canoe or kayak.

MORE INFORMATION

Open dawk to dusk. Seasonal entrance fees may apply from Memorial Day to Labor Day—check the park's website to see if fees are in effect before you go. Batona Trail was constructed by the Batona Hiking Club of Philadelphia. It was expanded and is now maintained by the Outdoor Club of South Jersey (ocsj.org) and the New Jersey State Park Service. The Outdoor Club of South Jersey also constructed and maintains Sand and Water Trail and 1808 Trail.

A footbridge spans a wet area of the cedar swamp along 1808 Trail.

Enjoy a peaceful walk through pitch pines to an old cranberry bog and placid Pakim Pond.

Features 🐕 ♿ 💧 👀 🏃 🎣

Location New Lisbon, NJ

Rating Moderate

Distance 9.4-mile loop

Elevation Gain 300 feet

Estimated Time 4 hours

Maps USGS Browns Mills; nj.gov/dep/parksandforests/maps/brendantbyrne-area.pdf

GPS Coordinates 39° 53.700′ N, 074° 34.490′ W

Contact Mailing address: New Jersey State Park Service at Brendan T. Byrne State Forest, P.O. Box 215, New Lisbon, NJ 08064; 609-726-1191; nj.gov/dep/parksandforests/parks/brendantbyrnestateforest.html

DIRECTIONS

Travel on NJ 70 until you reach Four Mile Circle. At Four Mile Circle, take the first exit (if heading east from Camden/Philadelphia) or the fourth exit (if heading west from Garden State Parkway) to merge south onto NJ 72. In 1.0 mile, turn left onto Mikes Crossway. In 300 feet, turn right onto Shinns Road and then immediately turn left into the parking lot of the Brendan T. Byrne State Forest Ranger Station. The parking lot has room for about 25 vehicles.

TRAIL DESCRIPTION

Brendan T. Byrne State Forest (formerly Lebanon State Forest) is a 37,242-acre property in the Pine Barrens. It was renamed in 2004 to honor former governor Brendan T. Byrne, who played a significant role in the passage of the Pinelands Protection Act in 1979. The act preserved the Pine Barrens as a large, wild area in the middle of the most densely populated state in the nation. The Lebanon Glass Works operated here (lured by the sand) from 1851 to 1867. In 1908, the state acquired the land and began reforestation. Today, white cedars, pines, woodpeckers, and turkeys enliven the surroundings. The white-sand trails dissecting the pure waters of flooded cranberry bogs (some of which are still farmed) provide a beauty like no other.

This hike follows Cranberry Trail, Mount Misery Trail, and Batona Trail in a large loop through the heart of the park to popular Pakim Pond. Start at the northern corner of the parking lot next to the ranger station, where a trail sign with a red blaze leads you through a gap in the fence and across the paved road to Cranberry Trail. This ADA-accessible, crushed-stone path provides a very easy walk through pine barrens forest. Take advantage of the lack of tripping hazards to scan the sides of the trail for pine warblers and chickadees. The trail turns right (0.7 mile) and passes through a cedar swamp, home to the Atlantic white cedar as well as the carnivorous pitcher plant and perhaps even the rare curly grass fern. Turn sharply left (0.9 mile) as the trail follows along one of the many sand roads in the park, crossing Shinns Branch (1.5 miles) before turning right to cross the sand road and continuing through the gate (outhouse to the left here if you need it). Blueberry bushes provide pretty blooms in spring, tasty treats in summer, and a fantastic red color in fall.

At 2.3 miles, leave Cranberry Trail for white-blazed Mount Misery Trail, which heads northeast. The trail emerges from the woods to cross dirt Coopers Road and follow dirt Muddy Road, staying left at the fork and curving around a conservation area until

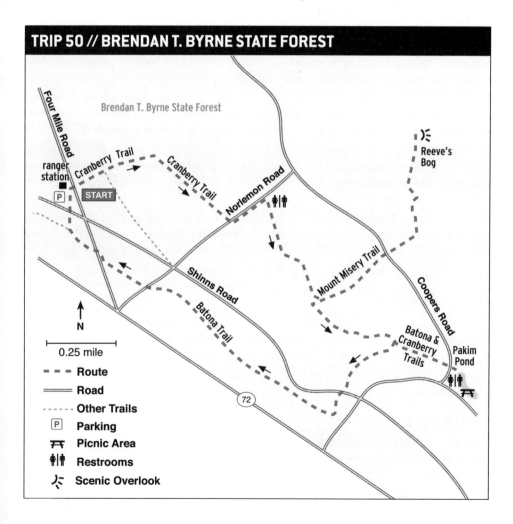

TRIP 50 // BRENDAN T. BYRNE STATE FOREST

Brendan T. Byrne State Forest

Four Mile Road

ranger station

Cranberry Trail

Cranberry Trail

Norlemon Road

Reeve's Bog

START

Shinns Road

Mount Misery Trail

Coopers Road

N

Batona Trail

Batona & Cranberry Trails

Pakim Pond

0.25 mile

- - - Route
=== Road
----- Other Trails
P Parking
Picnic Area
Restrooms
Scenic Overlook

72

reaching the wide-open water of the Reeve's Bog, a former cranberry growing area. Wander a bit farther down the white-blazed trail along the old cranberry dike to admire views of the water. Keep watch for red-tailed hawks. Listen for their cry, which sounds remarkably like a bald eagle cry in Hollywood films. This is because filmmakers don't like the call of the bald eagle and often substitute the call of a red-tailed hawk instead.

When you have had your fill of the wide-open views, retrace your steps to the intersection with red-blazed Cranberry Trail (5.0 miles). Turn left to head southeast on this trail. In a short while, the pink blazes of Batona Trail appear and overlap with the red blazes of Cranberry Trail (5.6 miles). Follow the dual blazes until you reach dirt Coopers Road. Cross the road and turn right, following the red blazes behind the guardrail and continuing until Cranberry Trail dead-ends at the Pakim Pond picnic area on the south side of Pakim Pond. (Batona Trail turns left to go around Pakim Pond and continues another 40 or so miles to Bass River State Forest.) This is a great spot for lunch or a snack. Bathrooms are also available.

When you are ready, backtrack down the Cranberry Trail/Batona Trail overlap, turning left to follow pink-blazed Batona Trail when it leaves Cranberry Trail (6.5 miles). Batona Trail drops slightly and then traverses a swampy area on a series of puncheons and small bridges. Listen for frogs in the warm seasons, but beware of mosquitoes. Also watch your footing, as the wood can become slippery. The trail climbs back out to cross paved Shinns Road before turning right to head northwest. Cross three firebreaks before entering "the hills section" of Batona Trail, which remains relatively flat for its first 45.5 miles, but starting here (7.3 miles into this trip) begins a stretch of slight ups and downs. Enjoy these minor elevation changes the rest of the way as you hike across more than a dozen firebreaks, which are used to help control forest fires (and are part of the course in the annual Scrub Pine Enduro race that is held here each October).

Notice the scorch marks on the trees, the result of a series of controlled burns that help prevent larger, out-of-control forest fires by eliminating the layers of organic materials that build up on the floor of the pine forests. Cross dirt Norlemon Road and then dirt Four Mile Road before reaching the blue-blazed side trail (9.1 miles) that turns right toward the ranger station and your car at the end of the hike.

DID YOU KNOW?

New Jersey is the third-largest cranberry-producing state, and nearly all the berries are produced in the Pine Barrens. Prime harvesting season is mid-September through mid-November. You can book a cranberry bog tour in October from Pine Barrens Native Fruits (888-272-6264). Sand from the Pine Barrens was used in Ipana toothpaste, popular in the 1950s.

OTHER ACTIVITIES

Tour the 36-building Whitesbog Village, once the family farm of J. H. White and now managed by Whitesbog Preservation Trust. The White family began growing cranberries

Sluice gates like this one were used for regulating water levels in old bogs, such as this one along Mount Misery Trail.

here in 1857. Pick up a map from the still-operating general store and explore the house and fields of Elizabeth White, responsible for the development of the blueberry as a viable crop. For more hiking, head to the far northwestern corner of the park and Ong's Hat trailhead, considered to be the beginning access point to 52.7-mile Batona Trail (state.nj.us/dep/parksandforests/parks/docs/batona14web.pdf, with an updated map due to be released in early 2024).

MORE INFORMATION

The first portion of this hike on Cranberry Trail, with crushed-stone surfacing, is rated as ADA accessible. Camping is available at Brendan T. Byrne State Forest; make reservations at njportal.com/DEP/NJOutdoors.

APPENDIX: OTHER HIKES IN NEW JERSEY

Briefly listed below, by region and county, are some hike-worthy trails not included in this book due to space constraints or extensive coverage in other publications. Research these gems on your own; maps are usually available from land managers' websites. Happy trails!

SKYLANDS
MORRIS COUNTY

Black River County Park (Chester): Four trails wind through this pretty 858-acre park. Take popular 2.3-mile Black River Trail along the Black River and past the Cooper gristmill.

Farney State Park (Rockaway): Hike a portion of 10.4-mile Four Birds Trail on a 7-mile moderate loop hike to Indian Cliffs. Check out the bat-viewing platform at Hibernia Mine in the 4,866-acre park. On Split Rock Road across the Splitrock Reservoir Dam.

Hacklebarney State Park (Long Valley): This 1,186-acre park is home to hemlock ravines and the Black River. Hike nine rugged but short trails, totaling 5 miles. Try the 0.1-mile waterfall trail. The park is known for brilliant foliage in fall. 119 Hacklebarney Road.

Negri-Nepote Native Grassland Preserve (Somerset): Enjoy the lake along a pleasant 2.9-mile loop that is good for beginners and especially for birders. March through December is the best time to visit; check for closures due to hunting season. 260 Skillmans Lane.

Pyramid Mountain National Historic Area (Montville): A moderate hike to Tripod Rock (a 180-ton boulder balanced on three smaller boulders) on the 3-mile loop via Mennen Trail is a must in this 1,534-acre area. Thirty miles of trails include a waterfall walk on the 5.2-mile Turkey Mountain loop hike. 472 Boonton Avenue.

HUNTERDON COUNTY

Ken Lockwood Gorge Wildlife Management Area (Annandale): Walk the unpaved road (closed to cars) that parallels the South Branch of the Raritan River through a deep gorge. This 498-acre preserve is one of New Jersey's most attractive wildlife management areas. Also try Columbia Trail. 203 Raritan River Road.

Musconetcong Gorge Preserve (Bloomsbury): Take moderate-to-strenuous Ridge and Highlands trails (views of the gorge) and Waterfall Trail in this 523-acre preserve. 182 Dennis Road.

Spruce Run Recreation Area (Clinton): Spruce Run Reservoir is the third-largest reservoir in the state, and 15 miles of recreational shoreline grace this park. All trails are easy to moderate, including 2.6 miles of the Highlands Trail. 68 Van Syckles Road.

Stephens State Park (Hackettstown): Follow an easy but rocky path along the Musconetcong River, which flows through this 805-acre park. Choose among six marked trails, ranging from flat to steep and rocky; includes 2 miles of the Highlands Trail. 800 Willow Grove Street.

Voorhees State Park (Glen Gardner): The Civilian Conservation Corps built many trails and structures in this 1,336-acre park. Twelve easy-to-moderate trails crisscross the property, including 2.3 miles of the Highlands Trail. 251 County Route 513.

Wickecheoke Creek Preserve (Stockton): Ramble along the creek on easy Wickecheoke Trail in this 4,000-acre preserve. Wear waterproof boots because the creek can get high after periods of rain. New Jersey's only covered bridge sits in the middle of Wickecheoke Creek Preserve. Built circa 1860, Green Sergeant's Covered Bridge crosses the creek at County Route 604. 33 Risler Street.

WARREN COUNTY

Marble Hill Natural Resource Area (Phillipsburg): This 288-acre park offers 4 miles of trails, including the beginning of the Highlands Trail. When complete, the Highlands Trail will stretch 180 miles from the Delaware River in New Jersey to the Hudson River in New York, with more miles in Pennsylvania (maintained by Appalachian Mountain Club). Plans include extending the trail into Connecticut. Highlights at Marble Hill include views of the "little water gap," the remains of the Fulmer Mine, and an old pump house. Trailhead at Loptacong Park, Upper Field Path.

SUSSEX COUNTY

Janet Van Gelder Wildlife Sanctuary (Sussex): Enjoy two rugged trails (each 3 miles or less) marked by white blazes and red plastic ties in this 221-acre sanctuary. Look for red-tailed hawks and search for Chewbacca's grave (a dog, one hopes). Take CR 515 to Lounsberry Hollow Road.

SOMERSET COUNTY

Lord Stirling Park (Basking Ridge): Adjacent to Great Swamp National Wildlife Refuge, this 425-acre park has 8 miles of hiking trails, which include 3 miles of ADA-accessible boardwalk through a sensitive marsh landscape. It is the former estate of William Alexander (who was never recognized as a lord by Parliament). 190 Lord Stirling Road.

Washington Valley Park (North Branch): Red Reservoir Trail provides easy hiking around the 21-acre reservoir. Enjoy hawk migration in fall. This 719-acre park is at the geographic center of Somerset County. Entrances on Miller Lane (hawk-watching) and Newman's Lane (reservoir).

GATEWAY
PASSAIC COUNTY

Apshawa Preserve (West Milford): Five miles of easy trails in the heart of the Highlands of northern New Jersey. 4 Northwood Drive.

Franklin Lakes Nature Preserve (Franklin Lakes): Take an easy stroll around a 75-acre lake. A universally accessible trail runs along part of the waterfront. 1 Nature Preserve Way.

High Mountain Park Preserve (Wayne): Challenge yourself on 11.5 miles of trail in this 1,300-acre preserve. Try the 4-mile summit hike on Summit Trail. This is the Preakness Range of the Watchung Mountains. 100 University Drive.

Pequannock Watershed (Newfoundland): Enjoy clear streams and ponds, and dramatic rock outcroppings in this 151,847-acre watershed. Try moderate Bearfort Ridge, Hanks Pond, and Firetower hikes. Permit required and fee charged. 223 Echo Lake Road.

HUDSON COUNTY

Stephen R. Gregg Park (Bayonne): Stroll this 100-acre park, named after a World War II hero. A half-mile promenade offers impressive waterfront views along Newark Bay. John Fitzgerald Boulevard off I-78 (Bergen County).

Hackensack River Greenway (Teaneck): Travel 3.5 miles along the Hackensack River (also known as "a bridge that saved the nation" because the Continental Army crossed here). Several public access points are provided, including one from Andreas Park. From NJ 4 East, take the River Road/Teaneck/Bogota/New Milford exit ramp on the right. Follow the signs for River Road at the bottom of the ramp. Turn left for the northern section of the Greenway or turn right for its southern section. To begin a hike at Andreas Park, travel 0.5 mile north on River Road from the NJ 4 off-ramp to Grenville Avenue and turn left.

Historic New Bridge Landing (River Edge): Stop at Bergen County Historical Society for this walking tour covering the American Revolution. New Bridge served as a battleground, fort, encampment ground, military headquarters, and intelligence-gathering post in every year of the war. 1201 Main Street.

Ramapo Valley County Reservation (Mahwah): In this 4,000-acre park, you can exercise your dog around Scarlet Oak Pond as well as take moderate-to-strenuous hikes, such as 3.75-mile Vista Loop and 3-mile Ridge Loop. 608 Ramapo Valley Road (US 202).

Ringwood State Park (Ringwood): Trails are moderate in this 4,444-acre park. Visit New Jersey Botanical Garden, Shepherd Lake, and Ringwood Manor, a mansion with relics from ironmaking days. 1304 Sloatsburg Road.

Saddle River County Park (Saddle Brook): Enjoy easy urban hiking along a stream in this 577-acre park. 1417 Saddle River Road.

Tenafly Nature Center (Tenafly): Seven marked trails and a butterfly house grace this 400-acre nature center. Try yellow-blazed Pfister's Pond Trail (10-minute walk, about 0.3 mile). 313 Hudson Avenue.

UNION COUNTY

Lenape Park (Cranford): Explore Lenape Pond and the Rahway River on easy trails that mingle rural and urban landscapes. Wander three adjacent local parks: Nomahegan, Echo Lake, and Black Brook via the Rahway River Parkway/Greenway.

Rahway River Park (Clark): Hike a 4-mile urban trail along the Rahway River. St. George Avenue off I-95.

ESSEX COUNTY

Eagle Rock Reservation (West Orange): Enjoy 400 acres along the Watchung Mountain ridge. Lenape Trail, an easy hike, skirts the eastern edge of the park. Visit the Essex County 9/11 memorial with extraordinary views of the New York City skyline. The main entrance to the park is on Eagle Rock Avenue, between Prospect and Mountain avenues.

Hilltop Reservation (Verona): Short, easy trails take you along a preserved ridgeline on Second Watchung Mountain. Try 1.3-mile Peace Trail and 0.3-mile More Peace Trail in the 282-acre park. Eastern entrance on Fairview Road between Valley View and Bolton roads.

South Mountain Reservation (West Orange): Hike six marked trails in the 2,110-acre reservation. Six miles of moderate Lenape Trail (see Trip 17) run through here and lead to waterfalls. An easy and pretty fall hike from the Tulip Springs parking area along Glen Avenue in the town of Millburn follows along the Rahway River to Hemlock Falls. Cherry Lane, off I-78.

JERSEY SHORE
MONMOUTH COUNTY

Gateway National Recreation Area–Sandy Hook Unit (Highlands): This national park property offers an 8.7-mile (one way) multiuse trail for walking and biking, as well as several shorter hiking nature trails. Climb the oldest lighthouse in the country, explore the abandoned military bunkers, and appreciate the diversity of nature on this exposed spit of land. Try to get on a ranger tour of the holly forest (visits are by ranger-led tour only). Bird-watchers, be careful where you aim those binoculars! The only legal nude beach in New Jersey is here as well. Fees Memorial Day to Labor Day, free the rest of the year. 128 South Hartshorne Drive.

Huber Woods Park (Locust): Explore 8 miles of hiking trails in this 367-acre woods, which includes an environmental center and a reptile house. 25 Brown's Dock Road.

Monmouth Battlefield State Park (Manalapan): Wander an 1,818-acre American Revolution battlefield (excellent visitor center). 16 Business Route 33.

Perrineville Lake Park (Millstone): Roam 5 miles of easy trails in this 1,239-acre park with several entrances. For a pretty amble, try 1.5-mile Lakeview Loop Trail. 23 Agress Road.

Turkey Swamp Park (Freehold): This is the largest park in the county at 2,261 acres, with a 17-acre lake and 9 miles of easy trails. 200 Georgia Road.

OCEAN COUNTY

Barnegat Branch Trail (Bayville): This rail-trail will eventually stretch more than 15 miles (one way) from Barnegat Township to Toms River. This was part of the old Central Jersey line. The Central section is reachable via William J. Dudley Park, Maple Street, and Sycamore Street.

Bass River State Forest (Tuckerton): Hike 23 miles of trails, including a white pine plantation started in 1928. Joe's Trail and Absegami Trail are also popular. Part of 52.7-mile Batona Trail also runs through here. 762 Stage Road.

Cattus Island County Park (Toms River): Take easy walks on 6.9 miles of well-marked trails on 500 acres, enjoying Barnegat Bay views. Visit Cooper Environmental Center. 1170 Cattus Island Boulevard.

Cloverdale Farm County Park (Barnegat): Stroll a 1.4-mile nature trail on a 90-acre working cranberry farm rich in history. 34 Cloverdale Road.

Double Trouble State Park (Bayville): Walk 8 flat miles in this 8,495-acre park in the Pine Barrens, which includes a historic district and cranberry bogs. An extensive trail guide is available online. 581 Pinewald Keswick Road (County Route 618).

Forest Research Education Center (Jackson): Opened in 1982 as the NJ Tree Nursery, this state property distributes more than 300,000 seedlings each year. Come explore 8 miles of trails and learn more about forestry. 495 Don Conner Boulevard.

Jakes Branch County Park (Beachwood): The hangar where the Hindenburg was kept is visible in the distance. Hike 8.6 miles of easy trails in this 400-acre park. Look for a five-story observation deck. 1100 Double Trouble Road.

Lochiel Creek County Park (Barnegat): An easy 1.75-mile trail in a 177-acre park travels through freshwater wetlands and pin oak uplands and includes a connector to the longer, flat Barnegat Branch Trail. 950 Barnegat Boulevard North.

GREATER ATLANTIC CITY
ATLANTIC COUNTY

Cedar Lake Wildlife Management Area (Williamstown/Buena Vista): The sandy trails of the Pine Barrens surround a beautiful natural lake. In winter, walk 0.2 mile north of the dam on the left side of Jackson Road and then cross a dike to the back of the lake to look for bald eagles. 117 Jackson Road in Williamstown.

Clarks Landing Preserve (Port Republic): This is a destination for nature lovers (especially those who appreciate pitcher plants and bald eagles). The trails in this 654-acre preserve (administered by New Jersey Natural Lands Trust) are not particularly well-marked, but a short, sandy path follows the Mullica River.

Egg Harbor Township Nature Reserve (Egg Harbor Township): The reserve offers 8 miles of trails that let you explore some typical pine barrens forest. A large lake populated by tons of birds marks the remains of a sand-mining operation. 318 Zion Road.

Hammonton Creek Wildlife Management Area (Hammonton): The trails at this 4,852-acre expanse are not well marked, but this is the former site of a large World War I ammunition company. Also thrilling are the remnants of a 1.5-mile-long elevated wooden racetrack loop, built by the Atlantic City Motor Speedway. (Please respect the private property boundaries.)

Hammonton Lake Park (Hammonton): This park (part of the Pine Barrens) has flat terrain, a lake, and wildlife (turtles are especially lively in spring). Hammonton is also the self-proclaimed blueberry capital of the world. You can manage a 2- to 3-mile hike if you combine Hammonton with the adjacent Smith Conservation Area. 100 Sports Drive.

KEEP Conservation Preserve (Port Republic): This little-known, local nonprofit preserve of 83 acres of woodlands and wetlands lies along Nacote Creek. See great horned owls, egrets, ospreys, and bald eagles. On Chestnut Neck Road off US 9 (New York Road).

Lakes Bay Preserve (Pleasantville): This secluded 24-acre peninsula (administered by the New Jersey Conservation Foundation) juts southward into Lakes Bay. Enjoy a marsh and share a half-mile strip of sandy beach with pelicans and sea lavender. Strong, steady breezes make it a great spot to watch wind surfers. The bay was named after Simon Lake, a Pleasantville native, who invented the submarine in 1894. Public access is by foot only. Lakes Bay Preserve is at the end of Baypoint Drive off Black Horse Pike.

Weymouth Furnace Park and John's Woods Preserve (Weymouth): No marked trails exist, but industrial-history buffs can wander the ruins of an 1800s furnace, forge, and paper mill. To make this a nature hike (and to see more ruins), cross County Route 559 (Weymouth Road), and walk the trails of 202-acre John's Woods Preserve, administered by New Jersey Natural Lands Trust. 2050 Weymouth Road.

SOUTHERN SHORE
CAPE MAY COUNTY

Cape May National Wildlife Refuge (Cape May Court House): Four easy trails cover about 3 miles through marshes and forests. Look for piping plovers. 24 Kimbles Beach Road.

Corson's Inlet State Park (Ocean City): Enjoy undeveloped land along the ocean-front. Four trails, each less than 1 mile, feature sand dunes and bird-watching. County Route 619.

Higbee Beach Wildlife Management Area (Cape May): Trails in this serene spot lead to a 1.5-mile beach at the tip of Cape Island along Delaware Bay. The six sites in this more than 1,000-acre wildlife management area are Signal Hill, Davey's Lake, Pond Creek, Sassafras Island, Hidden Valley, and the magnesite plant. Take County Route 626 to New England Road (County Route 641).

Lizard Tail Swamp Preserve (Cape May Court House): Hike 3 easy miles within Cape May forest on trails created and maintained by The Nature Conservancy. The nature preserve protects a globally rare Cape May lowland swamp community. 460 Court House South Dennis Road.

CUMBERLAND COUNTY

Bivalve Wetlands Walk (Port Norris): Take a 4-mile out-and-back hike across salt marshes near a town that during New Jersey's oyster boom had more millionaires per square mile than anywhere in the country. Don't miss the Bayshore Center, which preserves and explores this unique area and houses New Jersey's official tall ship, the *Meerwald*, an old oystering vessel. The best times to visit are during late fall, winter, and early spring to avoid mosquitoes and biting flies. Park at the Bayshore Center, 2800 High Street.

Egg Island Wildlife Management Area (Fortescue): The hikes are short and easy on a quiet beach, passing salt marshes and tidal creeks, in this 6,714-acre expanse, home to diamondback terrapins and horseshoe crabs. Take County Route 553 to Maple Street.

Eldora Nature Preserve (Delmont): Hike 5 miles of marshes, swamps, and wood-lands on three trails. A boardwalk overlooks West Creek and a marsh. The preserve is on the southern end of the Pine Barrens and is the site of The Nature Conservancy's first property created specifically to protect rare moths. 2350 NJ 47.

Harold N. Peek Preserve (Millville): Hike wetlands around the Maurice River and observe a wild rice marsh in this 344-acre preserve. As you roam 3 miles of easy trails, you may spot an eagle. 2100 South Second Street.

Thompson's Beach (Maurice River Township): Thompson's Beach was once a vaca-tion destination, but storms wreaked havoc on this Bayshore town. (One storm in the 1950s, classified as a "tidal wave" by some insurance companies, reduced the town from 107 buildings to just 7. The town was finally purchased and demolished.) Walk a half-mile out to the island and explore the beach in each direction. Be very careful to check the tides, or your trip might be a lot longer than you planned! Nearby Moore's Beach offers a similar, shorter hike.

DELAWARE RIVER
MERCER COUNTY

Abbott Marshlands (Bordentown): Tidal freshwater wetlands can be found in the congested Trenton-Hamilton-Bordentown area, amazingly enough. Several trails exist in Abbott Marshlands. Bordentown Bluffs Trail is of moderate difficulty and is part of Delaware and Raritan Canal State Park. The attractive, wooded trail follows Crosswicks Creek. Easy routes include Roebling Park Trail in Spring Lake, Tidal Water Trail, and Towpath Trail. The Bordentown Bluffs Trail entrance is at 180 Orchard Avenue.

Jacob's Creek (Hopewell): This picturesque 1.5-mile (one way) trail features wildflowers, mature forest, and a creek (hop over the water on stones). Park in the small lot just west of Jacob's Creek on Pennington-Titusville Road.

Ted Stiles Preserve at Baldpate Mountain (Titusville): Make this an aerobic workout (9 miles round trip) or a leisurely stroll around the lake and through the stewarded meadows and native plant preserve. Enjoy views of Philadelphia's skyline and the Delaware River. This area is also popular with cyclists. 327 Fiddlers Creek Road.

Stony Brook–Millstone Watershed Association (Pennington): Hike 3 to 5 easy miles past a farm, meadows, and a pond. This sometimes-whimsical trail features a Haiku Station, a Hobbit Tree, and a Lonely Tree. 31 Titus Mill Road.

BURLINGTON COUNTY

Batona Trail: Carranza Memorial to Apple Pie Hill (Tabernacle): Hike 4.1 miles (one way) through Wharton State Forest on the Pine Barren's famous Batona Trail through scrub pines, past beaver lodges, through a cedar swamp, and up Apple Pie Hill, one of the tallest points in South Jersey. From the top of the fire tower, look for Philadelphia and Atlantic City on a clear day. The fire tower is open only when staffed or on scheduled days; call 609-726-9010 for information. Drive 8.9 miles on Carranza Road from US 206 to reach the Carranza Memorial. Parking is behind the memorial.

Crystal Lake Park (Bordentown): This 370-acre park includes 8 miles of moderate trails through woods and past wetlands and a lake. 240 Axe Factory Road.

Historic Smithville Park (Easthampton): Hike about 4 miles of easy trails (one of them floats) past Smith Mansion and an old factory complex. 801 Smithville Road.

Rancocas State Park (Hainesport): This 1,252-acre park provides about 8 miles of easy trails in a 58-acre natural area of forests with an extensive freshwater tidal marsh. Enter on Rancocas Road or Deacon Road.

Franklin Parker Preserve (Chatsworth): The largest New Jersey Conservation Foundation property at more than 11,000 acres, Franklin Parker Preserve protects the old DeMarco cranberry farms. More than 20 miles of trails highlight the beautiful former bogs. Red Trail (6 miles) is the most popular and features a swinging bridge over the Wading River and a pair of oversized Adirondack chairs. White Trail

(2 miles) offers a good chance to spot a bald eagle. A 7.2-mile stretch of Batona Trail crosses the preserve but cannot be reached from the rest of the trail system. The Chatsworth entrance is at 1450 County Route 532.

Whitesbog Village at Brendan T. Byrne State Forest (New Lisbon): Take a 7-mile hike here past active cranberry bogs (some access restricted during growing season), through an old farming town, and through the fields that Elizabeth White used to develop blueberries into a commercial crop. 120 West Whitesbog Road #34.

CAMDEN COUNTY

Pennypacker Park (Haddonfield): Hike lovely, easy, wooded trails near Cooper River, Hopkins Pond, and Driscoll Pond. Search for the commemorative stone that marks where William Foulke discovered the first nearly complete dinosaur skeleton in 1858. Pennypacker Park is bounded by Kings Highway, Park Boulevard, and Grove Street.

Timber Creek County Park (Blackwood): This park was created from an old horse farm. It features a half-mile paved loop and more than 2 miles of unpaved trails that offer a surprisingly secluded walk through the woods along Timber Creek and by an attractive pond. The site also includes a popular, 9-acre, fenced, unleashed dog park. 236 Taylor Avenue.

Winslow Fish and Wildlife Management Area (Hammonton): Go through calm, peaceful hardwood and upland forests, fields, and swamps, and pass a section of the Great Egg Harbor River. A 1.6-mile round-trip hike follows Blue Hole Trail. (Blue holes are rumored to be dark blue, deep-water hangouts for the Jersey Devil, which will pull you to the bottom in a flash if you so much as dip a toe.) It's an interesting place to wander and eat blueberries.

GLOUCESTER COUNTY

Piney Hollow Preservation Area (Newfield): In this property right next to Unexpected Wildlife Refuge (see below), visitors can hike several miles of moderately difficult trails through woods and over bogs, dikes, and swamps. 1394–1526 Piney Hollow Winslow Road.

Tranquility Trail (Woolrich Township): An hour-long hike through wildflowers and fields, and briefly through woods, leads to a vista of Raccoon Creek. The name of the trail was chosen from hundreds of student projects submitted by the township's schools. 300–331 High Hill Road.

Unexpected Wildlife Refuge (Newfield): Explore and observe nature and swamps in about 10 miles of moderately difficult trails (tricky bridges, blowdown). All visitors must make an appointment (call 856-697-3541). 110 Unexpected Road.

SALEM COUNTY

Elephant Swamp Trail (Elk Township): A 12-mile out-and-back hike travels along an old railroad line, built in 1978 and demolished in the 1990s. Features include farmland, swamps, Atlantic white cedars, and open fields, with some nature signage.

(Legend has it that when a circus was traveling by train through Elk Township in the 1800s, an elephant escaped, got loose in the swamp, and was never seen again.)

Oldmans Creek Preserve (Auburn): South Jersey Land & Water Trust's only property, this former Boy Scout camp features 2 miles of trails in an expanding trail system along Oldman's Creek. The hike is in Auburn, but use 21 Main Street in Swedesboro to get to the parking lot next to the Land & Water Trust's headquarters.

Supawna Meadows National Wildlife Refuge (Pennsville): In spring, hike short Forest Habitat Trail through a forest and around a pond to hear a symphony of spring peepers and southern leopard frogs. Grassland Trail provides sightings of northern harriers and American kestrels in winter; an observation platform overlooks a finger of tidal marsh. 197 Lighthouse Road.

INDEX

O

Oakland, hikes near, xii–xiii, 122–126
Ocean City, hikes near, 271
Ocean County, additional hikes in, 269
Old Bridge Waterfront Park, 120
Oldmans Creek Preserve, 274

P

Palace of Depression, 218
Palisades Interstate Park, xii–xiii, 80–84
Parvin State Park, xvi–xvii, 242–246
Passaic County, additional hikes in, 267
Paterson Great Falls National Historic Park, 79
Paterson Museum, 79
Peanut Leap Cascade, 80–84
Pennington, hikes near, 272
Pennsville, hikes near, xiv–xv, 194–198
Pennypacker Park, 255, 273
Pequannock Watershed, 267
Perrineville Lake Park, 269
Phillipsburg, hikes near, 266
Pine Barrens Jamboree, 141
Pine Barrens region, 143–144
  cryptids in, 180–181
  hikes in, 138–141, 225–228, 247–250, 256–259,
    260–264, 269–271
Pinelands National Reserve (PNR), 225–229
Piney Hollow Preservation Area, 273
Piper's Corner Preserve, 228
Plainsboro Preserve, xii–xiii, 100–104
Pleasantville, hikes near, 270
Point Rear Range Light, 198
poison ivy, xxiv
Pompton Lakes, 126
Port Norris, hikes near, 271
Port Republic, hikes near, 270
Prallsville Mills complex, 41
Princeton, hikes near, xiv–xv, xvi–xvii, 230–233,
    234–237
Princeton Battlefield State Park, xiv–xv, 230–233
Princeton University, 233
public transportation, trips accessible by
  Delaware River region, 251–255
  Gateway region, 75–79, 80–84, 90–93,
    122–126, 127–131
  Jersey shore region, 154–158
  Southern Shore region, 215–218
Pyramid Mountain National Historic Area, 265

R

Rahway River Park, 268
Ramapo Mountain State Forest, xii–xiii, 122–126
Ramapough Lenape Nation, 126

Ramapo Valley County Reservation, 267
Rancocas State Park, 272
Rattlesnake Swamp Trail, x–xi, 65–69
Ringwood, hikes near, xii–xiii, 96–99, 267
Ringwood State Park, 126, 267
River Edge, hikes near, 267
Rockaway, hikes near, 265
Rockhopper Trail, x–xi, 13–17
Round Mountain, 30–33
Rush Holt Environmental Education Center,
    100–104

S

Saddle Brook, hikes near, 268
Saddle River County Park, 268
safety considerations, xxiii–xxv
Salem County, additional hikes in, 273–274
salt marsh ecosystem, 199
Sandy Hook, 149
Scherman Hoffman Wildlife Sanctuary, 24
Scotch Plains, hikes near, xii–xiii, 85–89
Scotts Corner Conservation Area, 104
Seaside Heights, 163
Seaside Park, hikes near, xiv–xv, 159–163
Shades of Death road, 44
Shamong, hikes near, xiv–xv, 225–229
Shawangunk Ridge Trail (SRT), 25–28
Six Mile Run Reservoir, x–xi, 61–64
Skylands region
  trip planner, x–xi
  region description, 1–2
  easy hikes in, 8–12, 30–33, 46–49, 57–60,
    61–64
  moderate hikes in, 3–7, 13–17, 30–33, 36–39,
    65–69
  strenuous hikes in, 13–17, 20–24, 36–39,
    42–45, 50–54
  other hikes in, 265–267
snakes, xxiv
Somerset, hikes near, x–xi, 61–64, 266
Somerset County, additional hikes in, 266–267
Somers Mansion Historic Site, 185
Sourland Mountain Preserve, x–xi, 3–7
South Cape May Meadows Preserve, xiv–xv
Southern Shore region
  trip planner, xiv–xv
  region description, 187–188
  easy hikes in, 194–198, 200–205, 211–214,
    215–218
  moderate hikes in, 189–193, 206–210
  strenuous hikes in, 189–193
  other hikes in, 271–272
South Mountain Reservation, 268

ABOUT THE AUTHORS

Priscilla Estes is a former medical editor, insurance marketing executive, yoga teacher, and award-winning journalist. She has been a member of AMC since 1996 and is past chapter chair and publicity chair for the AMC Delaware Valley Chapter (AMCDV). Priscilla has guided hikes for AMCDV and has led weekend hiking and yoga retreats at Mohican Outdoor Center. She retired to the mountains of western North Carolina and is an active trail worker with the Carolina Hiking Club—as well as a hiker—and enjoys playing the dulcimer and gongs. Priscilla volunteers with Friends of the Library in Waynesville, North Carolina, and has been a professional book reviewer for *The US Review of Books* since 2009.

Michael McCormick is a lifelong resident of New Jersey and has been exploring the state since childhood. His time in Boy Scouts gave him the opportunity to develop a passion for the outdoors as he worked his way to Eagle Scout. As a schoolteacher, scout-master, and father, Michael enjoys sharing his enthusiasm for the outdoors and local history with others. He began his *South Jersey Trails* blog in 2013 to record his adventures and to encourage people to explore those trails. Michael, his wife, and their five boys enjoy roaming near and far, from creeping down a nature trail at a toddler's pace to backpacking in the Pine Barrens. They are taking camping trips across the country in pursuit of their goal of visiting all 63 national parks (so far they have made it to 36!).

AMC BOOK UPDATES

AMC Books strives to keep our guidebooks as up-to-date as possible to help you plan safe and enjoyable adventures. If we learn after publishing a book that relevant trails have been relocated or that route or contact information has changed, we will post the updated information online. Before you hit the trail, visit outdoors.org/books-and-maps and click the link in the Book Updates section near the bottom of the page. While hiking, if you notice discrepancies with the trip descriptions or maps, or if you find any other errors in this book, please let us know by submitting them to amcbookupdates@outdoors.org or to Books Editor, c/o AMC, 10 City Square, Boston, MA 02129. We will verify all submissions and post key updates each month. AMC Books is dedicated to being a recognized leader in outdoor publishing. Thank you for your participation.

ABOUT AMC IN NEW JERSEY

AMC'S DELAWARE VALLEY CHAPTER

The Appalachian Mountain Club's Delaware Valley Chapter offers a wide variety of hiking, backpacking, climbing, paddling, bicycling, snowshoeing, and skiing trips each year, as well as social, family, and young member programs and instructional workshops. The chapter also maintains a 15-mile section of the Appalachian Trail between Wind Gap and Little Gap, as well as trails at Valley Forge National Historical Park. The Delaware Water Gap is also home to AMC's Mohican Outdoor Center, a frequent base for AMC's outdoor leadership workshops. A 90-minute drive from New York City, Mohican offers front-porch access to the Delaware Water Gap, with self-service cabins, comfortable bunkrooms, and the river, wetlands, and Appalachian Trail a stroll away. To view a list of AMC activities in Pennsylvania, central and south New Jersey, northern Delaware, and other parts of the Northeast and Mid-Atlantic, visit activities.outdoors.org.

AMC'S NEW YORK-NORTH JERSEY CHAPTER

The New York-North Jersey Chapter of the Appalachian Mountain Club hosts more than 1,000 outdoor recreation activities per year. The chapter offers its members outdoor events on most weekends, many for beginners. The New York-North Jersey Chapter of the Appalachian Mountain Club celebrated its 100th anniversary in 2012, and was the first AMC chapter to be formed. Members come from the New York City metro area, southeastern New York, and northeastern New Jersey area. To view a list of AMC activities in the New York-North Jersey region, visit activities.outdoors.org.

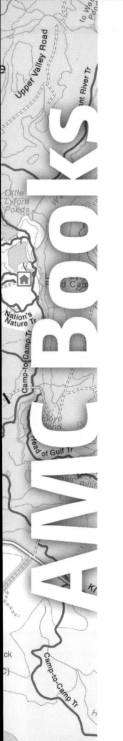